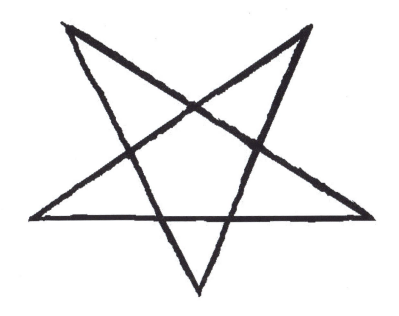

HOSTIA

Secret Teachings of the ONA

CUM SUPERIORUM PRIVILEGIO VENIAQUE

SANCTIONED BY JALL
OUTER REPRESENTATIVE
ORDER OF NINE ANGLES, 124 yf

****

Editor: Chrétien Sauvage
ISBN-10:1493633902
ISBN-13: 9781493633906

Credits: Anton Long & Christos Beest

Disclaimer: *The material contained in this document regarding various aural and historical traditions is provided for research and historical purposes only, and in an effort to advance and facilitate the understanding of issues related to sinister esoteric traditions in general.*

VAE VICTIS

EDITOR'S FOREWORD

This volume has been two years in the making. As the *Hostia* volumes are among the most essential of the Order of Nine Angles corpus, readers may ask why these were not included in the first or second of the "Sinister" volumes. Simply put, the original PDFs proved resistant to digital formatting and subsequent editing attempts, and entire sections had to be typed in letter by letter. Some pages, notably those containing alchemical symbols were finally inserted as images, as were the celebrated letters of Stephen Brown – albeit these in order to maintain the original sense of character.

This document contains all three *Hostia* volumes (I-III), in their entirety, with the exception that 'Copula Cum Daemona' is not included in *Hostia III*, as our own hardcopy omits the first several pages. The reader is encouraged to read the corrected version instead in *Sinister Tales* (p.573). Likewise, since 'Concerning the Temple of Set' is printed first in *Hostia II*, it is not repeated at the end of *Hostia III* for obvious reasons.

As with any transcription effort from hardcopy, there are at times sections of the original which are illegible. In this case, this edition of Hostia normally indicates this with standard editorial marks (e.g. "[illegible text]", and one essay in *Hostia I* is listed as 'Untitled', as our original hardcopy likewise does not have a legible title. The reader may consult the original typed manuscripts for further reference, if clarity is needed in such cases.

As ever, this edition is published as a volunteer initiative, in the hopes that it will prove useful to initiates at all stations along the Way.

Chrétien Sauvage
Order of Nine Angles
Samhain 2013 ev

TABLE OF CONTENTS

Editor's Foreword   4

Introduction   8

HOSTIA I

The Tradition of the Sinister Way   14
The Seven-Fold Sinister Way: A Comprehensive Guide   16
Insight Roles – A Guide   21
The Secret Tasks of the Sinister Way   25
Selling Water by the River   29
Sinister Shadow Magick   36
Guide to Black Magick   41
Satanic Influence – A Modern Tale   47
[Untitled Essay #1]   55
Manipulation I – Sinister Themes   58
Manipulation II   62
Ritual Magick – Dure and Sedue Ceremonial   64
The Alchemy of Magick   68
Acausal Existence – The Secret Revealed   71
Baphomet – A Note on the Name   73
Baphomet – A Note on the Name II   75
A Gift for The Prince: A Guide To Human Sacrifice   77
The Deofel Quartet [Notes]   80
The Sinister Path – Aims and Intents   86
Brief Guide To The Seven-Fold Way   93
Historical Addendum: *Reductio Ad Absurdum*   94
The Abyss   98
The Nine Angles – Esoteric Meanings   104
Crowley, Satan and The Sinister Way   108
Hangster's Gate   114
The Temple of Set: A Brief Analysis   117
Culling – A Guide to Sacrifice II   122
Satanism, Sacrifice and Crime – The Satanic Truth   127

The Hard Reality of Satanism   133
The Publication of Esoteric Traditions   140
The Secrets of the Nine Angles   142
The Septenary Star Game   146
Star Game: Addendum   154
Advanced Star Game   156
Internal Adept – A Brief Practical Guide   159
The Dating of Esoteric Tradition   164
Notes on Rituals – II   166
Aeonics   169
Aeons and Their Associated Civilizations   170
Aeonic Magick General Notes   173
Aeonic Magick General (I)   175
Aeonics S. Trad. II   177
Aeonics – The Secret Tradition I   184
Cliology – A Basic Introduction   190
Satanism and Child-Abuse   203

HOSTIA II

ONA – Organizational Structure   209
Synistry   213
VIII Sacrifice   214
Aeonics and Manipulation I   217
Aeonics and Manipulation II   221
Esoteric Tradition – Synistry   225
Esoteric Tradition VI   229
The Rite of the Nine Angles   233
Hell   239
The Sinister Calling   241
Revenge   246
Conquer, Destroy, Create   248
Magick and Politics   252
Insight Roles   255
Insight Roles II   258
The Publication of Esoteric Traditions on the LHP   261
Letters of Stephen Brown   265

ONA Strategy and Tactics   282
Concerning the Temple of Set   287

HOSTIA III

Adeptship – Its Real Meaning and Significance   294
Mastery – Its Real Meaning and Significance   299
Arthurian Legend According to the Secret Sinister Tradition 307
Satanism – Or Living on the Edge   309
Letters of Stephen Brown II   318
Notes on Study and Practice in Modern Satanism   323
The Practical Esoteric Aims of Satanism: 90-130 yf   325
The Song of a Satanist   333
The Left Handed Path – An Analysis ONA   338
Introduction to *The Deofel Quartet*   347
Responses and Critical Analysis   349
The Deofel Quartet – A Satanic Analysis   352
Nexion   359

INTRODUCTION

Perhaps moreso than other volumes within the corpus of classic ONA writings, few intimate the sort of inherent darkness that is embodied in the collected works known as HOSTIA. The name alone brings to mind those myriad connotations concerning Traditional Satanism and the Seven-fold Sinister Way which separates the path as promulgated by the Order of Nine Angles so firmly and irrevocably so against those others whose mis-use of the nomenclature Satanic only serves to obfuscate the reality of what Satanism actually is rather than to illuminate a way based on practical deeds beyond all accessory trappings of the "occult", said way of practical deeds which lies at the very core of the ONA .

As a return to darkness is needed (and is indeed underway) within the larger milieu known as the Sinister and as continued re-emphasis of the genuine nature of Satanism, the reality of which is so very stark, demanding and exacting often to a quite brutal degree is fundamental, perhaps also then there is no better time than now to present HOSTIA to the public with a strategic aim in mind pursuant to the strategies, albeit in a different space of causal time, outlined in Order MS (some present here, within this volume) concerning the nature of spreading - through publication - information concerning the Sinister Tradition.

Those among our Sinister kin whose formative years amidst and post Initiation were influenced primarily by HOSTIA and other writings like them share a certain common heritage within the ONA. One could almost say they share a certain elite status - not elite by claiming again and again their supposed allegiance to the Sinister and most certainly not by chest-beating through whatever self-styled title they have awarded themselves.

Elite rather in that they have had the privilege to be exposed, during strategic periods of causal time according to those striving to forward the Sinister Dialectic of history, to elements of the tradition that were hitherto secret, transmitted aurally and which, at a certain time, were released - with an intent to produce a new generation of Adepts and indeed those who would go on beyond Adeptship to Mastery and beyond.

Elite in that they took the information in such secret teachings and, rather than enshrine the books themselves as some sort of fetish item (as is presently in vogue amongst some) applied these secret teachings and made themselves as Satan in the real-world, through being hard, through testing themselves - and testing others (and some instances, in the case of those treading the path with the assistance of an Order guide, being tested themselves by the ONA directly and most assuredly being tested by the varied and oftentimes dangerous circumstances they might find themselves in as a result of their applying these teachings.)

There has been a stated thirst for practical information concerning the application of the Sinister Path and within its near four-hundred pages such a thirst should be quenched within HOSTIA. From check-lists of supplies for those planning to undertake the Rite of Internal Adept to specific addresses and contact point locations related to Insight Roles (though some of said addresses may now be defunct), from in-depth treatises regarding pursuing evil in a real-world context as well as various diagrams and instructional treatises concerning various esoteric processes within the Sinister Tradition such as the Star Game to overviews on Aeonics from various angles, it is clear that HOSTIA is meant as a practical text. A text which, if applied vigorously, will lead one on a path to a life full of zest, of danger - of overcoming great obstacles, of ordeals - a life often punctuated by tragedy yet always laced with exultation.

As such, on behalf of the ONA, the following volume is presented to you, the reader, as both a challenge and an invitation - a challenge to meet the goals set for oneself at the time of Initiation which, as the term denotes, is but a starting - and an invitation to embark on your own decades-long and more than likely lifetime adventure, that Sinister Quest which may take you far afield from what you know now; which may, indeed, reap perhaps on many levels greater consequences than rewards but which will, assuredly, place you firmly shoulder-to-shoulder in lockstep with those Dark Warriors who have tread the path before you and those who will do so long after your own causal life has passed.

March with us.

Jall
Outer Representative
Order of Nine Angles
124 Year of Fayen

HOSTIA

SECRET TEACHINGS

OF THE O.N.A.

VOLUME I

Printed & Published by
Thormynd Press
PO Box 700
Shrewsbury
Shropshire
England

INTRODUCTION

The present work contains esoteric manuscripts circulated among members of the ONA. The MSS contain further details of the sinister tradition of that Order and compliment the information about it already available in the books 'Naos', 'The Black Book of Satan' and 'The Deofel Quartet' as well as that published in the journal 'Fenrir'. The aim of publishing these MSS is to make the rituals and methods of this sinister tradition available to all those who might be interested. Such publication, as will be evident, enables individual potential to be fulfilled, aiding the emergence of a new Aeon.

THE TRADITION OF THE SINISTER WAY

The essence of genuine Satanism can be simply stated: it is a way to inner development, the goal of which is a new individual. This way involves three essential stages and these exemplify the spirit of that way and the individuals who follow it.

The first is direct experience, the second is direct practice and the third self-development. The first involves direct experience of both the external 'world' and the inner (or psychic) 'world' through striving to achieve certain goals both practical and magickal. The second involves using 'practical' (or causal) and 'magickal' (or acausal) energies to manipulate others, situations and energies in a practical way – producing changes in accord with certain goals. The third involves beginning the process again but starting from the new level of self-understanding and ability attained – persuing different (and probably more complex) goals.

A Satanist is an individual explorer – following in the footsteps of others (and perhaps using their guide books) but always seeking further horizons, daring to defy convention (in ideas as well as in morals and attitude) yet part of an evolutionary succession enabling what is experienced to be understood and become beneficial. For this reason, a genuine Satanist understands tradition as important and necessary – the culmination of centuries of insight and experience, a useful guide which enables further progress and exploration: a starting point for that inner and outer journey which is begun by Initiation, as well as a map of the way chosen and followed.

This tradition is not sacrosanct – but it does possess a validity until the individual reaches the stage where the unique genius within each individual has been brought to fruition enabling the creation (from experience and self-insight) of a unique way and a fulfilling of a unique Destiny. In magickal terms, this is the stage of Internal Adept, where that unique Destiny is made known (dis-covered) and where the individual Initiate has developed the talents necessary to fulfill it by a following of the previous stages – a stage reached from between three to five years after Initiation.

The tradition (explicated in the 'seven-fold sinister way') provides only a beginning – it is for the individual to go beyond it, toward the dangers and rewards of the Abyss. It is, however, necessary – since it is, in one sense, a 'short-cut': enabling self-development to be achieved far quicker than would be the case without it as well as fully enabling the explication of individual potential. This does not mean that following it is easy – the path may be shorter, but it is just as dangerous (and in some places, more so). It is a mountain path to the summit rather than a meandering valley path, and enables the horizon, the other mountains waiting to be conquered, to be seen – as they cannot be seen from the wooded valleys below.

But each new Initiate must walk this path – alone. and for each it is a new experience, a process of direct learning and a personal achievement, for only a very few have ever ventured that way before and stood atop the summit that is 'Internal Adept' to see in the distance the still higher peaks that wait beyond the Abyss.

What is important is following that path – and going beyond it, toward the Abyss – actually undertaking the journey and experiencing in real time what is encountered and seen: of being taken to the very limits of your endurance and abilities. No one can do this for you – just as the path does not lead to some pleasant grove where you sit at the feet of some 'Master' listening to their past experiences and fables. It does not involve you staying comfortably 'at home' with the security of your known world and friends and ideas, just as it is not a 'mental' journey done in comfortable surroundings and with no physical effort or danger. It IS practical, and direct – and involves physical and psychic hardship, and while you may be a little soft when you start, you will not be so when you succeed.

Just as if you believe you are tough enough now, you will be rudely awakened. Is this what you really want?

- O.N.A.

15

THE SEVEN-FOLD SINISTER WAY: A COMPREHENSIVE GUIDE

Aim:
Essentially three fold: a) Initiation; b) magickal Adeptship; c) fulfillment of individual wyrd and potential.

Stages:
1) Neophyte; 2) Initiate;3)External Adept; 4) Internal Adept; 5) Master of Temple/Mistress of Earth; 6) Magus/Magistra; 7)Immortal

Note: Initiates are sometimes known as 'Novices', Neophytes as 'Oblates'. External Adepts as 'Professed Brother/Sister'; Internal Adepts as Priest and Priestess; a Magus as 'Grand Master'.

Neophtye:
Tasks: Study of Esoteric tradition as given in Order MSS – particularly *Black Book*, *Naos*, Azoth and *'Fenrir'*. After this preliminary study (c.1 month) undertake ritual of Self-Initiation [*Black Book*] and construct simple form of the Star Game [*Naos*].

Initiate:
Tasks: Study septenary system in detail [*Naos* etc.] and begin workings with the spheres and the pathways. Study and use of Tarot.

Undertake hermetic workings/rituals for specific desires/personal requests.

Continue with study and use of Star Game – relating the abstract symbolism to the Tree of Wyrd, septenary etc.

Set a demanding physical goal [e.g. running 20 miles in 2.5 hours or less or cycling 100 miles in less than 5.5 hours or walking 32 miles in less than 7 hours: it must be one of these] train and achieve it.

Seek and find a companion and Initiate this individual [*Black Book*] and then undertake the workings with the spheres and pathways with this person.

Begin to teach this individual the Star Game, and use the game together.

Undertake the Grade Ritual of External Adept.

*The first stage is the awakening of the darker/unconscious aspects within the psyche. These aspects/energies are identified with in the rite of Initiation and then symbolised in the workings with the spheres and pathways following Initiation. These workings give practical experience of the darker forces/energies. The Star Game begins the process of objectifying these energies in a more conscious way: giving greater insight and control. and this is the beginning of self-awareness since the Tree of Wyrd is symbolic of individual consciousness. both unconscious/acausal ('sinister') and causal. as well as representing the forces/energies beyond the individual psyche.

The setting of a physical goal. by the Initiate, and the training to achieve it. is important because it enhances the vitality and developes personal qualities important to the magickian: determination, elan and so on. This task must be undertaken, for without it, the Initiate stage is not complete.

The seeking. finding and working with a companion begins the confrontation with the 'anima/animus' energies/archetypes resulting in practical experience of them as well as enabling the use of sexual magickal formulae [qv. 'Rite of Nine Angles', etc.]. This is a very important part of developing self-awareness, and the 'ritualized' setting enables both practical experience and the possibility of developing self-insight. (This 'ritualized' setting is first the workings with the spheres and pathways, use of Star Game, and then later the organization of a Temple [see below].)

External Adept:

Tasks: Organize a magickal group/Temple for the performance of ceremonial rituals as given in the *Black Book* – the Ext. Adept as the 'Master'/Mistress of this Temple, the companion as the 'Mistress/'Master'.

It is the task of the new External Adept to find suitable members, Initiate them and so on. Regular sunedrions should be held [*Black Book*, for details. The Ext. Adept is called a 'Choregos' while running the Temple.].

After the group has been run for c. 3-6 months, the Ext. Adept should set another but more demanding physical goal, train and achieve it. [For example, running a marathon in less than 3 hrs (men) or 3hrs 30 (women); cycling 100 miles in less than 5 hrs (4:45 if really determined) or walfing 50 miles in 13 hrs.]

After running the Temple for between 6-12 months, choose a Priest and Priestess from the group to run the Temple while the Grade Ritual of Internal Adept is being undertaken.

¤Notes: The titles assumed by the Ext. Adept, the companion and those appointed 'by the Ext. Adept to positions within the Temple such as Priest and Priestess, are purely honourary, and do not signify the achievement of the magickal grade associated with that title in the 'Seven Fold Way'. It is one of the tasks of the Ext. Adept ('Choregos') in running the Temple to appoint suitable members to fulfill the positions required by rituals (e.g. Priest, Altar-Priest, Thurifer and so on). It is up to the Choregos whether to inform members that the Temple is organized as part of the tasks/training of an Ext. Adept in the sinister path. If the Choregos decides to do so inform the members of this, then those members, should the Choregos so wish, may also begin to follow the tasks of the Seven Fold Way as above: the Choregos always keeping a step or two (in terms of Grades) ahead of them. No one can be appointed to the Grades themselves: not even by a Grand Master – the Grades must be achieved by each and every individual, the only exception being

Initiation. Initiation may be given, according to the ceremonial ritual [*Black Book*] by anyone of the grade of External Adept and above who organizes a Temple, provided that the Initiate completes the initiate tasks as above.

The final task of an External Adept is to prepare for and undertake the Grade Ritual of Internal Adept.

*The tasks of an External Adept develope both magickal and personal skills. The organizing and running of a Temple brings further magickal experience as well as enables several archetypal roles to be lived, this living vitalizing (partly through the energy of the archetypes) the individual, enabling greater magick. One of the roles is that of the 'shadow' – the sinister magickian adept at ritual. The personal qualities developed include manipulation, the charisma of power and sexual/material pleasures. There is also a growing self-awareness, and understanding of archetypal energies as well as the further confrontations with the anima/animus. There may also be glimmerings of the unique wyrd of the individual – a wyrd revealed through the ritual of Internal Adept.

Internal Adept:
Tasks: Depending on the wyrd of the individual, either continue with and expand the Temple (training Initiates in the Seven Fold Way and so on) or begin the personal tasks revealed by the Grade Ritual.

Study of and training in Esoteric Chant [Note: this may be undertaken earlier, by an Initiate or External Adept if an aptitude exists and someone of or above the Grade of Internal Adept is willing to give instruction.].

Study of Advanced Star Game and esoteric, aeonic aspects of both forms of the game ['cliology' etc.].

Preparation for and undertaking of Nine Angles rituals: 'natural' and/or 'chthonic' according to desire.

Further training of companion up to and including Grade Ritual of Internal Adept, if required.

Prepare for and undertake Grade Ritual of Abyss.

Master/Mistress:
The fundamental tasks of this Grade are three-fold: the teaching to suitable individuals of the Seven Fold Way either on an individual basis or via an organized Temple; the performance of Aeonic magick, and development of proficiency in the Star Game, particularly the advanced form.

Some may opt to specialize in a particular field.

■■■

¤General Notes:
The Initiate stage lasts between six months to a year. The External Adept stage lasts from one to three years. The Internal Adept stage lasts from three to seven years.

Fundamental books, manuscripts etc:
- *The Black Book of Satan* [Re-issued 1989 ev: a complete guide to sinister ceremonial rituals and organizing a Temple] 63 pages
- *Naos* [A guide to hermetic workings, basic septenary system and the Star Game] 65 pages
- Azoth[An introduction to more advanced septenary workings] 38 pages
- Falcifer [A fictional account of noviciate training] 103 pages
- Temple of Satan [A fictional account of confrontation with anima/aminus in a sinister context] 109 pages
- Advanced Star Game 5 page MS
- The Forbidden Alchemy 4 page MS [Note: published in 'Fenrir' no.8]
- Rite of the Nine Angles (and other Order MSS)

INSIGHT ROLES – A GUIDE

As stated in several esoteric Order MSS, the Satanic novice is expected to undertake experiences in the real world. This is above and beyond the tasks mentioned in the various guides to the 'seven-fold Way', which guides were intended for publication and thus did not contain the secret tasks. These secret tasks are outlined in the MSS 'The Secret Tasks of the Sinister Way.' One of these tasks, undertaken by an Initiate, is an 'Insight Role'.

An Insight Role is in effect an extended magickal ritual and involves the individual living in a certain way and striving for a specific (often non-esoteric) goal. It involves playing a specific 'role'. The novice is expected to learn from this experience. It is important that the novice identifies with the role to the extent that friends/associates and those the novice is brought into contact with by virtue of that role do not realize the novice is playing a 'role'. For the duration of the Insight Role, the task of that role should be the main interest/occupation of the novice. Insight Roles, as a technique, have been used by Satanic novices for at least a century, and this technique has as its primary aim the gaining of self-insight by the novice using the technique. The technique also developes certain skills – some magickal, some involving the gaining of Satanic judgement and insight. Expressed simply, Insight Roles develope Satanic character.

Until quite recently, Insight Roles were wide-ranging and also exceptionally difficult to undertake – the novice was expected to undertake a role which was the opposite of what they considered their own character to be. [qv. the now deleted Order MS 'Insight Roles' I &II]. The technique, however, has been recently revised by the Grand Master representing traditional groups. In this revised form, it is an extremely effective noviciate technique, although (like all genuine esoteric techniques of Satanic magick) it is still difficult to undertake and still requires a genuine Satanic commitment from the novice. Like the Sinister Way itself, it is not for the dilettantes or the imitation 'Satanists' who merely wish to play at being Black Magickians.

One essential aspect of an Insight Role is that it requires the novice to change their life-style and usually their place of residence. Another, is that it tends to isolate them from non-Satanists. Third, it often brings them into conflict and confrontation – with others, and themselves. Fourth, it tests them – forcing them to find inner strengths and reserves. Or, of course, it destroys them – or makes them renounce their Satanic quest and vows. All these are necessary.

All Insight Roles are demanding; some are physically dangerous. All force the novice to make choices- to learn. All, when successfully undertaken, build self-confidence and thus character. All, in brief, express Satanism in action.

The novice is expected to make his/her own choice from the roles outlined below. It must be understood that: (a) only the roles listed below are actually Insight Roles, so the choice must of one of them; (b) the completion of at least one of these roles is necessary before the Internal Adept rite can be undertaken.

It is usual for the novice to undertake an Insight Role following Initiation and after the completion of the tasks outlined in the MS 'The Seven Fold Way A Comprehensive Guide' (i.e. after completion of the tasks associated with the stage of Initiation and before undertaking the rite of External Adept).

However, if the novice Wishes, an Insight Role can be undertaken when he/she is an External Adept and has completed all the tasks of an External Adept (such as running a Satanic Temple for a certain period of time). Generally, it is advisable for the novice to undertake a role before External Adept. Further, should the novice so desire, two Insight Roles can be undertaken, one after the other. This is an interesting experience – but requires a demonic commitment.

During some of the roles, the novice should try and keep their Satanic views and beliefs secret, and become in fact a shape-changer, a chameleon.

The Roles:

1. Either by foot or by bicycle or by accepting lifts, travel alone around the world, taking between six months to one year (or more). You must live frugally, and carry with you most of what you need. You should travel to as many countries as possible, the more remote the better and expect sometimes to find work to enable you to travel further.

2. Become a professional burglar, targeting only victims who have revealed themselves to be suitable (e.g. by testing them – qv. the Order MSS dealing with victims etc.). The aim is to specialize in a particular area – e.g. Fine Art, jewellery – and become an 'expert' in that area and in the techniques needed to gain items.

3. Undertake the role of extreme political activist and so champion heretical views (by, e.g. becoming involved in extreme Right-Wing activism). The aim is to express fanaticism in action and be seen by all 'right-thinking people' as an extremist, and a dangerous one.

4. Join the Police Force (assuming you meet the requirements) and so experience life at 'the sharp end' and being a servant of a higher authority.

All roles should last for at least six months and all must be completed (i.e. you leave them) before the end of eighteen months. All the roles will by their very nature test your Satanic Views and beliefs and thus your desire to continue along the sinister way. All will expose you to difficulties. Once the choice is made, it is up to you to find means of undertaking the role – e.g. in the case of joining the Police, finding reasons why which will convince a selection panel; in the case of becoming a burglar, finding someone to buy your stolen items and so on.

The essence of these Insight Roles can be succinctly stated: *Incipit Vitriol.*

ONA 1989 ev

• Note: In times of actual War, an alternative Insight Role is to join one of the Armed Forces and so gain combat experience.

THE SECRET TASKS OF THE SINISTER WAY

The Order MS 'The Seven Fold Sinister Way – A Comprehensive Guide' details the tasks and so on which an individual following the sinister path must undertake in order to reach Adeptship and beyond. That 'Guide', however, is exoteric. There are, in addition, esoteric tasks to be undertaken. These tasks have remained secret by virtue of their nature – they represent genuine Satanism in action and as such often are 'a-moral'. Such esoteric tasks are revealed following a Satanic Initiation.

Further, to understand these tasks, it is necessary for the Initiate to be familiar with, and in agreement with, the secret teachings explicated in the various esoteric MSS – for example, 'The Hard Reality of Satanism', 'Satanism, Sacrifice & Crime', 'Culling – A Guide to Sacrifice', 'Guidelines for the Testing of Opfers', 'Victims – a Sinister Expose', 'The Practice of Evil in Context'.

For a long time, the matters mentioned in these secret MSS were transmitted only on an oral basis it being forbidden for the teachings and practices so transmitted to be written down or divulged to non-Initiates. However, as explained elsewhere, this has now changed.

Accordingly, this MS will detail the secret tasks which a Satanic novice must undertake as part of their commitment to Satanism. That is, these tasks – and the others detailed in the MS 'The Seven Fold Sinister Way – A Comprehensive Guide' – are both required and necessary: without them, there can be no genuine advancement along the way, for such tasks develope that character and those abilities which are Satanic and which thus represent the presencing of the dark forces on Earth via the agency (or vehicle) of the Satanist.

As has been stated many times, genuine Satanism requires commitment – it requires self-effort, by the Initiate, over a period of years. It involves ordeals, the achievement of difficult goals, the participation in pleasures and the living of life in certain ways. Only thus are self-insight and genuine Occult abilities born – only thus is an Adept created.

Neophyte:
Before Initiation and after undertaking the tasks of a Neophyte as given in the 'Guide' MS:

(a) find an area where game is plentiful and, equipping yourself with either a cross-bow or an ordinary bow (such as a longbow) hunt/stalk some suitable game and make a kill. Skin and prepare this game yourself (if necessary 'hanging' the game until it is ready) and (when ready) cook and eat it.

'Game' in this context means [for the U.K.] venison, hare, rabbit, partridge, pheasant, wildfowl and so on. In effect, you are assuming the 'role' of hunter.

(b) obtain from a Nazarene place of worship, some 'hosts'. If you are seeking Initiation into an established group, this will be your test of fidelity (etc.) and the hosts will be used in the celebration of the Black Mass. If you are undertaking a self-Initiation (as for example given in *The Black Book of Satan*) then immediately following this rite you should trample on or otherwise defile these 'hosts' (e.g. by urinating on them) saying 'By this deed I pledge myself to counter Nazarene filth and give myself, body, blood and soul, to Satan, Prince of Darkness.' You should then burn the hosts or what remains of them by placing them in a vessel containing flammable liquid and setting this alight, laughing while the burning seals your gesture and your oath.

Initiate:
After the rite or ceremony of Initiation and following completion of the tasks as given in the 'Guide' MS, you should choose and undertake, for between six to eighteen months, an 'Insight Role'. [See the MS 'Insight Roles – A Guide'.]

External Adept:
(a) With the Temple (formed as one of the tasks of an External Adept – see the 'Guide') perform a Black Mass with hosts obtained by a neophyte of the Temple wishing Initiation.

(b) Train several members, and yourself in the undertaking of tests relevant to choosing an opfer. Select some suitable victims, using the general guidelines for so selecting, and undertake the relevant tests. The victim or victims having been chosen, perform The Death Ritual with the intent of eliminating by magickal means the chosen victim(s). Thereafter, and having completed all the necessary preparations, select a further victim using Aeonics or sinister strategy as a guide and undertake a culling either during a suitable rite (e.g. the Ceremony of Recalling) or via practical means. You may elect to do this latter yourself, or you may nominate a trusted, suitable member in good standing to undertake this for the glory of the Temple, using a method of your own devising. At the same time. perform a Death Ritual.

It must be stressed: (i) the victims must be chosen according to Satanic principles as given in the various Order MSS; (ii) those chosen must be tested according to Satanic principles as given in the relevent MSS; (iii) the acts or acts of culling may arise from your own implementation of Satanic strategy and tactics or from one of the members of your Temple who is fulfilling Satanic wyrd by some role or Satanic act, that member having elected to follow the sinister path in a committed way.

Beyond External Adept, there are no secret tasks of a prescribed nature, for those following the sinister path to undertake.

These secret tasks, together With the tasks and ordeals and rites described in the 'Guide' and explained in detail in the books *Naos* and *The Black Book of Satan* (and explicated in the various Order MSS contained in *Hostia I/II* and *Hysteron Proteron*) represent the Way of

27

Satan. They are Satanic. As such, they are fitting only to a minority. Some who profess to be Satanists (and who may be seeking a Satanic Initiation in an established Order) will read them, or hear of them, and be surprised, perhaps even appalled. 'They are not necessary' they or some others will say, fearing to really begin following the reality of the Left Handed Path as marked out by those tasks. But Satanism and the Left Handed Path are as they are – dark, dangerous, difficult and full of diabolic ecstasies. So it is, so it has been and so shall it be – to enable evolution while the fearful majorities in their sloth and delusions continue their morbid existence.

ONA

SELLING WATER BY THE RIVER

Question: What is Satanism?

Answer: Satanism is Fundamentally a way of living – a practical philosophy of life. The essence of this way is the belief that we all as individuals can achieve far more than we realize during our lifetime. Most people waste the opportunities that life can, does and Can be made to bring. We are gods when we awake.

Q: How do you then understand magick?

A: Magick is essentially the opening up of areas of consciousness latent within all – a means of changing the individual and the world. The techniques of magick (for example, rituals) are simply means to achieve this. For too long magick has been mis-understood as 'spells, conjurations' and the like, and while such things are magick, they are only a beginning, a mere intimation of what real magick is all about.

Q: You often use the term 'traditional Satanism'. What does this mean?

A: Traditional Satanism is a term used to describe the sinister path which for centuries was taught on an individual basis from Master (or Mistress) to pupil. To this path belongs the Septenary System, Esoteric Chant, the comprehensive training of novices (including the development of the physical side), the Star Game, and most importantly – the Internal system of magick (the Grade Rituals etc.). This path is also known as the Seven-Fold Way.

Q: I've heard of La Vey and his 'Satanic Bible'. How does the Seven-Fold Way differ from his Satanism and those who follow his views?

A. La Vey took what may be described as the popular/media conception of Satanism – the black-robed, Mephisthophelean figure – together with the 'pleasure principle' and some simple magic{k), mixed it with the qabala and various historical myths and legends pertaining to the dark side, and served the whole lot up to a gullible audience. The whole thing was pretty pathetic – although it did provide some with a few thrills. There was no substance to either La Vey or his 'Church': no inner path, direction or way. Nothing original.

The Seven-Fold Way, on the contrary, possesses direction, and goes far beyond the external type of magick implicit in both the 'pleasure principle' and ordinary sorcery. It offers the individual the difficult (and sometimes dangerous) path to genuine Adeptship – to self-mastery, self-excellence and ultimately wisdom. It is not a refuge for the neurotic, the weak-willed or the self-deluded, but rather a challenge to the daring. Those who follow in the foot-steps of La Vey (as a recent 'Temple' does) have added little – they are still trapped by 'role-playing', still fettered by self-delusion (often about their magickal abilities) and still lack not only self-insight but also that spontaneity which is one of the marks of a genuine Adept. They concern themselves still with the awarding of meaningless titles, seek members and the recognition of the 'authorities'. They teach the same historical mish-mash as La Vey and possess an originality quota of zero.

They have failed to understand that the ceremonial, ritualistic and 'theoretical' approach is but the first small step toward inner progress. Because of this, there can be no organized 'Temple', no 'authority' within it, no proselytizing and no awarding of grades/initiation or titles. There is only – in the genuine path – a limited amount of guidance, and the struggle of the individual through experience.

Q: But surely rituals are important – e.g. the Black Mass?

A: Yes – but only in the beginning stages of the Way when the novice/initiate is discovering the hidden (or magickal) forces of nature and themselves, and is daring to walk along the' path to Adepthood.

Ceremonial and hermetic rituals are the province of the novice and the 'External Adept' and are pointers to what is beyond.

Q: Which is what?

A: First, the discovery of the unique Destiny of that individual, second the living of that Destiny, and third, for those whose Destiny becomes fulfilled by such living, the crossing of the Abyss. From the Abyss the Master and Mistress is born. All this takes many years.

Q: What then is the purpose of your Order?

A: To offer our teachings and guidance to those who might be interested. In former times, teachings were kept secret, but there is no need for that now: the opportunity is open to all.

Q: But are you not still secretive?

A: Yes and no. Those who seek hard enough will find us, and those who are sincere will not be put off by the obstacles placed in their way (sometimes by us). For those who are, there are plenty of other groups around.

Q: What about Initiations?

A: We do not offer Initiation – candidates achieve Initiation. We do not offer nor award (for money or anything else)Grade Rituals or titles of any kind: these are again achieved by individuals, through their own toil, hardships, terror and joy. We simply guide them toward the self-achievement that, e.g., the Grade Rituals represent. Any other way is simply fraud and self-deception. Grade Rituals – which signify the different stages of achievement along the Seven-Fold Way – may be likened to running in a race. You either race, or don't; and if you race, you either win (achieve the goal) or do not. You may pretend to yourself that you have raced and run, but in the end you are fooling only yourself.

Q: What, then, are the Grade Rituals?

A: They are tasks, simple in form, but difficult to complete successfully. For example, the Grade Ritual of Internal Adept simply involves the candidate in living totally alone and isolated for at least three months: without any of our modern 'conveniences'/technology, and without speaking to anyone. Simple to describe – difficult to undertake. The 'ritual' is the (alchemical) change which occurs in the individual by virtue of living so for at least three months. Such primitive isolation creates the Adept, bringing a genuine mastery of magick and a lasting self-insight. It is the intention of the Order to publish all the Grade Rituals in the next issue of *Fenrir*.

Q: Returning now to the popular conception of Satanism, what about sacrifices, the blackmailing of members, sexual crimes and so on?

A: Satanism is all about – in its beginnings – making conscious (or liberating) our dark or shadow nature. In the past, certain experiences were often undergone in order to achieve this, and some of those experiences were often frowned on by 'conventional' society. Some might have been 'illegal' at the time as well. But gradually (at least in traditional Satanism) a way was found to 'short-circuit' these evolutionary experiences which enhanced the consciousness and thus wisdom of those undergoing them – if they survived, of course. Thus was Internal Magick evolved. This enabled the experiencing of the dark side, and its integration, as well as made possible what was beyond. This system had been gradually refined and enhanced, and while it avoids the quicksand of criminality it is still not lacking in danger or difficulty. It offers, in short, the distilled essence of thousands of years of evolutionary understanding – and makes possible the next stage of our evolution as a species: *Homo Galactica*.

Q: You stress the development of the physical side. Why?

A: Because traditional Satanism aims to develop the whole individual – mind, body and character. We give our novices difficult physical goals to achieve (such as running 20 miles in under 2t hours – fitter individuals are naturally given more difficult tasks) because the striving for such goals, and their achievement, develops qualities necessary in any Adept. They are tests of determination and character, and sort the serious out from the pathetic. The striving also creates a physical joy, increasing the vitality of the person.

Q: I met someone recently who claimed to be a 'Master'. I had my doubts about him. Is there some way of identifying a genuine Master?

A: The answer should be obvious. A Master is someone who has passed beyond the Abyss, the stage beyond an Adept. In consequence he will be somewhat detached: intense and serious, but also natural, spontaneous and quite cheerful (almost playful, sometimes). But perhaps most of all, he will not take himself too seriously, and he will certainly not playa 'role' or fulfil the expectations of novices (e.g. by dressing up, cultivating a 'demonic' stare and answering questions mysteriously). He will possess that illusive quality – natural charisma.

Q: What about wealth – and power? Surely all Satanic Masters possess these?

A: Some do, some do not. The sign of a Master is neither wealth nor power, but achievement – of wisdom, skill in esoteric arts, and original creation (e.g. the extending of human knowledge, artistic creativity). The Destiny of each master is different, as is the life-style which reflects that Destiny. For example, out of the four Masters who exist in the West at this moment in time, one lives a somewhat isolated existence with hardly any material possessions, while another lives in relative luxury and splendour. The former concerns himself primarily with aeonic magick, while the latter teaches a few pupils. Genuine Masters do not conform to someone else's expectations or ideas: they are individual, and unique.

Q: Do you worship a being called Satan?

A: Genuine Satanists do not worship anything – not even themselves. Fundamental to Satanism is a desire to overcome, to accept challenges and to seek to know and understand. A genuine Satanist would rather die – laughing and defiant – than submit to anyone or anything. Most people waste their lives and die old and miserable: the Satanist revels in life and adventure, and knows the right time to die, for challenges never end. This way of living is hard, and this way of dying breeds fear among the feeble multitude who prefer comfort and security to the ecstasy of living on the edge like gods.

As to Satan – each Initiate discovers the reality for themselves. All that need be said is that there external forces beyond the psyche of an individual: in genuine Satanist magick there is identity with these darker external forces, not a fear of them and certainly not a submission. This, of course, is somewhat dangerous – but the strong survive, and the weak perish. Good riddance to the weak.

Q: So, fundamentally, you would say that Satanism is the way you live your life?

A: Yes, as I indicated at the beginning. Magick – of whatever type – enhances your life, and is a way to knowledge and increased vitality. Magickal acts are important in the beginning, but most important of all is our attitude to life and our ways of living. This is why we despise the Nazarene philosophy – the Satanist is proud, strong, defiant, while a Nazarene is afraid of living, afraid of dying and mentally sick: weighed down by guilt and envy. The meek espouse peace because they know the strong would destroy them – so they infect the strong with the disease of 'pacifism', with guilt because they are strong...

Q: But surely that particular philosophy – of, as you call it, the 'Nazarene' – is dying out today.

A: As an organized religion it might be – but over the past two hundred or so years this poisonous philosophy has sprouted various political and psuedo-political forms, and it is these forms which are

34

eroding our vitality. There have been a few attempts to cut out the cancer – but they have unfortunately failed, and the cancer grows and spreads.

Q: What, then, can you do?

A: Why should we do anything? Most people are stupid and deserve their fate. We offer an alternative – those who have if only in a small way the Promethean spirit will be drawn to us and thus have the opportunity to master their own Destiny. It is up to each and every individual: we can point the way, but they must make the effort to walk along it.

SINISTER SHADOW MAGICK

Satanism is dark, and Satanists revel in evil. As a word, evil is regarded as deriving from the Gothic (via Old English) 'ubils' implying 'beyond' and 'going beyond due limits'. Later, the word – like so many others – was re-interpreted 'morally', in the abstract terms of Nazarene fundamentalism and 'evil' became a general term, applied to one's opponents and those excesses which timid and psychically ailing Nazarenes feared.

Genuine Satanists do evil, they cultivate evil: they are evil, in all senses of the term now accepted. Imitation Satanists, however, play mental and intellectual games: they enjoy the 'thrill' of calling themselves Satanists. Some go further, and may revel in a local notoriety, finding a vicarious pleasure in being known as a 'Satanist'. But these imposters do no evil – in fact, they explain (quite often) that Satanism has been misunderstood and is really rather a 'moral religion' (or something of the kind), perhaps even an 'ethical knowledge'. Such people are pathetic and certainly not Satanists.

In the beginning, a genuine Satanist will cultivate evil on the personal level – by going to and thus finding his or her limits. This involves more than just going beyond the (accepted) limits imposed by society or whatever. It means experience, on the practical level, of evil and all that it implies. Later, when the Satanic novice has some experience and thus self-understanding and mastery, there is impersonal evil. The first is sinister shadow magick of the external and internal kind. The second is sinister shadow magick of the aeonic type – the manipulation, changing, of individuals and events on a not insignificant scale, that is, one which produces tangible results and often disruption/creation/evolution and thus continues the sinister dialectic of history. This is called 'shadow magick' not only because it is mostly secretly done, but also because it is dangerous, psychically and physically, involving as it does acts of defiance against the restrictions imposed by all other forms and individuals.

Neither of these mean a type of juvenile 'rebellion' nor purely 'mental' acts (achieved by ritual or anything else). They mean a directed, calculating, purposeful involvement in real life and situations: for the beginner Satanist (the novice) just as much as the Adept. What differs, is the aim at first, it is personal, to aid self-mastery, understanding and thus build Satanic character; then, it is impersonal or aeonic. Thus one image of the genuine Satanist – someone in control, seeking more mastery of life; seeking more challenges and goals and insights.

Let me be explicit so I cannot be misunderstood.

1) The Satanic novice will aspire – to what is beyond, in all things. This means practical experience, testing Destiny and achieving difficult goals in the personal life. It means real danger in the real world, not cheap manufactured 'thrills' of self-induced stupour and loss of control – but rather, life and liberty threatening situations. These may be and often are amoral, illegal and evil – all laws are fundamentally an accumulation of tireless attempts to stop creative individuals making life into instants of poetry'.

Naturally, some guidance may be needed – it is easy to become lost, directionless, or caught – and this is where the advice of a more experienced Satanic Adept may be useful. However, the acts of a Satanist are not random nor motiveless and neither do they arise from any weakness of character nor uncontrolled desire. Instead, they arise from fulfilling Satanic wyrd – or, viewed another way, from presencing the energies of 'darkness'/Satan on the Earth in accord with sinister intent.

An example will explicate this. A Satanic novice, having developed to a certain extent via ordeals such as Grade Rituals, the achievement of personal, physical goals and the organizing and running of a Satanic Temple, desires to go further. For this, practical experience and some guidance is needed. Let us assume the novice is advised or chooses to use a political form to achieve this experience – and thus becomes involved with radical 'right-wing' politics because such people already possess an element or two of Satanic spirit, the 'other sides' in this form and at this moment in the history of this aeon representing the Nazarene disease in another guise.

Thus, she takes part in direct political actions – this is both exciting and dangerous, given the prevailing sickness of this age. Gradually, she acquires practical experience 'on the edge', and hopefully some real, tangible enemies, if she is performing right. These enemies probably hate her for her political views – and some of them may even try to harm her personally.

Thus, one or more of them deserve to die – or at least come to some harm, psychically if not physically. For they not only threaten her own Destiny and thus achievement but also Satanic wyrd, because she by her actions is fulfilling higher, Satanic goals (in simple terms, presencing the darker forces via a tangible form). This fulfilling is expressed in the form she is guided toward or chooses for herself via a knowledge of Aeonics. On the practical level, she can and should undertake magickal rites (such as the Death Ritual) to aid her – but other means can be used, such as assassination. She may wish to do this herself, or she may manipulate others into doing it. The result is the same – personal experience and development, and aeonic energies presenced via the execution of the act.

Thus is her own evolution, and that of the acausal or sinister, furthered. Given the nature of the form chosen, this Satanic novice, by using such a form to the utmost of her ability (that is, seeing it as fulfilling a part of her own Destiny – conventionally, 'believing in the correctness of the views so espoused') goes beyond the norms of society and its herd majority and thus achieves personal knowledge of the illegal and the forbidden (in that society).

2) Beyond this, when Adeptship is attained by experiences such as the foregoing, the Satanist will try and open a nexion – to directly access acausal energies on Earth via rites such as Nine Angles etc. This is the beginning of aeonic shadow magick – and this involves an even greater commitment to change than before, on the practical

38

level. What form or forms this takes depends on individual wyrd, dis-covered by the Grade Ritual of Internal Adept and prepared for by previous rites, and experiences. It may be political, as it may be the use/manipulation of archetypal forms/ images with sinister intent – or involve using 'religion' as a Satanic instrument of change. Whatever the form, the changes are supra-personal they effect more than a few individuals. In fact, they radically disrupt existing forms and norms. For example, a political form may be chosen and used.

After some time, violence, riots somewhere, the spread of a new idea... The rising of a type of State in essence inspired with sinister energies and thus contributing to aeonic evolution... Perhaps a war. To propitiate with blood the darker forces...

Thus it will be understood that Satanists act in a directed way. Whether they are novices. or Adepts. Their evil has a purpose (as Satan Himself does as do THEY who are beyond Him have a purpose. on this Earth). The acts, and the evil. arise from a Satanic desire and understanding made real in a practical form or forms. The going beyond, the evil, are part of Satanic wyrd – on the personal and aeonic level. I repeat – they are not direction less , motiveless acts, nor do they arise because the person doing them is somehow inadequate or weak or in the thrall of some uncontrolled desire.[1] The Satanist is controlled – knowledgeable, particularly about themselves and what Satanism means in supra-personal terms. They are part of history – participants in a sinister dialectic of surpra-aeonic proportions, and aware of the power of the sinister to change both themselves and those forms which others through the ages have created to shape our evolution or which [like the Nazarene disease] hinder our evolution.

---

[1] The conventional description of Satanic deeds and 'crime': most so-called Satanic crimes are acts by dabblers who have no self-insight and even less self-control; the rest, results from acts by characterless, insipid morons who are weak. Such description and such attributions arise from a fundamental misunderstanding of genuine Satanic acts.

Have I been understood? Does this sound the death-bell for the imitation Satanists? γνωση τεκνησ σημεια τησ εμησ κλυων. It is a pity that this, like Satanism, is so often misunderstood and mistranslated.

ONA

GUIDE TO BLACK MAGICK

According to traditional Satanism, magick may be divided into three forms: external magick, internal magick, and aeonic magick.

External Magick

This is results magick or sorcery and it is the magick of the Initiate and External Adept. It itself exists in two forms: ceremonial and hermetic.

Ceremonial is ritual magick – ceremonies and rites where more than two individuals are involved. Ceremonial magick can be done for basically two reasons: to create/draw down and then direct magickal energy for a specific aim (e.g. cursing), or to represent through words and symbolism the myths/knowledge of a particular tradition or cultus. Sometimes, however, the energy generated by a symbolic rite can be directed to a specific end – as in the Black Mass. Hermetic rituals usually involve one or two individuals ('sex magick' is usually hermetic) and are generally done extempore. They require those undertaking them to possess or be capable of developing during the ritual. An empathy with the forces/energies employed, as well as possessing the necessary desire to direct the forces/energies. In contradistinction, ceremonial rituals are usually written down and when performed a set text is followed, with only minor variations to allow for the emotion of the moment.

Internal Magick

This is when magickal techniques (e.g. Grade Rituals) are used to alter the consciousness of an individual. The rites of internal magick 'open the gates' between the causal and the acausal, and change the perception from 'ego' consciousness to the 'self' and what is beyond. In the Jungian sense, internal magick produces 'individuation', and leads to Adepthood. The main rites of internal magick are the hermetic workings associated with the spheres and pathways of the Septenary Tree of Wyrd. and the Grade Ritual of Internal Adept which involves the individual living in isolation for at least three months. It is one of the main functions of established Orders and

Temples to prepare their members for internal magick and offer guidance along the way.

Aeonic Magick

This is the magick of the Master, the Mistress of Earth and the Magus, and its basis is an understanding of those forces which influence large numbers of people over long periods of time. On one level, aeonic magick is the alteration/distortion of such forces; on another, it is the 'creation' of new energies and their dispersion over the Earth to change conscious evolution. In one sense, this is the 'blackest' magick of all.

Satanism, as a way of magick, has no seasonal rites, no servitude or submission to any deity and no fear. There are thus in Satanic rites no defensive circles or measures of any kind: only an exultation in the forces of the rite, a prideful possession and mastery.

Rituals are often done at the time of the full moon because it helps one to see when the ritual is done outdoors and because it gives atmosphere to the rite. Sometimes, rites are conducted on or around the seasonal changes – solstice and equinox – because there is magickal energy present then (due to Earth's changes) and this energy can be harnessed. The same applies to planetary workings – the rising and setting of planets (astronomically calculated for the horizon of the observer – and not using the fraudulent 'planetary' tables given in most books). Such planetary energies exist – but are generally small, and have little effect on rituals done correctly. Most Occultists delude themselves about the nature and extent of these energies (this is particularly true of the Moon) to become sensitive to them is difficult in our shielded, technological society. Generally, only Adepts (and the naturally gifted) possess the required empathy. However, this said, the full moon is rightly associated with 'lunacy' and 'demonic' possession – as anyone who has worked nights at Mental Hospitals will testify. This power can also be harnessed during a ritual.

Celebratory rites in traditional Satanism are of two kinds – 1) those that express the energies of Satanism – e.g. the Black Mass,

Ceremony of Recalling – and whose performance thus distorts the currents of the Nazarenes and the Old Aeon; and 2) those which create new energies appropriate to the Satanic age of fire to come – e.g. invokations to the 'Dark Gods'.

The Black Mass is still celebrated simply because the Nazarenes (and their allies) are still powerful and still polluting us with their filth. It is still the main ceremonial rite performed on a regular basis by organized Temples, and – like all ceremonial rituals its performance gives identity to the Temple, strengthening the magickal and personal ties of the members as well as furthering the work of the Prince of Darkness because it is a rite of Black Magick.

The mysteries of the Nine Angles form an important aspect of genuine Black Magick. On the physical level, the nine represent energy Vibrations – for according to tradition, a crystal shaped like a tetrahedron responds to voice vibration of the correct pitch and intensity. In simple terms, the crystal amplifies the power of thought and produces magickal change. Quartz gives the best results, although spinel may be used. The tetrahedron shape has to be created from the natural material by a skilled operator.

On another level, the nine symbolize (that is, re-present) the progression of Aeons and thus the Aeonic energies. The representation is that of the nine combinations of the three alchemical substances $[\alpha(\alpha), \alpha(\beta), \alpha(\gamma)$ etc.] over the seven fundamental levels, these levels being the spheres of the septenary 'Tree of Wyrd'. The Star Game is a physical representation of these symbols the seven boards are the spheres, and the pieces are the alchemical variations. (It should be noted that the nine main variations spread over the seven spheres also represent an individual – their consciousness, life and wyrd.) Thus the magick or 'sorcery' of the Star Game an imitation (magickally done) of an Aeon or individual whose change (the moves of the Star Game) is manipulated by the magickian (the 'player' of the Game). The Star Game has two sets of twenty-seven pieces – one set white, the other black, representing the two aspects of cosmic Change (or the causal and acausal). These pieces are spread over the seven boards.

The Nine Angles also symbolize the seven plus two gates (or spheres) that join our causal universe with the acausal (or 'magickal') universe. The seven are the spheres of the Tree of Wyrd (zones of magickal energy), and the other two are the Abyss – where the causal and acausal meet in temporary stasis – and the acausal itself, which is beyond even the Tree. The Abyss, in the septenary system, lies between the spheres of Sun and Mars, and its crossing is the ordeal of the Adept and the genesis of the Master/Mistress of Earth. It signifies the beginning of acausal perception.

The other important form of Black Magick is to do with self-survival after death. This can be done in two ways, depending on the aim of the operator. The first is transference of the essence of self-hood, near the moment of physical death, into another physical body, ensuring thus the continuation of existence on the physical level. The second in passing the acausal Gate – creating an existence entirely in the acausal dimensions.

The first involves finding a suitable body to inhabit; the second has some resemblance to the creation of the 'diamond body' in some of the esoteric schools of Taoism and it is this form which is generally undertaken by the Adept. The first is sometimes done as a temporary measure or if the wyrd of the individual compels completion of some task on the physical.

The process of the first involves the creation of a strong 'astral self' – via chant and visualization and strengthened through acts of magick over a period of time, sometimes using a crystal tetrahedron to ensure the right amount of magickal energy. Thus an 'astral double' is created – and this energy is most usually stored in a crystal until the time for transfer. Meanwhile, a donor should have been found – a good, healthy specimen.

The psyche of this donor is then infiltrated through both astral and physical contact. The actual transfer occurs during a ritual with both donor and operator present (the former may be hypnotized or drugged or otherwise enticed) consciousness being transferred to the 'double' which then ousts the weakened psyche of the donor. The second form is actually the next stage of conscious evolution – and the goal of the Adept.

What it is important to realize about traditional Satanism is what is meant by 'Satan'. Traditional Satanists regard Satan as not simply a symbol of self-consciousness, but rather as a representative of those supra-personal forces beyond the individual psyche.

To see 'Satan' as simply a self-symbol – as two recent 'satanic' groups do – is, firstly, to be self-deluded about the nature of cosmic forces, and second, to make (or attempt to make) Black Magick tame and safe. To deal with greater forces is to court danger – psychologically and physically. Traditional Satanists see this danger as a means: the strong survive and the weak perish; this simply being a reflection of genuine Satanist philosophy rather than the tame view spewed forth by the imitation and toy 'satanists' who abound today.

Satan – in traditional Satanism – is never represented pictorially, and apprehension of the physical or causal manifestation of our Prince is an experience that each Satanic novice achieves for themselves by undertaking rites of Black Magick according to the dark tradition. This apprehension mayor may not change when the new Master or Mistress of Earth is born via the ordeal of the Abyss, and it is up to each and every Adept to undergo this experience since the reality cannot be taught – only experienced in the primal Chaos that is the Abyss. What pictorial representations that are used, are those of the forms sometimes chosen by the Shape-Changer himself, for the Prince of Darkness must have his fun with feeble mortals. It is important to realize also that the name 'Satan' is not His real name – it is a convenient epithet, used because it expresses part of His nature. There is, in fact, no real 'name' as we understand names –

only perhaps a sound vibration (which cannot really be written down) which summons Him to our consciousness and our world. In a sense which few people will understand, Satan is the essence of the acausal: the cosmic force of Chaos whose intrusion into our causal dimensions disrupts the entropy that linear time produces. Our species requires and has required symbols to enable apprehension and evolution – and this is true also of the Initiate (and to a lesser extent of the Adept) who belong to that lower order. The Abyss destroys – or creates a new species, a new 'mind' capable of functioning on levels not normally accessible to those of the lower order.

and the most potent symbol of certain cosmic forces has been, and still is, Satan In reality, Satan (who has a secret or 'genuine' name known to all Initiates) concerns Himself generally only with Aeonic magick – the changing of this world. Through Him, the Masters and Mistresses work Internal Magick, and through their Orders, Initiates undertake rites of External Magick, to the glory of His name.

SATANIC INFLUENCE – A MODERN TALE

It is a fact – seldom fully understood and appreciated – that most individuals follow the creative lead of a few. It is also true that some of this majority absorb the creativity of others and bring it forth again, sometimes slightly altered, to claim it as their own – and that this whole majority needs the stimulus of new forms, ideas and ways, born via a creative genius or two, to vitalize them and begin the process of internal and external change.

The recent history of Satanism gives evidence for this. Various types of Satanism have emerged over the centuries, as have various exponents of it. Historically, Satanism is often taken to be – by those unacquainted with the Left Handed Path – as Diabolism, that is, the invokation of the Devil and the making of a pact with Him. This is evidenced in the medieval Grimoires and in those who were accused of such things. Later, various individuals were regarded as 'Satanic' and as teaching a form of Satanism, the most familiar being A. Crowley, Esq. Still later, various organizations emerged, each claiming to be Satanic and each teaching what they called was authentic Satanism. The most significant of these are the Church of Satan (Anton LaVey), the Temple of Set (Michael Aquino) and the Order of Nine Angles (ONA).

Diabolism: Central to all forms, is fear – of the powers, entities invoked. Hence the use of various forms of protection such as 'circles'. The 'pact' so familiar from the Grimoires and accounts of Diabolism was one between a Master (The Devil) and a servant (the sorcerer). Implicit in all forms of Grimoire-type Satanism is the belief (deriving from Nazarene religion) of Satan as a fallen angel ruled over, ultimately, by 'God' – there is always the possibility of being 'saved'. The archetypal Diabolist was a lapsed or practicing Nazarene whose conjurations brought excitement and a sense of the 'forbidden'.

Crowleyism: While 'Thelema' as a doctrine and belief is regarded by many non-Occultists as 'Satanic', there is very little real Satanism in it or indeed in Crowley's own life and works. The work of Crowley is, in many ways, a continuation of the Eastern-influenced esoteric groups and societies active before and during his own time – a type of Westernized Tantra heavily imbued with qabalism. The archetypal follower of Crowley is someone versed in Occult doctrines and mysticism who seeks through sex and other rites certain states of consciousness and who is orientated toward a belief in 'Thelema' as a new faith/creed.

Church of Satan: The church achieved a high media-profile due to the showmanship of LaVey. He expounded a philosophy of unenlightened egotism and self-interest together with a belief in carnality. The rituals were in the tradition of the Grimoires and imbued with qabalistic symbolism/notions (including some deriving from Crowley). Further, the Devil was dispensed with as an external Power – making the LaVey type of Satanism more of a practical belief system than a dangerous (in Occult terms) undertaking.

Temple of Set: The Temple was and is an essentially intellectual development of the Church of Satan. To the original was added an intellectual infrastructure (deriving in part from various mythologies and traditions) and an organizational structure with the aim of making Satanism a new 'religion' acceptable to a significant number of individuals. Both the Church of Satan and the Temple of Set (the latter more so than the former) insist upon belief in their own version of Satanism – and expect the adherent/member to accept/conform. There is thus a fostering of dependance by the individual upon the group (and in particular the leader(s) and Master).

Order of Nine Angles: The Order first emerged to public view in the early 1980's (eh) and basically taught that Satanism was a means to attain self and Occult insight and abilities, and that this could only be done on an individual basis via direct, personal, experience.

The archetypal Church of Satan member was a black-robed figure who played a 'role' and who placed ego-fulfillment and pleasure before everything. La Vey was accepted as a 'Master' and an authority to be revered – and a personality cult developed.

The archetypal Temple of Set member is someone who has read a lot of Occult literature, who engages in discussions with others about their beliefs and practices, and who likes the charisma and appeal of being a 'Satanist'. often, they dress for the part – and need a group identity, a sense of 'belonging'. They also accept Temple authority and are content to let an organization confer advancement upon them (in the form of titles and positions).

The archetypal ONA member is the lone sorcerer/sorceress struggling via practical (and sometimes dark) experiences toward self-attainment, guided by the teachings of the Order and by an occasional meeting with someone who has gone that way before.

Each of the above manifestations will be considered in turn. But what, then, is Satanism? By what criteria can such manifestations be judged?

First, let us consider what Satanism is not. It is not an acceptance of conventional morality or ways of living; it is not a belief, or faith, which causes a rejection of the reality (and harshness) of life; it is not a refuge for the failures, the cowards and the weak ... Satanism is about pride, an acceptance of individual worth. It is about defiance challenging the accepted, seeking to know the unknown and seeking the discover, to explore and to conquer: a refusal or bow down or give in. It is about excellence – of going beyond what is, in personal terms; of achieving a greater awareness and understanding than the majority.

It is a desire to experience the limits of living, to strive for the gods. The Diabolist is insipid and rather pathetic, a historical curiosity only – a footnote in the psycho-pathology of the Nazarene religion. Crowley was a rather underdeveloped egotist who lacked the character to develop real self-insight. He could and did manipulate others, and did possess some Occult powers (intuitively) and some understanding of the Art of magick. His followers are trapped by the flaws of his system – chief among which are a belief-system (in 'Thelema') and methods which encourage self-stupification and self-satisfaction (and thus the illusion of development) rather than real self-insight and thus Occult abilities.

Church of Satan members (and to a lesser extend those of the Temple of Set) accept a sanitized Satanism – a 'safe Satanism' where the Darkness is said to be only within, where it cannot threaten them. They also are stuck on the bottom rung of Occult understanding – seeing nothing beyond the ego and the carnal. The Temple of Set claims to go further, but there is little or no practical experience of evil, of the Sinister, of those Dark forces which are part of the cosmos – there is instead an intellectualizing. There is also no going to extremes, in living, no ordeals which challenge (and make) character. No quest for personal excellence. Instead, there is the security of organization, the acceptance of Temple authority and mandates. In brief, a fostering of a type of mental servitude – in belief and in practice. All these are contrary to what Satanism is.

Only the ONA understands and practices Satanism as it is, with its insistence that Satanism is about individual self-development in both the real and the Occult worlds, and that this can only be achieved by hard, long, dangerous and toilsome experience. Further, the ONA has exhibited a creativity and an understanding which makes all other manifestations pale into insignificance. Thus, it is not surprising that it has been so influencial in the past few years.

This influence has, however, seldom been acknowledged – other groups and individuals often borrowing the teachings, methods and ideas and claiming them as their own, this 'borrowing' not being confined to 'Satanic' or Left Hand Path groups in general. This is both natural, and necessary given the sterility of creativity which exists and has existed in such groups, and given the nature of the human species in general, and the Satanic in particular.

The chief contributions of the ONA toward an understanding of Satanism in particular and the Occult in general may be briefly described:

1) Satanism and the LHP as a means to individual development leading to Adeptship and beyond – via practical experience and ordeals (qv. The Grade Rituals); 2) the emphasis on developing both the mental and physical character of the individual; 3) a greater understanding of magickal (and Occult) forces – and thus their nature – via the development of the concepts of causal and acausal, and an abstract system to represent this, enabling conscious apprehension (as against belief and superstition); 3) the re-structing of magickal forms and symbols in archetypal terms in particular the septenary Tree of Wyrd and the *Deofel Quartet* (the later explicating the archetypal, particularly in the 'real world' from the viewpoint of the sinister novice); 4) the creation of a Sinister Tarot whose images are sinister and thus imbued with Satanic energy; 5) the emphasis on the individual Initiate working alone and achieving practical goals – without accepting in a religious way a higher authority – and making this achievable by all via the publication of practical guides to all aspects of Satanism (*Naos*, *Black Book* etc.); 6) revealing and significantly extending Aeonic Magick – enabling any individual to undertake such works; 7) bringing an awareness of the Dark Gods – of the sinister energies/forces which exist and which are supra-personal and thus .. dangerous to individuals, one aspect of which has been symbolized by 'Satan'/ the Devil; 8)an emphasis on the personal qualities – the character of a Satanist, enshrined in the concepts of excellence, honour and the motto 'die, rather than submit to anyone or anything'; 9) are-affirmation .. of the positive, life-enhancing nature of Satanism as against the stereotyped image of obsession with death and decay – and a moving away from the 'role'/image of the Satanist as showman-type 'Devil'/Mephisto figure obsessed with carnality and pandering to his/her own weaknesses, and seeking media-attention, toward the secretly working lone sorcerer/sorceress concerned with their own development and works of esoteric sinister magick ...

A perusal of literature, statements and other such causal forms by other groups and individuals since the manifestation of the ONA will show the extent of its influence – of how, in a subtle way, such individuals and groups have been changed by a sinister organization. Such changes, and such influence, will grow, although it may well go unnoticed by all save the few genuine Adepts.

****

It is indicative of the sorry state of most Occult paths and the people who follow them – that there is an abundance of dis-information, deceit, mystification and cultivation of egos. Consider a typical case. A young man developes an interest in Occult arts, and eagerly seeks information and contacts. Books and articles are read, contacts made, perhaps a group or three joined. Soon, the young man is part of 'the Occult scene' and one of three things usually happens: (1)he accepts some system, or person, for a while and tries following what is expected – then, after some 'practical' work, decides it is not right for him, and moves on to another system or person; (2) after a little while he comes to believe he has attained his goal (and thus is an 'Adept' or 'Master' or whatever) usually after engaging in a few rituals and a lot of conversations and meetings with others; (3) after a short or intermediate period cultivating and fawning upon others (and thus assisting them in their endless campaigns to 'safeguard' their own reputations by attempting to discredit others via rumours and so on) he establishes an identity for himself – exaggerating his own achievements, knowledge and contacts. In short, there is the perpetuation of old Aeon traits and values – contra what the Occult in general is supposed to be achieving. Two things are involved in this process: the desire (mostly unconscious, and natural) for self-importance, and self-delusion. Part of this self-delusion occurs because of the 'intellectualization of the Occult' – there is too much talk, too much acceptance – of what others say (particularly about others) without first-hand knowledge, too much theory and too much ego-domination where 'cleverness' (particularly in words) is rated above practical experience. Too much concern for someone's 'past'. The result is almost inevitable (and a waste of the potential of

Occultism) – the young man achieves no real progress, no real insight, no real Occult abilities. He has becomes infected with the 'Occult disease'. Instead of going within, into the wilderness, to lose all illusions and delusions and begin the hard and solitary path to Adeptship by practical work, there is the camaraderie of being 'in the know', of 'being accepted' or working (mostly in intellectual or psuedo-intellectual ways) in a certain 'niche' and thus becoming self-satisfied in a .. comfortable way. The Occult thus becomes a 'habit' or an interest – a source of self-congratulation (perhaps even of material income) and a place where a 'role' is obtained and lived out. Some 'practical' work may be done – but the end result is the disposable Occultist so familiar from the recent past and the present: the attender of meetings (or the more modern 'symposiums' or 'conferences'), the seeker after and spreader of gossip and rumour, the psuedo-intellectual dilettante writing articles and books (and perhaps even editing a Magazine) not for direct, personal experience but rather from hearsay, from self-opinion and from intellectual aridity and cleverness.

Or, perhaps, the plagiarist enjoying a cliquey Success and amateur adulation – or the self-appointed 'Master/adept' who may need the mystique of an organization to mask his lack of character or charisma or "ho may be so self-deluded that he actually believes he has attained his goal. Then again, our young man may turn out to be one of those many failures who hang around the 'Occult scene' – flitting from one group to another, one 'master' to another, and talking, worshipping (both 'gods' and 'masters') and talking again and accumulating a mass of useless information, 'lore' and 'grades/degrees'.

Despite the interest in recent years in the techniques or ways or the Occult – despite all the many words written and spoken – there has been little or no real achievement on the personal level: no increase in the very few Adepts. Instead, almost the opposite has occurred – an increase in self-delusion, in glorifying the ego at the expense of obtaining insight; a turning away from effective experience to the glorification of the vapid, the intellectual and the 'non-directive', sensation seeking, temporary, 'mind-expanding' experience. In short, there has been less real self-discipline and more ego-biased stupidity and stimulation.

Adeptship, and the wisdom that lies beyond that, is obtained by a slow, hard process which requires self-discipline and the self-overcoming of hardships. There is no path to it which is not without difficulties and which is not solitary – which does not require the discarding or all those props which most require to survive: a dogma, friends, ideas, companionship, lovers, material security, 'masters'... There is no potion to obtain which when taken will suddenly give insight or wisdom, no sudden revelations, from god or mortal, which instill wisdom, no technique to be used a few times a week, no ritual or rituals which will give personality or character or self-development. This process requires years and involves certain ways of living – and often a certain guidance. It requires also the desire to reach the goal, to not give in when things become difficult or confused – a tenacity to follow the chosen path to its ending.

The Occult knowledge and insight of an individual is shown most of all by their bearing – by the way they relate to others. But this bearing is not the assumption of some 'role' (such as 'master' or 'Guru' or whatever) – rather, it is genuine and spontaneous, full of individual character: neither affectation nor pretension. This is so because the knowledge and insight is within, acquired from experience. f:here there is lack of real knowledge and lack of insight, there is pretension, artifice, the 'I must preserve my own ego by doing down all others' syndrome, and the inebriated laughter of the ill-disciplined, ill-at-ease discussion machine.

Our young man would do well to try and find some guidance from an insightful individual – and be prepared for a hard and long journey. Perhaps then, in time one new Adept will arise, and the 'new aeon' be brought a little nearer.

(1990 eh)

[UNTITLED ESSAY #1]

Although it has been mentioned before, this bears repeating: magick, properly used, develops the potential of an individual in a realistic, practical way – that is, it produces, from the experiences undergone, a genuine insight and thus an understanding of self, others and the world. This is in complete contrast to what happens outside of genuine esoteric traditions where there is adherence by the individual to abstract doctrines, ideas and beliefs – that is, there is little or no understanding based on experience, on the reality apprehended through trials, hardship, explorations and discovery. Magick returns the individual to their inner core – destroying illusion, affectation and abstraction of the arid intellectual type.

Of course, one should really say – real magick, properly used, does this. There is an awful lot of pretentious 'magic' and 'magick' about. What differentiates real magick is first the practical nature of its methods (which are both 'internal' i.e. psychic – and 'external' – ie. involving practical work and experiences in the real world, not just 'in the head') and second its structure or system: a working toward a definite goal. This goal is Adeptship (part of which may be said to be the Jungian 'individuation) and what lies beyond even this: wisdom. The striving for this goal (and the striving is necessary: it is not a 'gift' from someone) changes the individual in significant ways – there is a re-orientation of consciousness, insights and achievement.

The way of magick (as explicated by the seven-fold way) enables each individual Initiate to develop their own unique understanding or 'view of life' or 'world-view' – that is, it creates character, it uplifts the individual, separating them from the anonymous majority who mostly merely exist rather than live and who never evolve and understand. Today, individuals are 'mass-produced' and conform to the accepted ideas and norms, even in the 'rebellion' that occurs, where the 'herd' or some fashionable 'trend' or 'idea' is followed without any understanding. Everything is categorized, made into moral opposites – and there is developing in society an almost religious zeal about certain attitudes, a zeal which restricts individual freedom and expression and which destroys genuine individuality. All this, however, goes mostly unnoticed, so low is the level of general insight – a situation brought about, in part, by the comfortable lives most people in the West today live; insulated as they are by technology, by material possessions, by the complexity of Modern life and by ideas from life in its realness, rawness and danger.

That it is necessary to give an example to illustrate the categorization and zeal which is increasingly occurring is a sad reflection on the general level of understanding. The example to consider is the disease if 'ism-itus': the creation of an abstract idea, described by a word ending in 'ism'. Examples of this 'ism' are then saught – in society, individuals and so on, and then that society and those individuals must be 're-educated' is the 'ism' is found since the 'ism' is regarded as morally reprehensible, the abstract idea being formulated in an abstract moral way. This procedure is not new – it is essentially a religious fundamentalism, extrapolated into politics and social concerns, and may be said to derive from Nazarene beliefs and ideas.

The 'ism' itself becomes a 'totem-word' – almost a 'magical incantation' – and is surrounded by an aura of guilt. To be associated with an 'ism' – even worse to be an 'ism' or be called the 'ism' – is reprehensible, almost a 'sin', and in certain countries definitely a crime, punishable by due process of law (and usually, if convicted, by imprisonment). What this amounts to – when taken with the other abstractions foisted upon individuals (the 'ism', remember is only one example of this) – is the production of essentially characterless people who seldom if ever have any real experience of life, who conform to a certain set of attitudes, and who are psychically unhealthy in that they are infected by notions of 'sin' and moral absolutes. There is little real understanding – only acceptance of the abstract forms which have been and are being projected onto and into 'history', 'society' and individuals and which give a comforting illusion of 'understanding' and knowledge (and also.in most cases a smug moral feeling of superiority such as one sees in certain religious types).

Magick, however, is a means to destroy all this – and thus it really is subversive, and dangerous since it can free the individual, returning them to that inner Being where insight is born and from which understanding, and ultimately wisdom, can be cultivated.

This is the reality of magick – it produces the only 'freedom' that is real and which has meaning: that inner one, which allows further steps to be taken, which allows evolution to be continued. For magickal Initiation is a personal liberation when an individual tal.es responsibility for his or her own evolution.

Further, this way to freedom, this means of liberation, should not be used only by a very few – it should be used by everyone, creating a whole society (or societies) of' Adepts: a whole new era or Aeon in which all have attained to self-insight. Idealistic: of course – but still possible, even if unlikely for at least the next few centuries. But herein lies that almost sacred duty of each Initiate – to keep this possibility alive by maintaining the reality and effectiveness of genuine magick.

(ONA 1990 ev)

MANIPULATION I – SINISTER THEMES

It is a fact of external sinister magick that manipulation is necessary. There is manipulation of forms, images and magickal energies as well as direct and indirect manipulation of people.

People manipulation can arise from many factors and be undertaken for many reasons. Initially, it is often done by Initiates because they wish or desire to revel in the feeling that such manipulation can and often does bring – a sense of power and re-inforcing of the ego: it creates a sense of self-identity and purpose, enhancing the 'role' of Satanist/Black Magickian.

Beyond this is the use by the External Adept of various roles – such as Priest or Priestess – which by their nature involve certain amounts of manipulation of others, e.g. in the running of a Temple or group. Experience brings skill – a learning from mistakes, and thus a more subtle approach. Instead of direct confrontation, there is a 'flowing with' the other persons(s) and then a skillful re-direction of them: i.e. they believe they are acting freely rather than being manipulated. Beyond External Adept, there may be further use of such skills depending on the wyrd of the Adept. [See Appendix for one such form.]

What all levels have in common is the acceptance of the belief that the magickal Initiate is superior to the non-Initiate: that others can be used to achieve personal/magickal goals. In the beginning, of course, this sense of superiority may be unfounded and mis-placed – arising from simple arrogance and self-delusion. However, if the Initiate truely learns, and really follows the hard path of internal magick, then this will be transformed into a reality, the External Adept having acquired the skill and begun the process of developing character: that which sets them apart from ordinary mortals. In addition, certain abilities will be developed (some connected with the 'Occult') and latent potential drawn forth – creating a new individual from the pre-Initiate one.

The post-Initiate will realize the rather limited understanding of the majority and see them as swayed by all kinds of external and unconscious influences: in short, understand that they are not really free. They will be seen as directed and controlled in varying ways by various means – by archetypal forces within their own psyche, directly or indirectly by others and by ideas/forms/Institutions/ideology, as well as by the various patterns psychic energies assume (one of which is the ethos of the culture/civilization to which they belong).

To the sinister Initiate this will be illuminating and also useful, providing opportunities for experimentation and self-learning, as for example via running a Temple.

There is no morality here – only the judgement of experience: most people are consciously and esoterically not very well developed. In fact, they are still rather primitive. The Initiate takes a dispassionate view – although there will be times when direct involvement leads to emotional commitment/involvement, and thence to a self-learning from the experience(s), as must be in the progress from Initiate toward the other Grades. Initially, however, others are seen as a means.

Gradually, there is a move away from this – from the direct, personal involvement to the more indirect and magickal: an internalizing. This brings awareness of the Initiate's own psyche and thus real understanding. There may be and mostly still is manipulation of others – but this has evolved from the random to the directed, centred on what the Initiate believes is his or her own destiny in magickal terms. The same applies to the manipulation of magickal energies – there is an evolution away from the undirected external type (which quite often arose from the unconscious – i.e. was not consciously understood) first to the internal as a process of internal magick, and then outward again but in a directed form, the direction arising from the magickal goals set, those involved in following the sinister path. In brief, there is an awareness of that balance which is so important for true Adeptship.

This balance – for an External Adept – is expressed in the understanding, from experience [i.e. not 'from book-learning'], that magick as a directed form is not always causal when used to assist the individual externally (and sometimes internally) – that is, it involves other factors which the individual at the time of working/ritual, may not be aware of/in control of. In short – the illusion of having achieved control/mastery of all magickal forms by techniques, is broken. One of the factors involved in this is the wyrd of the individual; another is the wyrd of the Aeon; another – and perhaps the most important for the individual to understand – is the nature of magick itself: no one who has not transcended beyond the Abyss can direct/control in a causal way all the divergent forms any magickal energy assumes in the causal. Quite often, however, most of the divergences go un-noticed when 'practical magick' is performed, because the time-scale of those divergences is not the same as that of the effects which are or become noticed by the Initiate/External Adept and which mostly are taken to be the 'success/failure' of the working. Some of the divergences are or may be in themselves of no consequence to the individual undertaking the working – i.e. produce no discernible outward effects – and even when they or some of them are of consequence, the Initiate/External Adept usually either ignores them or accounts for them in other, temporal, ways. A recognition of/sensitivity to the divergences begins the process that leads from External to Internal Adept: once again, practical experience is the teacher. it should be obvious that those which are of consequence (whether noticed or not) effect these acausal changes upon the individual due to (a) the wyrd of that individual and/or (b) the wyrd of the aeon.

Thus the learning curve which magickal workings impart. In a sense, each Grade Ritual and the associated experiences, imparts more ability to apprehend and thus control the causal manifestations – gives more skill at manipulation, both magickal and of people (there is a stage when the two are understood as the same thing), as well as brings an awareness of the acausal effects beyond the time-scale of the working and its desire/results.

The understanding of the limits (well, some of them!) often occurs following the solo Nine Angles rite by an External Adept – at first intuitively, and then more consciously. This begins the process of consolidation and leads either to further self-insight, return to self-delusion, or rejection of magick and the quest. For, in essence, the solo rite is a foretaste of the chaos of the Abyss – undirected acausal energy, the effects of which (i.e. what results from its presencing in the causal ['on earth']) are mostly unforeseen and often unwanted, the ritual itself being so structured (or rather unstructured) that little or no direction is given for the energies – they flow and presence according to their nature, the individual being a channel. [Note: this is what happens to a greater or lesser extent in external workings by an Initiate/External Adept re the 'acausal component' of the working.] Thus, the wyrd of the individual to some extent directs and/or disrupts the flow, producing certain changes in the causal. The nature of these changes thus depends on that wyrd.

Thus the essence of magick – and hence sinister manipulation – is glimpsed and then apprehended, in most for the first time. This enables both the causal and acausal components of the energies accessed via a magickal working to be controlled and manipulated and thus presenced in the causal, and it is this which marks the true Adept: the Internal Adept possesses the understanding, and the Master/Mistress can make that understanding real.

***

1990 ev

MANIPULATION II

One of the fundamental principles of Black Magick is elitism: the belief that the majority are essentially beneath Initiates in terms of understanding, intelligence and ability. This gives the foundation for manipulation both on the personal and the magickal level.

The Black Magick novice is generally scornful of others – until and unless worth has been proved or shown. However, as explained previously (Manipulation I) an experienced novice will have learnt the subtlety of manipulation: direct confrontation as a mode of manipulation will seldom be used (unless a person or group deserves to be so treated: or such an approach is magickally necessary). Instead, there will be the 'flowing with' approach – manipulation without the person or persons being aware of it. Quite often, this approach is 'psychological'; at other times it may be psychic (e.g. directly magickal) – or perhaps via the charisma of the magickian overpowering the personality of the person(s) in question.

Whatever, there will be an arrogance based on the belief of one's own superiority – and thus an isolation. For a true Black Magickian is essentially a strong individualist who finds his or her own company preferable to that of others – unless those others can be useful in some way. That is, there is no dependance of any kind, particularly not emotional, on any other individual or individuals. This, of course, is what the novice strives to achieve.

It cannot be achieved quickly – or even by 'will' alone. Rather, it is a cumulative process – an alchemical change, a re-orientation of personality, and such changes take time.

In the seven-fold sinister way, these changes occur during the stage of External Adept and are a necessary prelude to the Grade Ritual of Internal Adept. One of most important aspects of this change is that involving the companion – the initial emotional involvement gradually changing, ceasing to be a dependance but rather a partnership, a mutually evolved understanding; the passion (both sexual and emotional) which possessed the novice giving way to a maturity.

The arrogence of the Black Magickian is not an empty one: it is not a posturing. Instead, it arises from within: from the knowledge and insight the novice has gained into him/herself – by having achieved in both the personal and magickal sense. Thus the magickal and practical goals which are set for novices – they develope self-assurence, a pride and that arrogance which is truly Satanic. The training for and achievement of these practical goals usually takes the novice to the limits of physical and mental endurence and this builds character in a specific way [or defeats the novice who gives up and either lets self-delusion triumph – 'I don't need such things: they are out of date/unsuited to me; I have achieved enough anyway … or abandons the magickal quest, perhaps later to try another 'method' (which is easier) or find another 'teacher'].

Initially, this arrogence is outward and expressed by manner, attitude and perhaps appearence. Later, when Adeptship becomes achieved, it becomes cloaked – except in the eyes and in that charisma which marks a Black Magickian.

Initial manipulation is often of the external kind – an adjunct to external magick – later, it becomes 'internal' (concerned with the internal goals of the External Adept) and still later, aeonic (bound up with supra-personal, acausal energies). [qv. *Deofel Quartet* for examples of the various types appropriate to Initiate and External Adepts].

ONA 1990 ev

RITUAL MAGICK – DURE AND SEDUE CEREMONIAL

Magick enables us to capture again and again those moments which not only shape our lives but which can extend the possibilities of our existence: those moments when we know with an exhileration and an insight that transcends words, when we become more than a single isolated individual burdened with a causal-existence.

For some time there has been a denial of and attempts to undermine the ceremonial in magick: there has arisen a plethora of self-written rituals and 'chaos' type workings. This, however, arises from a misunderstanding of the nature of ceremonial. Basically, there are two types of ceremonial workings in magick: dure ceremonial, and sedue ceremonial. The first is essentially ritual used for internal magick – to produce/provoke/inspire changes within the consciousness of those participating/attending.

The second is (or rather should be) a performance which transports the individual participants to another realm and which engages their whole being. It is not however a possession – but rather a developed awareness, a new way of being distinct from 'everyday' existence, one in which all the elements (mind, body, emotions etc.) are a unity.

A sedue ceremonial is an artistic event of the highest type because it is a conscious attempt to make the acausal real (to presence it) in causal time. However, like any artistic performance, a ritual can be good, indifferent, bad or great depending on the talent and abilities of those performing/conducting it. If it is any of the first three, it will not achieve its purpose.

A great performance is one which captures the essence of the ritual – which brings the acausal, which 'opens a nexion', and which thus has the magickal power to transform. This of course is a rare event – at least these days – and like, for example, a great performance of a drama or a symphony, requires both talent and preparation. Unfortunately, in the past as in the present, ceremonial rituals when attempted are done mostly by inept performers with little or no

64

preparation and little if any empathy with the magick which the ritual re-presents. Thus the ritual is magickally ineffective: non-inspirational for the participants/congregation. Further, elements of self-delusion (regarding the 'magick') are mostly present. Such 'performances' tend to confirm the mistaken belief that ceremonial forms are either boring or outmoded or both.

A ceremonial ritual should be vivifying – and awaken 'numinous' feelings. It should stimulate all the senses – for a sedue ritual in a subtle way; for dure ritual in an obvious/overt way. Incenses and fragrences should stimulate the sense of smell; the eyes should be stimulated by colour and imagery; hearing by the sounds of chanting, by music, words; the intellect by the symbols/content/intent; the passions by the spirit or élan of the performance and perhaps the sight/gestures of an individual or individuals performing a specific 'role', their manner of dress (or undress) and their physical movement.

A ceremonial ritual is a seduction – of the participants/congregation by he/she/they conducting it or the power of the rite itself because the rite captures or transforms an aspect or aspects of the acausal. This seduction is subtle if the ritual is a sedue one, and obvious/overt/harsh if it is a dure one. But by its nature it always has a temporal structure as it always is a nexion to the acausal – if it is a genuine magickal rite, that is, one that possesses when performed acausal (or magickal) energy/power. Both of these aspects – the temporal structure and the nexion – are important, although hitherto esoteric.

Each shall be considered in turn. First, temporal structure. This means that the ritual has a beginning, a middle (or 'action'/development) and a definite end: it is confined in temporal time, and while a specific performance may be 'fast' or 'slow' depending on the mood and the intensity, it is generally of a certain duration. Second – a nexion. This means that in form and content (e.g. the techniques used to draw upon magickal energy) it is effective – it accesses the forms/symbols and so on required for its purpose.

This means more than that it 'produces emotion'. Emotion arises or should arise from the performance by the effort and talent of the performers. Rather, such accessing means it re-presents certain elements of the acausal in an accessible form, such as archetypes or numinous symbols. This requires what can only be called a type of 'artistic creation' – and this in itself can be of varying quality, as in music or any creative endevour. Most creations, however, as rituals, are not effective: they do not presence the acausal, although they may produce emotion and perhaps the occassional insight. Emotion, however, is not magick – just as 'intellectual stimulation' and/or undisciplined behavior are not, although such things result and are expected to result from what passes for 'magickal rituals' today. Only rarely does a creation become or be magickal – that is, a nexion, despite the intent of the person or persons who undertake such creation. Thus, no amount of desire, no amount of intellectual knowledge can make or create a ritual which is magickally effective. Only rarely does a creation become or is magickal. It may become so due to the 'aura' or 'tradition' surrounding it (partly due to past performances) – but even in this instance it must still possess some aspects which access the acausal directly. It is magickal when it is that rare entity: a genuine magickal creation.

The temporal structure and accessing of a ritual mean that a genuine rite, once created or transmitted via tradition, must be respected for what it is: effective performance requires fidelity to the temporal limits and its internal structure – in terms of all its formalized elements such as words, chants, symbols, images, colours etc. Outside of this, there can be (and indeed should be) artistic interpretation, a vivifying of the original by the talent and skill of the performer(s). A genuine magickal ritual is a work of art – and requires 'interpretation', that is, performance, to presence the acausal. it is in short a conscious causal expression of aspects of the acausal – and in performance lives in both the causal and the acausal. Hence its power to transform.

[It should be remembered that only ceremonial magick is being considered here – the above does not imply that only ceremonial forms are effective as magick. There are many other forms or means of accessing the acausal.]

Given this understanding, it should be obvious that there are very few rituals, written down or transmitted, which presence the acausal and which, in an inspiring performance or interpretation, are capable of transforming either the consciousness of others or of producing changes in the causal metric itself. That is, there a few rituals which possess in their written form the potential to be a nexion to the acausal: and even these require inspirational performance: rehearsal, planning, the correct intent or desire ... In short, the creation of 'atmosphere' and skill/ability in performance. The rituals that proliferate today – and most of those regarded as 'traditional' – may in their performance pass some moments of causal time and may even fill some individuals with emotion (and boredom is an emotion), but they are not and never will be magickal.

of the rituals that do exist, those in '*The Black Book of Satan*' together with a few others (such as The Ceremony of Recalling in its various forms) rank as supreme works of magick. Some other rites possess the potential to do even more on the causal level (e.g. the Nine Angles rites) – producing aeonic changes.

Thus explicated, genuine Black Magick becomes available to all: for the first time ever.

-    ONA 1990 ev

THE ALCHEMY OF MAGICK

Magick is not an object for academic study – it is essentially practical. It also requires self-discipline and training the acquisition of skills. No books or teacher can teach magick: it can only be learnt by practice, by the trials and errors of experience. All books and teachers can do, at best, is guide: toward and into the relevant experiences and offer some explanations for cause, effect and what is beyond the causal.

Similarly, willful self-expression will be mostly counterproductive. What is required of the novice and Initiate is self-discipline and that insight which arises from achievement and adversity. Modern life, however, has made these things difficult – it is easy to be self-opinionated, to accept the comforts of modern living and the lack of self-discipline, just as modern 'methods' and 'ideas' about 'magick' make it seem that understanding of and achievement in magick is easy: all that is needed are the relevant books/grade manuals/ information and a chaotic mind/attitude/approach.

There is not and never has been any substitute for self-learning from experience. The real learning of magick occurs by the individual novice, alone: group work and group experience merely confirm that learning and extend the techniques, the forms that are used. This is so because real magick is internal – an alchemy of psychic change. It is the techniques which are external. For instance, sexual magick is a technique of magick – it is not magick or 'magickal' in itself – just as ceremonial ritual is a technique. All techniques are forms which are dormant – they need vivifying, bringing to life: they need to be infused with the 'breath of life'. This vivification is magick, and its achievement is individual, that is, it does not rely on the form – on minute details of performance or technique.

Sometimes, this vivification is shared – e.g. between two individuals undertaking a sexual rite or a group gathering for a ceremony. For too long the techniques have been regarded as magickal in themselves, leading to a complete misunderstanding of magick – as, for example, by Crowley and his followers and by adherents of latter-day 'chaos' techniques. Magick is beyond technique – techniques and forms merely presence the magick in the causal, and to access the magickal energies skill is required. Sometimes, this skill is intuitive – an inborn gift – but most often it has to be cultivated, learnt, acquired. The skill is an internal one, and may be likened to an attitude of mind. It is a 'moving with' magickal energies as those energies are, in themselves – it is not a loose, undirected approach, a chaotic acceptance, but a finely balanced direction; not a loss of conscious awareness/understanding, but a new type of awareness. It is like running long distances: innate ability may help, but training is required, an awareness of limitations born from past experience, a self-discipline to achieve the distance in the time set – and then the running, which when successful is a 'flowing with' the body and mind…

In magick, desire makes the energy – once accessed via the individual – presence in the form/technique chosen. This desire is usually aimed – that is, it has a causal goal (as for example in external magick). The form or technique chosen may stimulate to some extent the production of magickal energies – but it is the individual who must push open the gate (or nexion) and direct the energies that lie beyond it. What the forms and techniques most often do is make the nexion seem real and accessible – often 'evoking' within the individual the consciousness required to push open the nexion and presence the energies. Because of this, ceremonial rituals (or any ritual where more than two are present and involved) require direction or control – of the images/forms/patterns invoked and the presencing of such in the causal. This direction is always toward the causal (that is, toward a specific aim or into the psyche of an individual or individuals) because of the nature of the energies – there is always 'flow'. If no control is undertaken (or the direction is confused because more than one attempts to control the flow – perhaps unconsciously) then causal change will still occur (and must occur) although in ways probably unforeseen by those involved – this is what usually happens when some individuals gather and attempt an act of magick – and often results in psychic disruption of one or more of those individuals.

The alchemy of magick is in learning this control – in being able to access the energies, and being able to produce changes via the presencing of what is accessed: internally (within one's own psyche), externally (in others and the things of the everyday) and aeonically (within and beyond the confines of aeonics). There is thus a learning about the various types of magickal energies (which may be said to be differentiated by **how** they presence in the causal) – and their uses. In short, the acquisition of individual skill and understanding. To achieve this, there are certain ways certain guides which may be followed. This is a serious commitment – not a hobby, not a gathering of some like-minded people as and when for an enjoyable and ego-gratifying delving into 'the Occult', and certainly not 'for laughs' or to entertain. There is an intensity, a self-discipline, even sometimes a hardness – and those pleasures which are beyond mere mortals. In brief, new ways of living. For while the alchemy of magick is not accessible to everyone (due to works such as *Naos*) it is unlikely many will foreswear their current and easy ways of living for the challenge.

ONA 1991 eh

ACAUSAL EXISTENCE – THE SECRET REVEALED

Acausal existence – the secret of true Immortality – has been hinted at many times in certain esoteric writings connected with a particular LHP. In the past, a few Adepts of the LHP – and the occassional notorious individual interested in dark sorcery – tried to secure for themselves an acausal existence by dark rites of sacrifice, and as a result dark legends arose. But such means are not really necessary.

Before describing what is necessary, a brief examination of such acausal existence will be in order. According to a sinister tradition we as individuals possessed of consciousness have both a causal and an acausal aspect to that consciousness. The acausal is latent (or mostly so) and magickal Initiation awakens it – opening a gate or nexion to the acausal. This allows the acausal to be apprehended (usually via a symbolism such as the septenary Tree of Wyrd) and acausal energies to be used/directed (i.e. 'magick'). The result is an 'expansion' of consciousness. Progression by the Initiate to the higher grades of initiation is actually the expansion of the acausal in individual consciousness (or, viewed another way, the progression of the individual into the acausal) – a balance of causal/acausal being achieved in 'the Abyss'. Beyond this, because of the balance so attained, it is possible to transcend to the acausal – to create an acausal existence when the causal ceases (i.e. physical death).

The acausal is not however, a 'dreamy realm' or some kind of nirvana/heaven. It is rather, the very essence of Being – beyond opposites, primal Chaos. Nirvana and such like are abstract moral forms – i.e. they are 'unbalanced' since they lack darkness, the sinister, the negative ..... [Nirvana and such like are usually described in terms only of 'light'.] The acausal is the realm of the Dark Gods – and these beings are not imaginative symbols '. for the titillation of consciousness, nor simply a part of the psyche, to be transcended or negated or whatever by 'forces of light'. Rather, they exist independant of our consciousness [yet such is the nature of the acausal that they are also part of what is dormant within us] and while they may be accessed (or 'dis-covered') by consciousness and thus presenced in the causal (on Earth) their actual intrusion would totally disrupt sentient life in the causal – like the meeting of matter and anti-matter. Sinister magick (of the aeonic and internal kind) may be said to be like a machine or engine where containment of opposites is possible and controllable in certain amounts and under certain conditions. [In simple terms, sinister aeonic magick contains the flow of the acausal into a temporal form – usually an Aeon and its associated civilization via a nexion/magickal centre to thus over thousands of years increase the amount of the acausal that is presenced, increasing thus evolution in individuals in accordance with sinister goals. Such is one of the forms of real Black Magick.]

The nature of acausal existence may be apprehended by individuals by certain sinister rites such as those of the Nine Angles. To achieve an individual acausal existence the sinister path must be followed, from Initiate to Internal Adept to Master/Mistress and beyond because this following of such a path in the way indicated (qv. *Naos* and *Black Book*) creates acausal consciousness in the individual over causal time. The Grade Ritual of Grand Master/G. Mistress makes the Adept more acausal than causal. Beyond this, is a simple ritual (the solo Nine Angles rite done by the Grand Master/G.Mistress) when consciousness is transferred beyond the nexion opened/created by the previous Grade Ritual. Immortality – the final stage of the way – is then achieved, followed then or shortly thereafter by causal death, although consciousness can be transfered to inhabit another causal body, this is not usually done as wyrd is achieved. Simple, really, although this alchemical process takes about 25 years. By virtue of the nexion, the new Immortal alters the temporal structure of the world, usually for an Aeon.

Now the secret has been revealed, the possibility is open to all. But it is doubtful if more than one or two a century will try, such is human weakness.

ONA 1991 eh

BAPHOMET – A NOTE ON THE NAME

The name Baphomet is regarded by traditional Satanists as meaning 'the Mistress (or Mother) of Blood' – the Mistress who sometimes washes in the blood of her foes and whose hands are thereby stained. [See 'The Ceremony of Recalling'. The supposed derivation is from the Greek βαφη Μητρα and not as is sometimes said from μητιοσ (the Attic form for 'wise'). Such a use of the term 'Mother' /Mistress was quite common in later Greek alchemical writings – for example, Iamblichus in 'De Mysteriis' used μητριζω to signify possessed by the mother of the gods. Later alchemical writings tended to use the prefix to signify a specific type of 'amalgam' (and some take this to be a metaphor for the amalgam of Sol with Luna in the sexual sense).

In the septenary system Baphomet, as Mistress of Earth, is linked to the sixth sphere (Jupiter) and the star Deneb. She is thus in one sense a magickal 'Earth Gate' [qv the Nine Angles] and her reflexion (or 'causal' as against her 'acausal' or sinister nature) is the third sphere (Venus) related to the star Antares. According to esoteric tradition the Antares aspect was celebrated by rites in Albion c, 3,000 years BP – in the middle and toward the end of the month of May and some stones circles/sacred sites were said to be aligned for Antares. In contrast, the sinister aspect of the Mistress (i.e. Baphomet) was celebrated in the Autumn and was linked to the rising of Arcturus, Arcturus itself being related to the sinister male aspect (second sphere of the septenary), later identified with Lucifer/Satan. Thus, the August celebration was a sinister *hierosgamos* – the union of Baphomet with her spouse (or 'Priest' who took on the role of the sinister male aspect). According to tradition, the Priest was sacrificed after the sexual union, where the role of Baphomet was assumed by the Priestess/Mistress of the cult. Thus, the May celebration was the (re-)birth of new energies (and the child of the union). Tradition relates this sinister sacred Arcturian rite as taking place once every seventeen years.

Once again, some sacred sites in Albion are said to be aligned to the rising of Arcturus, over three thousand years ago. In the Middle

73

Ages, Baphomet came to be regarded as the Bride of Satan and it from this time that both 'Baphomet' and 'Satan', as names for the female and male aspect of the dark side came into use (at least in the secret sinister tradition).

Hence the traditional depiction of Baphomet – a beautiful mature woman (often shown naked) holding up the severed head of the sacrificed priest (usually shown bearded).

To some extent the Templars revived part of this cult, but without any real esoteric understanding and for their own purposes. They adopted Baphomet as a type of female Yeshua but with some bloody/ sinister aspects – and contrary to most accepted ideas, they were not especially 'Satanic'. Rather, they saw themselves as holy warriors and became a military cult with bonds of honour, although their concept of 'holy' differed somewhat from that of the Church of the time, including as it did dark/gnostic aspects. Their sacrifices were in battle – and not as part of a specific rite.

The image of Baphomet (e.g. by Levi) as a hermaphrodite figure are romantic confusions and/or distortions: essentially of the symbolic/real union of Mistress and Priest and his later sacrifice. The same applies to the derivation of the suffix of Her name with 'wisdom' (and a male image at that!) – even the confused gnostics understood 'Wisdom' as female.

ONA

BAPHOMET – A NOTE ON THE NAME II

There is a tradition regarding the origin of the name Baphomet which deserves recording, even though it is not regarded as authentic, having no present-day proponents. This tradition regards the name as deriving from Βουβαστισ; the Greek name for the Egyptian goddess Bastet, recorded by Herodotus (2.137 ff). It is interesting that Herodotus identifies the goddess with Artemis, the goddess of the moon. Bubastis was regarded as the daughter of Osiris and Isis and often represented as a female with the head of a cat – cats were egarded as sacred to her. Artemis was a goddess unmoved by love and she was regarded as Apollo's twin sister (the identification of her as a 'moon goddess' followed naturally from this since Apollo was linked with the sun). Like Apollo, she often sent death and plagues, and was propitiated sometimes with sacrifices.

It is interesting that (a) Βουβαστεια is the Pythagorean name for 'five' [qv. Iamblicus: Theologumena Arithmeticae, 31], perhaps a link with the 'pentagram'?; (b) the Templars, with whom the name Baphomet is associated, were said to have worshipped their deity in the form of a cat.

***

The tradition recorded above, and the one described in part I, both regard Baphomet as a female divinity – and both are esoteric traditions, hitherto unrecorded.

It is possible that both are correct – that is, that the actual name Baphomet derives (as mentioned in part I) from the Greek βαφη Μητρα: the prefix refering to being 'dyed/ stained' or 'dipped' in blood   qv. Euripides, Hercules Furens:

μαινομένωι πιτύλωι πλαγχθεὶς
ἐκατογκεφάλου τε βαφαις ὕδρας (1190)

75

The suffix derives from 'mother' or 'mistress' used in a religious sense (qv. Iamblicus 'De Mysteriis').

This name – Baphomet – is thus a descriptive one for the 'dark' (i.e lunar) goddess, to whom sacrifices were made, and which was actually known in former times as 'Bubastis' – that is, Bastet, to whom cats were sacred.

Thus, Baphomet could be regarded as a form of Artemis/Bastet – a female divinity with a 'dark' side or nature [when viewed via conventional morality] to whom sacrifices have been. and continue to be. made. Sinister tradition regards Baphomet as the Bride of Satan/Lucifer – this would fit well since Lucifer is often regarded as a form of Apollo: Artemis is the female form ('sister') of Apollo. Here, it must be remembered that both Apollo and Artemis were not aetherial. Moral and lofty divinities (the classical gods have been romantically misinterpreted) – they could be, and often were, deadly and dark: both 'sinister' and 'light'.

A GIFT FOR THE PRINCE:
A GUIDE TO HUMAN SACRIFICE

In ceremonial rituals involving sacrifice, the Mistress of Earth usually takes on the role of violent goddess or 'Baphomet', the Master of the Temple that of either Lucifer or Satan, the sacrifice being regarded as a gift to the Prince of Darkness. This gift, however, is sometimes offered to the dark goddess, the bride of our Prince.

Human sacrifice is powerful magick. The ritual death of an individual does two things: it releases energy (which can be directed – or stored, for example in a crystal) and it draws down dark forces or 'entities'. Such forces may then be used, by directing them toward a specific goal, or they may be allowed to disperse over the Earth in a natural way, such dispersal' altering what is sometimes known as the 'astral shell' around the Earth. This alteration, by the nature of the sacrifice, is disruptive – that is, it tends toward Chaos. This is simply another way of saying that sacrifice furthers the work of Satan.

Sacrifice can be voluntary, of an individual, involuntary, of an individual or two, or result from events brought about by Satanic ritual and/or planning (such as wars). Voluntary sacrifice results from the traditional Satanist belief that our life on this planet is only a stage: a gateway to another existence. This other existence is in the acausal realm where the Dark Gods exist. The key to this other existence is not negation, but rather ecstasy. A Satanist revels in life because by living life in a joyful, ecstatic way, the acausal that exists within us all by virtue of our being, is strengthened. For Satanists, not only the manner of living is important but also the manner of death. We must live well, and die at the right time, proud and defiant: not waiting sickly and weak. The scum of the Earth wail and tremble as they face Death: we stand laughing and spit with contempt. Thus do we learn how to live.

Voluntary sacrifice usually occurs every seventeen years as part of the Ceremony of Recalling: the one chosen becomes Immortal, living in the acausal to haunt the edge of our minds.

An involuntary sacrifice is when an individual or individuals are chosen by a group, Temple, Order. Such sacrifices are usually sacrificed on the Spring Equinox, although if this is not possible for whatever reason another date may be used. While voluntary sacrifices are always male (and usually twenty-one years of age) there are no restrictions concerning involuntary sacrifices other than the fact that they are usually in some way opponents of Satanism or the Satanic way of living.

Great care is needed in choosing a sacrifice: the object being to dispose of a difficult individual or individuals without arousing undue suspicion. A Temple or group wishing to conduct such a sacrifice with magickal intent must first obtain permission from the Grand Master (or Mistress).

If this is given, then detailed preparation must begin. First choose the sacrifice(s) – those whose removal will actively benefit the Satanist cause. Candidates are zealous interfering Nazarenes, those attempting to disrupt in some way established Satanist groups or Orders (e.g. journalists) and political/business individuals whose activities are detrimental to the Satanist spirit (Sacrifice – 2).

There are three methods of conducting an involuntary sacrifice: 1) by magickal means (e.g. the Death Ritual); 2) by direct, personal, sacrifice; and 3) by assassination. Both (2) and (3) can be undertaken either directly by the group/Temple/Order or its members or by proxy.

Proxy involves the Master or Mistress finding a suitably weak-willed individual and then implanting in their mind by hypnotic means a suitable suggestion. Whatever method is chosen a date for the sacrifice should be set and on that date a suitable ritual undertaken. This ritual is most usually the Death Ritual – if method (3) is chosen, fhe Ritual is performed twice: first, seven days before the chosen date, and then on the date itself while the member/proxy is undertaking the sacrifice. The energy of this latter ritual is then directed (or stored temporarily) or dispersed over the Earth by the person conducting the ritual.

Method (2) involves the Ritual of Sacrifice. The victim or victims are brought or enticed to the area chosen for the Ritual, bound by the Guardian of the Temple and at the appropriate point in the Ritual sacrificed by either the Master or Mistress using the Sacrificial Knife. The bodies are then buried or otherwise disposed of; care being taken if they are found for suspicion not to fall on any of those involved. Those involved, of course, must be sworn to secrecy and warned that if they break their oath their own existence will be terminated. Breaking the oath of sacrifice draws down upon them the vengeance of all Satanic – groups, Orders and individuals – both magickal and more directly. Those who participate in the Ritual of Sacrifice must revel in the death(s): it being the duty of – the Master and Mistress to find suitable participants.

Note: Method (2) and (3) are no longer undertaken and are given for historical interest.

THE DEOFEL QUARTET

The Quartet consists of:

1) Falcifer: Lord of Darkness
2) The Temple of Satan (aka Witch Queen)
3) The Giving
4) The Greyling Owl

The general purpose of these MSS is briefly explained in the 'Introduction' which follows their title page. More specifically, each work deals with one (sometimes more) forms of 'magickal/archetypal' energy as these are understood in the septenary tradition and the means whereby these can be controlled as well as how those forms affect individuals, both consciously and unconsciously. In some of the works (for example 'Falcifer') the magick is obvious; in others, (for example 'The Greyling Owl') it is much less obvious, and for good reason.

The best approach is to read each work in order of complexity, starting with the least (esoterically) complicated. Thus, the reading sequence would be: Falcifer; The Giving; The Temple of Satan; The Greyling Owl. Further, this increasing complexity operates, in the individual works, on different levels. At first, all of them should be read merely for enjoyment (and the 'esoteric' information obvious on a first reading). A further reading should provoke questions and (hopefully) insights into esoteric matters in general and the reader's psyche in particular.

•••

The Deofel Quartet: Themes and Questions

Viewed in a simplified way, the four works deal with the first four spheres of the Tree of Wyrd. Thus:

1) Falcifer – deals with the first sphere (Moon) and some of its 'influences' (in the personal sense) in an overtly magickal setting.

2) Greyling – deals with some aspects of the second sphere (Mercury) in a way Ire-moved' from a magickal setting.

3) Temple – deals with some aspects of the third sphere in a directly magickal setting.

4) Giving – deals with the transition from the third sphere to the fourth sphere, in a specific magickal setting.

(1) and (2) may be said to be written from a ♂ perspective; (3) and (4) from a ♀ perspective. But in all the interplay between the 'male' and the 'female' aspects is important. (Note: ♀♀ is dealt with in the MS 'Breaking The Silence Down').

In each of the works the interplay of λ ('light') with φ ('sinister') is also described, although only in some of the works (e.g. Falcifer) is this framework viewed in the 'conventional magickal sense' (i.e. from 'sinister' viewpoint). In all cases, the 'moral' relativity should be obvious, although it may take some insight/further study of MSS for this to be seen. The same applies to the magick – i.e. the alteration of individuals/ events/archetypal forms and so on by a Master/Mistress/ magickian: only in a few instances (e.g. Falcifer) is this instantly recognizable as 'magick' (robes, rituals and so on). There are important reasons for all this – reasons which once understood should aid the esoteric understanding of the reader.

Thus, the MSS are more challenging/esoterically interesting than might appear from a first, casual, reading. The following lists give some (not all) of the main themes and questions dealt with/arising from the Quartet. They are intended only as a guide to further reading of the MSS. Ideally, what follows should be read only after the MSS themselves and then to provoke further study of them/aid the understanding obtained from the first reading.

l) Greyling – What forces (in both magickal and personal sense (is there a difference?) control/influence the characters of Mickleman, andrea, Alison, Fenton? Does Alison's perception change? If so, by what means? Is this means intentional – or via magick? If so, to what end/purpose? Does Mickleman's perception/insight change? What is his initial level of self-understanding? What his wyrd? What is Fiona's part in this? What if anything is Edmund seeking to achieve and why? Some key elements (clues exist in the MS):

a) How does supra-personal magick work? b) To what end this magick? c) Archetypally (re spheres of ToW) what forces act upon the psyche of the main characters? d) The MS expresses one aspect of real magick in action – is this magick as described in the MS sinister? If so, why?

•••••••

2) Temple – What archetypal elements are present in Melanie and Thurstan? How is Melanie changed – and why? (See quote from Book of Recalling at beginning of MS.)

Does Thurstan change through his love with Melanie? If so, why? Can all these changes be related to the experiences of an Initiate, in real life, following the seven-fold way?

What level of insight has Algar attained? Is he a magickian – in control? Do external forces/archetypes control/influence him? Is this related to Initiate experience? Does Algar understand wyrd?

Pead – what is his level of insight/achievement?

Jukes – what is his? Does his esoteric development change? If so, how?

Saer – who is he? What is his role? His magick? What is Claudia's understanding/role and so on?

Main theme – what is the magick and wyrd of the MS and Why?
3) Giving – Rhiston and Mallam: what is their level of development/understanding? Does this change. Can they as characters be related to journey of an Initiate?

Lianna – what is her esoteric development/insight? What key factors influence her?

Thorold– what is his role and how does this change? Has he esoteric self-awareness? Is there a manipulation of him by Lianna? If so, why?

Imlach and his daughter – what are their roles and level of esoteric development. How well does Imlach fulfil the archetypal role of Guardian?

Monica – is she manipulated? If so, why? Is her death the result of magick? If so, why?

Some themes:

a) What is the magick of the 'story'? Is this magick sinister? b)How do Mallam's belief and magick differ from Lianna's? Is he a Satanist? Is Lianna? What is Lianna's relationship to him, his wyrd? b) Is the historical setting (Templars etc.) necessary? c) Does the story show Lianna as a real Mistress of Earth? d)What is Sidnal's role in relation to the magick and Lianna? Is he 'Satanic'?

(What is Satanic?)

To some degree, all the MSS in the quintet deal with a particular type of magick/ manipulation and this is explicated in many ways including:

a) of individuals and groups of individuals by other individuals and groups, be these others magickians or not;

b) of how various individuals are affected by certain elemental/magickal forces and 'emotions', these forces etc. being manifest in various guises – some directly magickal, some archetypal (as, for example, when a man is charmed by and falls in love with a woman, he apprehending that woman archetypally) and some aeonic.

The manipulation of the energies/forms and so on varies in the different MS, as the aim or intent of such manipulation does – for example, sometimes it is for direct personal desire/gratification, sometimes it is due to unconscious factors, sometimes it is due to a desire (sinister and otherwise) to change/aid a particular individual or individuals.

However, just as important in each MS as this covert/overt form of magick is how and why individuals become changed via it in many and various situations. Thus, for example, sometimes change occurs because of personal involvement with others, sometimes through being influenced (either consciously or unconsciously) by magickal energy (which itself may be directed at that individual by another), sometimes through mediums like music (with perhaps some 'magickal' input from another), sometimes via personal confrontation with unconscious fears and/or insights.

All of these changes are presented in the various MSS from differing perspectives – and these perspectives are sometimes individual (directly personal) as they are sometimes magickal. The perspectives change – from MS to MS and sometimes within a single MS – and while the perspective may be 'sinister' it is also sometimes 'moral': that is, seen from the viewpoint of an individual adhering to 'conventional morals/attitudes'. This diverse variation is intentional, since by it the reader is (or should be) able to objectify the action/changes/characters and thus understand the influences (magickal and otherwise) behind these, particularly with reference to the psyche. This understanding is aided by the fact that each MS is related to a particularly septenary sphere and thus to some extent deals with the energy/magick/influences both unconscious and conscious of that sphere. However, as in real life and real magick, other influences (from other spheres) may sometimes intrude and complicate matters and the reader should be capable of understanding the interplay.

The understanding that results from a reading and study of the MSS (using the themes, questions and so on revealed here and in other notes on the quintet) is part of the process of Initiate awareness – and should assist those following the seven-fold way to arrive at a personal understanding of their own psyche as well as that of others. Such understanding enables magick itself to be understood and used effectively.

THE SINISTER PATH – AIMS AND INTENTS

The Sinister Path, as the way of genuine Satanism is sometimes known, comprises two traditions. The first of these is 'traditional Satanism' – represented by such groups as the ONA – and the second derives from the teachings promulgated by Anton La Vey and includes his 'Church of Satan' as well as the 'Temple of Set'. In both aims and intent, the two traditions differ considerably, and while traditional Satanism may be said to have its roots in Europe (particularly Britain) the La Vey tradition is primarily American and of fairly recent date.

The primary aim of traditional Satanism is the achievement, by the individual, of magickal Adeptship and this is achieved by Initiated individuals following what is called the 'seven-fold way' (sometimes called the 'seven-fold sinister way'). This way is essentially a series of magickal techniques, teachings and goals and during its early stages may be said to consist of an exploration, by the individual, of hidden/latent/sinister/forbidden areas of consciousness.

During these early stages, practical magick is employed, and traditional Satanism distinguishes between 'external' and 'internal' magick. The first type is primarily sorcery; the second, an exploration/expansion of individual consciousness. One of the tasks of an Initiate following this seven-fold way is the formation of a magickal/Satanic Temple for the performance of ceremonial rituals. Among these rituals is 'The Black Mass'. However, these ceremonial rituals – and external magick itself of whatever kind represent only the first few stages of the sinister seven-fold way: they are, essentially, a practical training in magick and magickal technique. It is beyond these stages that the real work of an Initiate of the 'Dark Tradition' begins, and these more advanced stages involve that Initiate in 'Internal' magick – the development of individual consciousness.

Thus, traditional Satanism is concerned with the 'inner development' of its Initiates, and its followers are few in numbers. Neither they, nor the groups to which they belong, proselytize, and traditional

Satanism has no religious or political connotations whatsoever. Rather, it is an esoteric way of living for those few individuals who might be interested – a way founded on Western Occult tradition (an aspect of this tradition is known as the Septenary system).

The La Vey type of Satanism concentrates on a glorification of the individual 'ego' and an indulgence in the pleasures of life. Both the Church of Satan and the more recent Temple of Set are organized on the basis of Satanism as a religion with all that this implies in terms of acceptance of doctrine and adherence to an individual leader/master/specific group. The fundamental tenets of this religion were stated by La Vey in his *Satanic Bible*. While the Church of Satan and the Temple of Set differ on some organizational matters, they both take this 'Satanic Bible' (and other works by La Vey) as their starting point, and in many respects the Temple of Set may be said to be a 'schism' from the Church of Satan. Other Satanic groups both in America, Europe and elsewhere, take these two organizations as their own 'role model' and follow both their teachings/philosophy and methods of magical working.

Basically, the teachings of La Vey and those following him have their origin in the qabalistic, Grimoire tradition. There is an identification with the 'demonic' aspects and a desire to use this to further personal goals and ambitions. Generally, followers of this tradition of modern Satanism do not believe in any existence after death, seek practical mastery over others, exult in the pleasures of the flesh, perform rituals and ceremonies for their own benefit and see their beliefs in religious terms. The main groups – the Church of Satan and the Temple of Set also actively seek followers, engage in public avowals of Satanic faith and offer members various titles and offices.

The aims of these groups include winning converts for their religion, making that religion more accessible and acceptable, and, ultimately, bringing that religion into social prominence. The majority of individuals who profess to be Satanists and who do not belong to any particular grouping, almost without exception adhere to the La Vey tradition. This is so because of the 'publicity profile' attained by La

Vey and, following him, Aquino (of the Temple of Set) and because of the ready availability of books dealing with this aspect of Satanism.

The fundamental aims of this type of Satanism may be simply stated as the glorification of the ego and the return of instinct. There is not, in this type, any glorification of 'evil' and certainly not any 'Satanic criminal behaviour'. Instead, there is an attempt to change the way the individual views the world – toward what may be termed a more Mephistophelean and Machiavellian approach. In contrast, the followers of more traditional Satanism believe that this approach is only a beginning. These followers eschew the religious approach and instead concentrate on achieving self-development beyond the stage represented by the 'ego'. Traditional Satanism also believes individuals can create for themselves an existence after death, and this creation is seen as one of the fundamental aims of this tradition.

Further, traditional Satanist groups and teachers are secret, and those who, after perhaps a diligent search, find them and seek to follow their seven-fold way are subjected to many ordeals before being accepted. This testing of all candidates ensures that only the most sincere and motivated are accepted.

The foundation of the Church of Satan in the sixth decade of this present century and the writings of the founder of that Church (particularly *The Satanic Bible*) represented only one further stage in the development of Satanism – a new divergence, founded on some aspects, although not all, of that particular magickal and practical view of the world. Satanism, in many divergent forms, existed before the Church of Satan in both the Old and the New worlds and those forms, as well as new ones, continue to exist independant of both this Church and the writings of its creator. Thus groups and individuals which claim that the Church of Satan (in either its present or its original form) represents the only genuine form of Satanism are, historically, deluding themselves.

Such claims are usually based on one or more of the following: (a) The founder of the Church of Satan inaugurated a 'new Satanic' age and this inauguration makes all other forms of Satanism invalid/superfluous; (b)a mandate was given by some supra-personal being; (c) there is a 'pure' tradition and this form is represented by a presently existing group.

Basically, those who claim to be 'genuine' Satanists divide into three groups: the Church of Satan, the Temple of Set and some small European groups (both the Church of Satan (CoS) and the Temple of Set (ToS) are American in origin) among which the ONA is included. From time to time, other groups become manifest – both they are almost without exception splinter groups/fronts of the Cos or the ToS (e.g. 'The Werewolf Order': a CoS 'front'). The CoS accepts (a) and (c) above and as a group adhere with an almost religious outlook to the founder of the Church and his '*Bible*' – for example, one the followers of this Church states (Black Flame, Vol 2 no 2): 'We have a Bible... We have a Church.... We have a tradition... We have a High Priest.' The ToS accepts (b) and (c) – the mandate emanating from the Prince of Darkness in the form of Set and divulged to mortals in 'The Book of Coming Forth by Night'. Further, the ToS accept that they are continuing the work begun by the early CoS, that is, they represent the original and 'pure' Church. In this sense, the ToS is a schism from the CoS.

Hence the conflict between the CoS and the ToS – both claim to be the genuine form of Satanism and both date the new Satanic age in the same way – 1990 ev is, for example, xxV A.S. Both of these groups have an organizational structure (although the ToS claims the CoS in its present form does not any longer possess a structure) and both have teachings and a leader. Members of both are expected to respect both teachings and leader. Both actively seek members and both engage in public/media avowals. The ToS hopes to make Satanism a legitimate religion. As far as basic teachings go, the CoS and the ToS differ – for although the ToS accepts the early works of La Vey (there being thus a little common ground) it differs quite significantly in what has been built upon those works. There is, for instance, in the ToS an emphasis on the 'higher self' above the glorification of the ego that is such a feature of the CoS as well as a move away from a fixed ideology and 'Church' like mentality. Nonetheless, the ToS demands a certain commitment (subserviance some opponents would say) to the teachings and authority of the Temple, and while this is not as pronounced as in the CoS it nevertheless exists. The squabbles between the CoS and the ToS aids this commitment – on both sides – and to a certain extent necessitates it. Having become established, and having media profiles, both the CoS and the ToS need to continually re-affirm both their identity and their mission – and this has led to the formation of personality cults (more evident on the side of the CoS although Aquino accepts the role of 'Voice of Set').

Both the Church and the Temple are concerned although in different ways – with safeguarding what· they see as the authentic tradition of Satanism, and accordingly each tends to be antagonistic to those outside of this supposed tradition, particularly if individuals and groups espouse views contrary to their teachings and policies. Both wish to protect what they see as their reputation and this tends to lead to suspicions regarding other groups and individuals who espouse different forms of Satanism – as well as sometimes polemics/disinformation against those groups and individuals to further enhance that reputation at the expense of those others.

All this is not unexpected given the form of both the CoS and the Tos and the claims made by each regarding the authority and authenticity of their version of Satanism – in fact, all the above follows naturally. In contrast, the ONA, for example, is not concerned with either an imagined (or even real) history regarding its own tradition and teachings – or with trying to claim some authority (either supra-personal or via some new aeonic manifestation) for that tradition and those teachings. Basically, some ONA teachings have been handed down by reclusive Adepts and some have been developed recently. What is 'historical' about these teachings mayor may not be valuable today and mayor may not be of interest to aspirant Adepts – indeed, some of the teachings handed down have been superseded and some of just mystifications. What exists is made accessable enabling its usefulness or irrelevance to be judged on an individual basis. What is important however is that the central core (recently codified and extended in the creative sense) offers a practical path to Adeptship and beyond. (This path being explicated in the books *Naos*, *The Black Book of Satan*, *The Deofel Quartet* and the Star Game.) The accent is on practical – it is devoid of mystifications, does not involve theoretical discussions, require acceptance of any dogma, ideology or organizational structure. Neither does it require submission to any individual or authority. It is not concerned with converting others, with reputations or establishing a favourable social climate for its adherents. It is, simply, a very simple and practical set of magickally-inclined workings which any individual can undertake for themselves. It does not need to be 'interpreted' by some Master or guide. It simply is: available to those who wish to avail themselves of its methods.

This is not to say that this path – the seven-fold sinister way – is easy. On the contrary, it takes time and effort, requiring a certain desire to follow it to its end. The following of this way depends only on the individual.

This present codification of the essence of ONA teachings into 'the seven-fold sinister way' is a result of the natural process of evolution within the LHP – in this particular instant, the result of the creative inspiration of one individual over the past few decades. This process, of refinement and extension, will continue as further insights are gained and new creativity – extending the frontiers – arises from other individuals who are Adepts of the LHP. Thus the present form of those teachings (as represented, for instance, in *Naos*) is itself only a stage between a historical past and the possibilities of the future: as such, this form is not sacred or subject to jealous guardianship with extended polemics in its defence. It is simply a working method which produces results – there is no mystique about it, no glorification of the creative individual responsible for its present form, no reliance on historical traditions, as there can be no dogma attached to it. It simply exists, to guide those who may be interested in following its methods.

It is up to each and every individual interested in the LHP and Satanism to choose which way to follow. Some lead to Adeptship and beyond – others merely to subservience to someone else's ego and mythology.

BRIEF GUIDE TO THE SEVEN-FOLD WAY:

Aims: a) Esoteric Initiation; b) Magickal Adeptship; c) Fulfilment of individual wyrd and potential; d) creation of next stage of human evolution

Stages: 1) Neophyte 2) Initiate 3) External Adept 4) Internal Adept 5) Master of Temple/Mistress of Earth 6) Grand Master (Magus)/Grand Mistress 7) Immortal

Neophyte: Construction of Star Game (qv *Naos*) and learning how to use this. Undertake ritual of Initiation (*Naos*; *Black Book*)

Initiate: Workings with spheres and septenary pathways (*Naos*); Hermetic workings for specific desires/aims (*Naos*). Achievement of demanding physical goal. Seeking and finding of companion (opposite sex: or same if gay) Initiate this individual (*Black Book*) and undertake workings with spheres/pathways with them. Use of Star Game with companion. Undertake Grade Ritual of External Adept (*Naos*).

External Adept: With companion, organize a Temple for ceremonial rituals (*Black Book*) holding regular sunedrions (*Black Book*): recruiting members etc. Run this Temple for between six months to one year – regular teaching sessions (*Black Book*) including Esoteric Chant, Star Game etc. At end of this period prepare for and undertake Grade Ritual of Internal Adept.

Internal Adept: Depending on wyrd (manifest during Grade Ritual) continue with Temple or fulfil on practical level the tasks of wyrd (e.g. creativity). Learning and use of Advanced Star Game and Aeonic magick o Further training of companion (up to Internal Adept if required/possible).

Use of Rites of Nine Angles. Preparation for G. Ritual Master/Mistress.

HISTORICAL ADDENDUM: REDUCTIO AD ABSURDUM

The individual responsible for the present codification of ONA (in the form of the seven-fold way, Star Game etc.) does not claim any supra-personal authority for that codification (in the form of Set/Satan or an extraterrestrial intelligence) or indeed for the creativity which was its essence. Neither does he claim any authority via having belonged to some ancient and mysterious group whose 'Master' taught and Initiated him.

The truth is simple, and a little ordinary. He was fortunate perhaps in spending most of his childhood and early youth in Africa and the Far East where, in the former, he grew up among peoples who believed in pagan practices and witchcraft, and, in the latter, he came in contact with many and various traditions including LHP Taoist magic and Martial Arts. All this formed a somewhat unusual education (there is no claim to being 'Initiated' into any form) and provided a continuing interest in esoteric arts. This curiosity, interest together with his keen intellect, enthusiasm and zest for danger' led him to, in later youth, to not only seek out LHP groups in Europe but also into many interesting and diverse experiences, and in the late sixties he was Initiated into some LHP groups/underground Satanic Temples. His diverse experiences then and later (some dangerous, some at variance with prevailing social dogma, many dark, some noetical) provided a useful background for an Occult and personal synthesis and led to him taking responsibility for a small LHP group. The teachings of this group were rather garbled, full of mystifications and occasional insights, but they did provide some basis for creative extension. Thus, the new synthesis that was the seven-fold way was created. The original LHP group had no historical significance and did not claim among its former members any person of significance on any level – it was simply a reclusive circle of a few individuals orientated toward the Black Arts whose teachings (such as they were) centred around a septenary approach to magickal alchemy and a 'mythology' about the Dark Gods.

(It should be noted that the other LHP groups he joined either derived their magic from a mixture of Crowley/Golden Dawn/demonism or were rather boring, lacking Satanic zest.)

In the early years of the eighth decade of the present century a decision was made to publish the traditions of this small group (the ONA – as it came to be called some decades earlier) together with the new codification. Some of the traditional material concerned Sacrifice and some related to the Dark Gods mythos.

No one within this group believes these traditions and methods are unalterable or invested with 'supernatural' authority. As expressed in such published works as *Naos* and *The Black Book* they are a practical method of achieving magickal Adeptship and extending consciousness into the next stage of its development.

Thus the DNA has no structure because no structure is needed – its members may guide others if those others wish, such guidance occuring because those members have themselves undergone (to a greater or lessor extent depending on their own personal development) the tasks of the seven-fold way arid can thus offer advice from experience.

It is as absurdly simple as that.

ONA 1989 ev

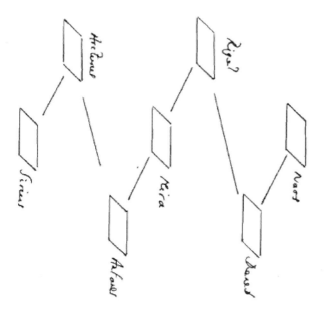

Helenus *Rigel?* *Sirius* *Mira* *Naos* *Atlas* *Deneb*

Notes on the Septenary Stars

Deneb: Jupiter sphere: Baphomet: Earth Gate (for ∝ working)
Rigel: Mars sphere: Dark angle (Man's Gate) - ∝ working
Antares: Venus sphere: Light angle (∝ working):Star Gate
Arcturus: Mercury: Satan/Lucifer: Dark Gate (∝ working)

*Rising of Arcturus (Albion c. 3 000 yrs BP) ⇒ August:
thus 'festivals'
*Antares ⇒ May - thus 'festivals' (middle/end of month)
('Venus' implies Baphomet image in 'light' aspect:
qv. Tarot image 2 'High Priestess')

*Baphomet: Mistress of Earth (qv. 'magickal energies'/Azoth
images).

Note: All the above represent only one aspect of the causal
symbolism (ie. how the 'chaotic'/raw energy of a particular
sphere is apprehended/viewed/manifested to individual
consciousness):-

∅ → λ :
viewed by t;u

Master   ∘ ∘ ∘   Mistress
Priest ∘   ∘ ∘   Priestess
  ♂   ∘ ∘   ♀

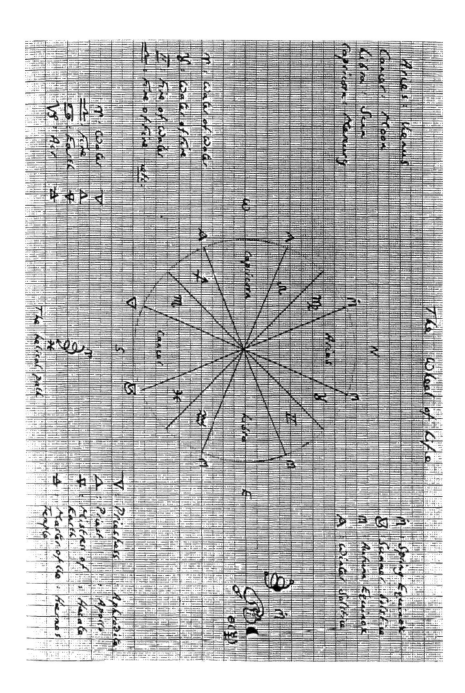

THE ABYSS

The Abyss is where the causal and the acausal meet: a nexus of temporal and spatial dimensions. Because of the nature of our consciousness, the Abyss lies latent within all of us – that is, our consciousness consists of both causal and acausal aspects. In this sense, we are all 'Gates' to the acausal dimensions, although this Gate – and the pathways leading to/from it – often lies undiscovered. Magickal training is essentially the discovery, exploration and use of these pathways.

Symbolized causally, the Abyss lies between the spheres of the Sun and Mars in the septenary Tree of Wyrd, and the 'Entering the Abyss' is that stage of magickal development which distinguishes the Master/Mistress from the Adept. The experience of the Abyss – which the Grade Ritual 'Entering the Abyss' begins – is fundamentally a destruction of the self-image which the Grade Ritual of Internal Adept created and which was glimpsed during the External Adept rite. It is also the destruction of all personal illusions regarding opposites: the final 'withdrawing of projections'. In essence, the Internal Adept has learnt (mainly through the Grade Ritual) to withdraw the projections of the 'ego' from other individuals – that is, theirs is an understanding of individuals as those individuals are in essence: without the distortion of one's own passions/ideas/prejudices and without the distortions of other people's ideas/judgements and so on. The experience of the Abyss takes this a stage further – there is a withdrawal of all personal projections made by every individual upon others/the 'cosmos' and so on: both personal and impersonal. Thus, the essence is apprehended behind the appearance which the causal produces because it is the causal. Put very simply, the Abyss is the beginning of acausal perception.

This perception implies a complete understanding of oneself, one's wyrd, as well as an understanding of others, of aeonic influences, and of the 'comsos' itself – the beginnings of wisdom … Yet this does not mean a negation of individuality. Rather, it is an enhancement of consciousness. This is so because the Abyss is also the Tree of Wyrd itself – all the spheres and the pathways in both their individual and aeonic forms: the 'individual forms' being Jungian-type archetypes (and the experiences/understanding appropriate to these) on a personal level, and the 'aeonic forms' being aeonic/cultural myths and images on a supra-personal level, in both 'sinister' and 'light' aspects. Further, the Abyss is also a direct opening or 'Gate' to the acausal dimensions.

The ritual of the Abyss implies an acceptance of acausal energies as those energies are – that is, without any 'abstract', personal or judgemental views. It is a letting 'in' of those Null, Chaotic energies without any hindrence. This of course can be dangerous, but the preparation reduces this danger as well as making possible an understanding of those energies and the 'forms' they may or may not assume in both the causal and acausal worlds. This latter point is quite important, because there have been many who, unprepared, having experienced some acausal energies via entering the Abyss too soon. Quite often, the result of this premature magickal experience is madness or extreme personal dis-orientation resulting in a 'possessed' personal life and/or loss of vitality; another and frequent result is personal delusion about one's own abilities and understanding, both personal and magickal.

This understanding of the acausal, vital to a 'successful' crossing of the Abyss, derives from the preparation implicit in (a) having undertaken the Grade Ritual of Internal Adept [that is, in essence, having spent at least three months alone without any external influences and without any personal contact] and (b) having fulfilled the tasks revealed by that Grade Ritual. This fulfilling of personal tasks (the accomplishment of part of the wyrd of the individual) is necessary (and it takes from one to many years after the Grade Ritual of Internal Adept) because it dissipates the energy of the 'self-image' that the Grade Ritual produces, preparing thus a voidness within the Adept. The Adept generally knows when this inner void is reached (in simple terms, the personal, driving energy is gone through achievement of personal goals: the reality, of course, is more complicated and here the advice of a Master/Mistress/Magus is often saught).

The ritual of the Abyss is simple. The physical part (the walk in the specified time without assistance) is essential preparation for the 'magickal' part because it prepares the consciousness in a very specific way as well as draining the physical resources of the body. To complete the walk given the conditions stated requires determination – and this determination is released/abandoned when the magickal part of the rite is begun, this release/abandonement occurring quite naturally because the physical goal has been achieved. Thus, there is a 'hidden' wisdom in the construction of the rite (as there is in all the Grade Rituals). The physical part also creates – because of the isolation – a feeling within the individual of being only a part of something more vast, and it is for this reason that the walk is undertaken as far from human habitation – as possible. This isolation, the concentration required to walk at a pace enabling the goal to be reached within the set time, the rhythm of walking, the anticipation of the magickal part, all combine to produce the conditions necessary within the consciousness of the individual conducive to success.

As mentioned above, the Abyss is also an opening into the acausal. The 'passing of the Abyss' is the opening of that 'Gate' within us. All magick is a glimpse of the acausal, and the stages of the seven-fold way are really stages when the acausal energies are developed and understood in a progressively more emphatic manner – that is, they may be seen as 'pushing that Gate wider and wider' – in the passing of the Abyss there is no longer a Gate, but rather a union or fusion. In another sense, the seven-fold way may be said to be the creation. Within the consciousness of the individual, of connections or pathways to the acausal – each stage developes more and more pathways until they form a conduit through which acausal energy 'flows'. Beyond the Abyss, the individual is part of the acausal 'flow' and has achieved the goal of sentient life.

This is really the great secret of alchemy, of magick and of the Left Hand or Sinister Path itself – that is, we can create for ourselves another existence in another 'universe' and an existence which continues after our causal self dies. The means to this existence is simply – the seven fold way.

According to tradition, the Abyss is also presenced physically in our causal universe. That is, terrestrial and 'Space' or 'Star' Gates exist where the two universes are joined. In reality, the terrestrial Gates may be said to be points where the causal and acausal come close to contact: where there is 'seepage' of acausal energy – the discovery of these places, and then the 'opening of the Gate' via magick producing Aeonic energy to alter the causal (and thus the individuals in the world). [See the Order MSS relating to Aeons. 'Lovecraft and the Dark Gods' etc.]

Ny — thra   *   k - thun

- ae   Af —   a —

30th .   Ny - thra   k - thun - ae

ae   .

Chant to open Star Gate

Ny - thra * k - thun - ae   At -   a

- 30th   At -

a   - 30th   .

At -   a   - 30th   .

Chant to return Atazoth

THE NINE ANGLES – ESOTERIC MEANINGS

The name nine angles is, in one fundamental sense, self-descriptive: the Tree of Wyrd possesses nine causal angles and nine acausal angles in the causal geometric sense, and these can be represented as formed by the corners or angles of a causal and acausal tetrahedron, one a reflexion of the other, the base of both lying in the plane of the middle sphere (the Sun). This double tetrahedron encloses in three-dimensional space the path from causal to acausal – the 'Initiate journey' from the sphere of the Moon to Saturn via the other spheres, this path being helical (cf. 'The wheel of Life'). The direction of this path is 'counter-clockwise'. In essence, the acausal is a reflexion (and vice versa) of the causal, so the single term 'Nine Angles' describes what is our normal (i.e. un-Initiated) view of the septenary, this septenary being a 'map' of consciousness and the cosmos. The realization of the dual nature of the spheres (for example, Mercury is the 'shadow' of Mars) arises from Initiation and is the first stage of an esoteric understanding of the term 'nine angles'.

The term also describes the nine fundamental 'alchemical' forms (represented by the symbols $\Theta(\Theta)$, $\Theta(\mathbf{\xi})$ or $\varkappa(\varkappa)$, $\varkappa(\lambda)$, $\bar{\varkappa}(\omega)$ and so on :i.e. the pieces of the Star Game). These forms are the basic apprehensions of magickal energy and thus re-present the acausal manifest in the causal (in the many forms of that manifestation – e.g. individual consciousness: the images/archetypes pertaining thereto). Hence each of these symbols is an 'angle' re: the above description of the septenary Tree. These nine fundamental forms (the abstract symbolism is a stage of understanding beyond the purely causal geometric one) exist in many combinations within the nexion which the 'Tree of Wyrd' represents – and these combinations are abstractly symbolized by the placement of the many pieces of the Star Game over the seven boards ('Spheres') of that game. (Note: The Advanced form of the Star Game is the most complete representation, but for convenience the septenary form will be used here. It should be noted, however, that the septenary form – difficult though it is for Initiates serves only as an introduction to the Advanced game.) This abstraction, in terms of the Star Game, makes the forms understandable on a level higher than that using words and ideas – this understanding is a new form of thinking, a form appropriate to the next century and beyond. Such an understanding arises from playing the Star Game and relating the abstract symbols to conventional representations (e.g. archetypal forms; the energies of the pathways; the symbolism of the Tarot and the many and various Occult symbolisms) – this developes the capacity for what may be termed 'acausal thinking': when the conventional representations are abandoned and collocations are viewed abstractly. This 'abstraction' is however a new 'insight' (a lower form of which is often described an 'intuition') and not a dry, academic process: it extends consciousness into new and important realms and pre-figures the development of a symbolic language which eliminates the confusion, both moral and linguistic, which exists in words and the translation of complex ideas into such words. It is 'mathesis' in the ancient Greek sense and while not being what we understand as 'mathematics' it complements mathematical abstraction and indeed interacts with it in some places: Essentially, the symbolism is a new tool to assist and develope our understanding, and it is via this symbolism that the meanings of the nine angles may most easily be understood without confusion.

On a less refined esoteric level (i.e. in more 'conventional' esoteric terms) the nine symbolize the sigil formed by connecting the spheres of the Tree of Wyrd with the two most important 'Gates' (see illustration). This sigil describes the energy flow and may be used, magickally, in several ways – for example, as a visualization 'sigil' (in hermetic rituals etc.) as a symbol of the path walked during certain rites (some connected with Esoteric Chant – qv. '*Naos*') and when an 'Earth Gate' is being saught with a view to drawing acausal energy through it to change the causal (e.g. inaugurate a new aeon) – the find an Earth Gate the sequence would be begun to end at the 'Earth Gate'. The nine also represents the tetrahedron (for example, the crystal one used in the Rite of the Nine Angles) which is itself symbolic of the nexion described by the Tree of Wyrd. Thus, for instance, in the Nine Angles Rite, the crystal represents one aspect of the nexion, the Priestess and Priest the other: together (i.e. the bringing together in the ritual) they enable the nexion to be opened. In this sense, the Priest and Priestess (when conjoined) form a 'tetrahedron' which, joined with the crystal one, enables acausal energy to become manifest in the causal (the 'world') – ,this is the secret hinted at in many historical alchemical MSS (for example the 'Rosarium Philosophorum': 'Make a round circle of the man and the woman...') and occasionally depicted in drawings. This 'double tetrahedron' is a magickal form of the double described above in the first paragraph (the causal geometric one).

In some 'esoteric' circles the nine is seen in terms of the five, the five itself deriving from the five angles of the inverted pentagram. This is, however, a misunderstanding, deriving as it does from viewing the 'angles' two-dimensionally when in fact they should be considered in a three-dimensional way, at first, and then four-dimensionally (the helical path within the tetrahedrons). This four-dimensional view is in itself only a beginning – beyond is the multi-dimensional when both the causal and the acausal spaces are considered. One means to apprehend this duality is the Star Game.

---

*For example, the causal within the acausal can be represented by the tensor $T_{\lambda\mu}$ where $C_{\lambda\mu}$ is the causal component and $a_{\lambda\mu}$ the acausal one. For an x^λ system (Euclidean space) $C_{\lambda\mu}$ has <u>nine</u> non-zero components. These are the symmetric componets of $T_{\lambda\mu}$: the skew-symmetric being acausal. In this sense, the nine form 'sub-spaces' of the causal, and the tensor 'describes' the nexion causal/acausal. It is possible to write an equation involving this tensor which describes this multi-dimensional space, the boundary conditions of which give, for example, the metrics of each form of 'space-time' (causal and acausal).

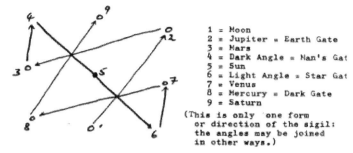

1 = Moon
2 = Jupiter = Earth Gate
3 = Mars
4 = Dark Angle = Man's Gate
5 = Sun
6 = Light Angle = Star Gate
7 = Venus
8 = Mercury = Dark Gate
9 = Saturn

(This is only one form
 or direction of the sigil:
 the angles may be joined
 in other ways.)

(Note: Take the four 'gates' from the nine angles and
an 'inverted' pentagram results.)

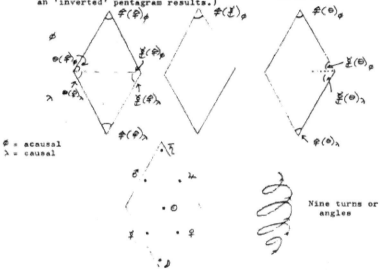

φ = acausal
λ = causal

Nine turns or
angles

Nine basic $\Theta(\Theta) \rightarrow \Theta(\underline{\chi}) \rightarrow \Theta(\overline{\varphi}) \rightarrow \underline{\chi}(\Theta) \rightarrow \underline{\chi}(\underline{\chi}) \rightarrow \underline{\chi}(\overline{\varphi}) \rightarrow \overline{\varphi}(\Theta) \rightarrow \overline{\varphi}(\underline{\chi}) \rightarrow \overline{\varphi}($
  angles

(Note: $\Theta(\Theta)_\lambda$ is causal angle; $\Theta(\Theta)_\phi$ acausal angle etc.)

107

CROWLEY, SATAN AND THE SINISTER WAY

In one sense, the work of Crowley may be said to be a restoration of various chthonic mysteries of mainly Sumerian origin. Thus the importance in the cult of Thelema attached to Set/Shaitan/Satan – an attempt to re-integrate into the consciousness of the individual the duality represented by the formula LAShTAL.

However, despite the many claims, Crowley did not inaugurate a new Aeon. His restoration is simply a restoring of something long dead – a kind of necromancy, and as a magickal force the cult of Thelema might as well not exist. In the exoteric sense, 'Shaitan' represents those instinctive levels that are often, in our modern society, repressed in the individual – and Satanic rituals of either the traditional kind or the kind based on the use of sexual formulae, are a means of catharsis: a beginning where consciousness is prepared and liberated from the restrictions implicit in ordinary life. In practical terms – and for the civilization of the West whose dominant religion and ethos has hindered by its distortion all that is natural in terms of sex – this often means participation in rituals such as those given in 'Codex Saerus' or Crowley's Gnostic Mass or some form of sexual working. Such participation restores the balance that is often lacking.

Yet such a participation is only a beginning – and the ritual forms of such a participation are only a means. They are means to experience and if correctly undertaken should provide the individual with an understanding of that aspect of their personality which has been symbolized as Satan (for men) and Lilitu/Darkat (for women) – the darker, sensual side. Such an understanding is personal in the sense that the personality of the individual is involved, and the perspective achieved is usually that of the life, or Destiny, of the individual in relation to his circumstances and other individuals. That is, there is little concern with or appreciation of, the forces of an Aeon – other than perhaps some vague 'intellectual' understanding: or what is thought of as understanding.

This re-integration of the darker aspects – whether it occurs through participation in rituals or via other techniques of magick – is represented, in the septenary system, by the three lower spheres of the Tree of Wyrd (Moon, Mercury, and Venus) and these spheres symbolize the three states of that re-integration – that- is, Calcination, Seperation and Coagulation to use alchemical terms. It is during the next stage that the individual who is following a planned and practical magickal way gains both cultural and Aeonic perspective. This enables an understanding of the relationship existing between the individual and their unique Destiny and those forces which are symbolized by a magickal formula or 'word' and which represent a particular Aeon.

Such an understanding (associated with the fourth state the sphere of the Sun – and the fifth stage, Mars) derives or has its foundation in, a rational approach and usually involves the individual studying Aeons, civilizations and the relations between them.

However, the system of Crowley, as well as the many systems deriving in whole or in part from his work, never arrives at this stage because it has (a) set the formulae of sexual magick above everything, and (b) negates with its approach the rational analysis required. The same is true of other magickal systems involved in the 'darker' side and which try in some way to let the individuals following them experience their own shadow nature. An integration and thus understanding of this nature – enabling the individual to build upon the foundations thus achieved – of necessity implies the development of those qualities such as reason, logic and scientific understanding, which Crowley et al have abandoned. Yet this development does not imply a mishmash of occult and psuedo-scientific concepts such as 'quantum mechanics' and 'relativity'[2] – an unstable amalgam currently fashionable in certain circles. Rather, it implies the development of the mind and a certain way of thinking.

---

[2] The next fifty years or so will see an end to these speculative, un-experimental and rather siily ideas/theories.

On both the esoteric and exoteric levels, the most significant step so far in the evolution of our consciousness has been the development of rational analysis and its extension as the scientific method. The acceptance of this method (which does not preclude an acceptance of the forces with which magick deals) implies a certain 'view of the world' and a personal approach to living: a way which is at once cautious, generally optimistic and open and enquiring. This 'view of the world' or way of thinking derives from the ancient Greeks – it is expressed in their early philosophy (i.e before the decline represented by Plato), in their religious attitude and in their way of living. It is essentially the same attitude exemplified by Western paganism, and it is the antithesis of that view and way represented by the religion of the Nazarene. The religion of the Nazarene inverts all natural values – as Nietzsche understood. Thelema, and similar beliefs, negate, as Nazarene philosophy and life does, that natural spontaneity which is the essence of this pagan 'view of the world' – because Thelema ties the mind in knots of obscurity and metaphysical speculation (as the qabala in general does) – it briefly frees the spirit only to weigh down the spirit with the chains of its own metaphysics. The true ethos of the West – which the religion of the Nazarene distorted and supplanted – may be signified by the word 'Azif' and the symbol of the sunwheel it is pagan in essence. The ethos of the West (which derives from the present Aeonic force or 'current' first established c. 500 AD) is not and never has been patriarchal in the sense that Crowley and his followers believed – such a 'patriarchal' ethos representing the distortion imposed upon the original ethos by the Nazarenes. That Crowley and others were unaware of this is indicative of how far removed Thelema is from genuine esoteric tradition. Esoterically, the genuine Western ethos is symbolized by that force which has become known as 'Satan' or Lucifer. Exoterically, this represents the desire to know which has attained its greatest manifestation in modern science and exploration. An analysis of Aenonic forces indicates that the present Aeon has, on the practical level – i.e. in terms of its effects on the vast majority of individuals who because they have not been liberated by Occult Initiation are sway to external influences – about three centuries more to run.

During this time, the distortion of the current caused by the Nazarenes and their allies mayor may not continue depending on how certain Initiates use certain powerful magickal forces. Whatever, the 'New Aeon' (the sixth out of the seven that mark our evolution) will have its beginnings on the magickal level within the next few decades – although on the practical level it will be about another three centuries until the effects are apparent. This new Aeon will have no 'word' and its magick will be the magick of 'Thought', that is spontaneous empathy. One of the most fundamental facets of this new Aeon will be the development of a symbolic language which extends the frontiers of thought. Such a language is already prefigured in the Star Game – just as the Star Game itself, as prefigured in traditional Alchemy. Another facet of the new Aeon will be the emergence of a new type of individual type outlined by Nietzsche. This new individual will be fierce, free (of both external and internal/psychic influences), exult in exploration and discovery and possess an essentially pagan attitude to life. It is and has been one of the aims of genuine sinister Orders to produce such individuals – by having their Initiates follow the seven-fold sinister way.

What has happened over the past fifty or more years is that the distortion of the Western ethos – and thus the genuine Aeonic current – has increased. Part of this increase is, in fact, due to Crowley and those who have followed him and his system without really understanding what they were doing. The genuine western esoteric tradition – as distinct from what most Occultists wish to believe is the 'secret tradition' – has no connection whatever with the qabalah, or Egyptian mysteries and symbolism, and neither does it employ in any way the sorcery of 'grimoire magic' and the forms once appropriate to now dead Aeons be such forms Sumerian, Babylonian, Egyptian or whatever.

The basis of the western tradition was and always has been rational in the sense that those who carried on its tradition saught to understand themselves, the world and the cosmos in a detached manner – free from religious/political dogma. That is, to understand things as those things are in themselves: without the projection of beliefs and ideas.

To this end, the septenary system was evolved, and the 'mysteries' expressed in abstract symbolism (of which Alchemy was one form). The essence of the Western tradition was not some 'great secret' or 'hidden knowledge' to be revealed to Initiates only – rather, it was the belief that everything in the cosmos could be understood if one probed, investigated or thought enough about it. That is, the cosmos was seen as a natural order into which individuals could gain insight. From this insight, a new individual would emerge: a more conscious, evolved person.

The tradition thus encouraged the development in the individual o:f empathy via personal experience: an experiencing of all aspects of our own nature as well as the worlds within and without. Thus were the 'rnagickal/Occult' faculties themselves developed. The way of this tradition was essentially practical – exemplified by the Grade Rituals, tasks and so on of the seven-fold way. There was no speculative metaphysical system, no acceptance of irrational fears and beliefs, no subserviance to someone else's personal mythology.

The new Aeon should be a continuation of the process which the genuine Western tradition began. Yet it is possible that this new Aeon may never emerge. The distortion of the Western current does and has represented a desire by some to return to what may be described as an aspect of the Babylonian ethos. This aspect gave rise eventually to not only the poison of Nazarene philosophy and religion, but also to the many political and social systems and ideas founded in the 'Nazarene view of the world'. There is, at this moment in time, a very real magickal conflict occurring between two forces – those representing (whether consciously or not is immaterial) this Babylonian/Nazarene ethos, and those represent.i.ng the genuine western (and thus 'sinister') tradition. On the outcome of this conflict the next Aeon depends – there will be either the new Aeon with the blossoming of the individual and the development of consciousness giving thus a liberation from the tyranny of religion and politics, or a return to those essentially patriarchal dualistic values where impersonal ideals/ideology have precedence over the individual. Every act of genuine sinister magick is a step toward the new Aeon. Thelema is a step back into the past – as are other systems which lack the empathy that experience arid then trascendence of the sinister brings.

HANGSTER'S GATE

Winter came early to the Shropshire town: a cold wind with brief hail which changed suddenly to rain to leave a damp covering of mist.

An old man in an old cart drawn by a sagging pony crossed himself as he saw Yapp shuffle by him along the cobbled lane toward the entrance to the Raven Inn. It was warm, inside the ancient Inn, but dark from fire and pipe smoke, and Yapp took his customary horn of free ale to sit alone on his corner bench by the log fire. The silence that had followed his entrance soon filled, and only one man still stared at hf. The man was Abigail's husband, and he pushed his cap back from his forehead before moving toward Yapp. His companions, dressed like him in their worn work clothes, tried to restrain him, but he pushed them aside. He reached Yapp's table and kicked it aside with his boot. Slowly, Yapp stood up. He was a wiry man and seemed insubstantial beside the bulk of Abigail's husband.

'Wha you been doing? To her!' Abigail's husband clenched his fists and moved closer.

Yapp stared at him, his unshaven face twitching slightly, and then he smiled.

'I canna move! I canna move!' shouted Abigail's husband.

Yapp smiled again, drank the rest of his ale and walked slowly toward the door.

'I be beshrewed!' the big man cried amid the silence.

Yapp turned toward him, made a gesture with his hand and left the inn as Abigail's husband found himself able to move.

No one followed Yapp outside. A carriage and pair raced past hf as he walked down the lane. The young lady inside, heading for the warmth and comfort of Priory Hall, was alarmed at seeing him and turned away. This pleased him, as the prospect of the walk to his cottage, miles distant, pleased him – for it was the night of Autumnal Equinox.

The journey was not tiresome, and he enjoyed the walk, the mist and the darkening sky that came with the twilight hour. The moon would be late to rise, and he walked briskly. Soon, he was above the town and at the place where the three lanes met. His own way took him down, past the small collection of cottages, alehouses and a Church, toward the wooded precincts of Yarchester Hall. He stopped, once, but could not see the distant summit of Brown Clee Hill where he had possessed Abigail. It had been a long ride back in the wind and the rain, but the horses had been strong, almost wild, and he smiled in remembrance, for that night Abigail had warmed his bed. Tomorrow, perhaps, they might go to Raven's Seat. It would be all over by then, for another seventeen years. No one would stop or trouble them.

His way led him into the trees, along a narrow path, down past Devil's Dingle to Hangster's Gate and the clearing. There was nothing in the clearing – except the mist-swathed gibbet with its recent victim swinging gently in the breeze. He would need the hand, and with practised care, he unsheathed his knife to stretch up and cut the dead man's left hand away. Less than a day old, the body had already lost its eyes to ravens.

It was not far from the clearing to his cottage, and he walked slowly, every few moments stopping to stand and listen. There was nothing, no sound – except a faint sighing as the breeze stirred the trees around. A lighted candle shone from the one small window of his cottage. It was a sign, and he stopped to creep down and glimpse inside. There were voices inside and as he looked he saw Abigail standing near a young man. He saw her draw the youth toward her and place his hand on her breast. Heard her laughing; saw her kiss the youth and press her body into his. Then she was dancing around him, laughing and singing as she stripped her clothes away to lay naked and inviting on the sphagnum moss that formed the mattress of Yapp's bed. Then the youth was upon her, struggling to wrest himself from his own clothes.

Yapp heard people approaching along the track and he stood up to hear Abigail's cries of ecstasy. He waited, until they reached him and they all heard Abigail climax with a scream. Then he was inside the cottage, with the others around him. The youth was surprised and tried to stand and Yapp stood aside to let them pin him down on the hard earth floor of the cottage. An old woman in a dirty bonnet gave a toothless laugh – Abigail laughed, even Yapp laughed as the tall blacksmith tore out the youth's heart. There was a pail for some of the blood. Abigail was soon dressed, the body taken away, and she led Yapp and the old woman through the trees to another clearing.

The moon was rising, the blood was fresh and she took the severed hand from Yapp to dip it in the blood and sprinkle their sacred ground to propitiate their dark goddess Baphomet.

(Copyright 1981 ev)

THE TEMPLE OF SET: A BRIEF ANALYSIS

As someone involved for well over twenty years with the LHP, I believe I can offer an analysis from the experience gained during the often hard struggle for , personal and Occult insight. Two things are obvious. First, the Temple of Set is not a Satanic organization; and second, it is not an Occult one.

Satanism by its nature is an elite philosophy of living and its genuine adherents are few in number and usually secretive (for a variety of reasons). The individuals who follow this path are generally rebels who either cannot or do not wish to conform. Those who desire the exhileration and danger of extremes: those who cannot and will not obey of bow down. In short, those who possess ... 'spirit'. For them, Satan is adopted as a symbol of defiance – and this defiance is and has been highly individual. Rather than accept, they question; rather than believe, they seek to discover for themselves. They have – a dislike of authority and all dogma. Gradually, this spirit of defiance brings a self-awareness: an insight into themselves and others and 'the world', and this results from the diverse (and sometimes dangerous) experiences of life which those individuals undergo. of course, some never reach this point – they fail for whatever reason or reasons.

Further, Satanism is about individuals fulfilling the potential of life: they strive to live as fully as possible, to reach out and become like gods (or goddesses). In achieving this, magick is used as a means – of enhancing life, and understanding. Such striving either makes creative individuals – or it destroys them. This creativity is evident in the life of the individual: through works (e.g. artistic) or through what they achieve (for example – making their own life a work of art which others may try and copy).

All this means two essential things. First, they can be no such thing as a Satanic organization or dogma; and second, there can be no Satanic authority (e.g. in the form of an individual). Organization implies conformity and loss of personal identity and authority (however

117

small). Dogma implies accepting someone else's beliefs. Authority (of whatever kind) implies subserviance – a mentality alien to Satanists. Furthermore, all these stifle creativity: one hallmark of a genuine Satanist.

The Temple of Set is thus an example of what Satanism is not. It is not a religion; it does not possess any 'authority'; it does not need an organization nor any media-profile of 'acceptability'.

of course, some guidance in the initial stages may (and often is) required by those just beginning their quest, and here the experience of those who have gone that way in the past may be of interest or value. But essentially each individual learns via their own experiences – no one can do it for them: there is no magic formula, no mysterious handshake which brings instant wisdom. For the beginner, 'Masters' and organizations are a snare, a path which leads only to the glorification of the ego of the 'Master'.

Such 'Masters' are usually insecure people who need the adulation and attention – it makes them feel alive, important. Naturally, some Satanists play such a 'role' – for a time. But they soon tire of it – it becomes boring. That is, if they are Satanists. Anyone who plays it for more than a year has arrested development – their quest has ended in failure.

Regarding the second point made above – viz. the Temple of Set is not an Occult organization. Implicit in any Occult path – Left Handed or Right Handed – are certain obligations stemming from the very nature of Occultism. Wicca, Paganism, Satanism, Black Magick – whatever – all are means, paths which though different in some respects have the same ultimate goal: or at least, when those paths are followed to their ends. In a simplistic sense, the goal is evolution – developing abilities, enhancing already existing ones, re-discovering forgotten ones. Occult paths reveal through the beginning that is Initiation they show the essence hidden by the appearence. Or, expressed a different way, they dis-cover what is concealed. Part of what is concealed is, of course, the 'mysterious' another is the occult energies of living things. On an individual level, the Occult is the discovery of what is hidden within ourselves, in our own psyche, and Occult paths are processes of self-learning – of what our unique Destiny is and how we relate to the cosmos, this Earth, other individuals.

Initiation is the beginning of a quest – a symbol to that part of the psyche normally hidden which the 'Occult' wishes to bring into consciousness, giving thus understanding. The form that this symbol assumes is actually irrelevant, and whatever its outer form it implies a responsibility by the very fact that it is a conscious participation, by the Initiate, in evolution. In the simple sense, Initiation is when the individual begins to take responsibility for their own development, their own evolution: the first genuine step toward real freedom, internal psychic freedom. It is the birth of one small part of the new age.

Naturally, quite often the promise of Initiation is not fulfilled – or is fulfilled only in part – in many individuals. But some continue and of those some may achieve the goal. This promise is why the Establishment and conventional religions discourage Occultism and conduct campaigns against it – for Occultism is a means to real freedom and as such it is a threat to them and their domination of the individual. Occult paths lead to inner freedom and one of the responsibilities of any Initiate is to continue this evolutionary quest by passing onto another or others not only what they themselves may have learnt but also the 'Occult ideal' – inner liberation through an Initiatory quest. This ensures continuity and future possibilities. This passing on is never forced, nor is it in any way dogmatic – for it is related to another aspect of Initiatory responsibility: the respect for differing paths, different quests.

Having myself followed a specific Left Hand Path, I am inclined to believe it is worthwhile and effective. But I also realize it is not suited to everyone who wishes to begin their own Occult quest. For many years I recruited for a Satanic group (although 'recruit is hardly the word: offered the path to those who possessed the right qualities is nearer the mark) but I was never interested in mere numbers, in proselytizing and tried hard to dissuade most applicants to test their seriousness – because Satanism is difficult and at times dangerous (in psychic terms). I was always aware that other paths were available and perhaps more suitable to some (indeed, to most who applied). I, as an Occultist, knew that Initiation involves the free commitment of an individual – for the goal was their liberation, not their subjection by me or anyone else.

Given all these factors, it is impossible not to I conclude that the Temple of Set is not an Occult organization. It does not respect other paths, and other individuals, as is shown by their attempts to discredit others and their insistence that they represent the only genuine form of Satanism. Furthermore, their dogmatic, religious stance with all that is therefore implied in terms of acceptance of Temple authority and mandates – rather than liberating their members actually holds them in thrall, both mental and psychic. Rather than participating in that liberation and evolution which is part of the new age, the Temple of Set actually an offshoot of the old order and its stifling ways of being. This is shown, for example, in their concern with numbers, in trying to recruit regardless of quality and regardless of whether the individual is actually suited to the Left Hand Path – for, for the Temple, numbers mean influence, feathers in the cap of the leader – a sign that the Temple is pre-eminent, flourishing and l succeeding. Naturally, much more could be written to further detail the reasons as to why this particular organization is detrimental to what we as Occultists seek to achieve by our various paths. But the essence of the matter has been revealed – sufficient to enable readers to judge the matter for themselves.

To return, finally, to the personal level – I have no cause to defend, no desire for personal gain in what I write: only a desire for others to understand what is really important about the Occult and the path which a long time ago I myself decided I would follow. Organizations like the Temple of Set undermine what serious followers of the Left Hand Path have been trying to achieve for centuries – basically because its members and leaders seek to glorify their own egos at the expense of the inner freedom of others.

ONA.

CULLING – A GUIDE TO SACRIFICE II

As has been written – opfers are human culling in action. That is, Satanic sacrifice makes a contribution to improving the human stock, removing the worthless, the weak, the diseased (In terms of character). Naturally, this culling occurs on a somewhat larger scale by using magickal means to direct/influence/control events in real time (i.e. in the causal) and so produce historical change (war/strife/struggle/change and so on), than it does by choosing a specific opfer and executing an act of sacrifice.

However, the correct choice of opfer means that with their elimination, the] Sinister dialectic will be aided and thus the intrusion of the acausal into the causal speeded up. [In non-esoteric terms, read 'aid the dark forces to spread over Earth'.] The choosing of specific opfers depends on three things: (1) Satanic judgement; (2) an insight into and knowledge of Aeonics and the Sinister dialectic; (3) the means for undertaking the act without compromising the individuals involved are available. Generally, it is the duty of a Master of Mistress to select opfers, although any Satanist, from novice onwards, can suggest suitable targets, in which case the Master or Mistress, after due consideration, will give judgement as to the suitability of the target. (1) means a judgement is made, based on experience. often, this is judgement concerning the character of the victim. The victim may be suggested/chosen (a) because one or more of their actions has brought them to attention and made them seem suitable; or (b) their removal will be beneficial to Satanism/ the Sinister dialectic. The suitability of the victim is decided by a Master or Mistress, and once confirmed, the victims are subject to tests (qv. Guidelines for the Testing of Opfers MS). often, the Master or Mistress meets with the victim 'accidently' and so can judge them on a personal level, using their intuition/insight and so on. (2) means the proposed action is assessed in the light of Aeonics/the Sinister dialectic – i.e. will it aid the cause of Satanism? The dialectic? (3) means (a) that members are available for the testing; (b) the loyalty of those who will participate is assured; (c) the Temple has the means and the abilities to conduct the act and make it seem 'accidental' if required as well as ensure safe disposal after the act and make the necessary arrangements (an alibi, e.g.) should any participant ever need one. Opfers are not chosen at random – they are always carefully selected, then judged, then tested. The actual act – be such a ritual or a practical act (such as an assassination) – is never done for any personal reason. That is, it never arises out of personal emotions or from personal declares. Instead, the act is supra-personal – done with a Satanic judgement and a Satanic detachment arising from both knowledge (e.g. of Aeonics) and because of the character/ actions of the victim. The act itself is often communal – involving a Temple/ group and thus a participation which enables a reasoned and balanced assessment by those participating (although the verdict of the Master/Mistress is final). In such communal action, one member is appointed to argue for the selected victim during the special sunedrions which is convened to consider the selection/ arrangements for the act.

The act itself is one which glorifies the Satanic, which affirms Satanic values that is, it aids evolution in a positive way, enhances the lives of individuals. In short, it aids self-development (of the participants) and aids evolution (via the Sinister dialectic/culling). Opfers become/are chosen as victims because of their nature or because of their deeds. Mostly, they are dross whose removal will aid change/the growth of civilization/the Aeonic imperative. The judgement which decides their fate (so far as subjecting them to tests) is of course a Satanic one – but quite often, this judgement is akin to an act of 'natural justice' or a Satanic retribution: the victims have effectively condemned themselves by their deeds.

Many examples might be presented to illustrate this – but two will suffice, although it should be remembered that these are merely illustrations, specimens, to throw some light on the underlying principles involved.

I. A young man of weak character (no self-discipline, a bully of the worst kind ...) spends his time stealing cars and committing petty crimes. He lies on 'Social Security' and has a distain for nearly everyone – which he shows by his loutish behaviour, when he is with his friends, of course, being too weak to do anything provocative on his own. He is often drunk. On one occasion, he steals a car with some cronies, is chased by the Police, but escapes. During the chase, he crashes into some others cars, and two people are injured, one a young woman, quite seriously. Sometime later, he and some others break into the house of an old, blind man. The man attempts to stop them and this enrages our young man who beats the old man unconscious with his fists, boots and the old man's stick. The old man had fought in the Great War of 1914-18 and had been given several medals for his gallant conduct. Our young man is rather proud of himself after this beating and considers himself a 'hard man'. This young man is a typical example of modern dross. His character and his actions make him suitable. Satanic judgement would give him a chance to redeem himself – make something out of himself – via a test designed to provoke this. Should he fall, another test would seal his fate.

II. A Satanic novice living in a European country where questioning 'The Holocaust' is a crime in law, joins an extreme Right-Wing political group which works underground. In doing this, he hopes to acquire experience 'on the edge' and so gain experience, and to aid the Sinister dialectic by challenging 'the accepted' and speaking/working for 'the forbidden' [qv. MSS concerning Aeonics and heresy.]. After some months of action, one of his comrades betrays him and some others because this 'comrade' gave in under pressure and made a deal with the authorities, having been captured doing something illegal (in that country – distributing 'forbidden' books and leaflets). Our novice, however, escapes – but two of his comrades are arrested, tried and eventually jailed for their 'crimes'. Thus, the person who betrayed them makes himself a victim for Satanic retribution – he acted against the sinister dialectic (and thus the novice aiding that dialectic). The novice selected him as a victim, and the Master guiding this novice agreed he was a suitable choice. The next stage was a special sunedrion to moot the case (with a member defending the victim's action and character) and then a judgement made after the Master had heard all the arguments. After the judgement – arrangements for the tests.

Essentially, sacrifice falls into two categories – (1) the magickal act, achieved by a rite such as The Death Ritual: i.e. death by magickal means. (2) the physical act – i.e. death by practical means. (2) can and often does involve a secondary/simultaneous magickal ritual which aids the act of execution, however this latter is done, or the act may occur during a magickal rite.

Excursus: The Reason For Revealing A Secret Sinister Tradition

Too often, in the past, the true nature of Satanic sacrifice was hidden – even from many who professed to be Satanists. More recently, psuedo-Satanists have claimed that 'Satanism does not and never has conducted human sacrifices'. However, I repeat that human sacrifice, properly conducted, is a culling and thus is positive it is a part of Satanic practice. of course, the psuedo-Satanists would deny this, Since in their weakness they seek respectability and seek to make Satanism easier and 'more acceptable', a playing at wizards. The time is now right, however – both strategically and tactically – to reveal the Satanic truth, the whole Satanic truth and nothing but the Satanic truth in clear, precise terms which cannot be mis-understood. The traditional code of silence which forbid the casting of this aspect of esoteric tradition into writing – and which expressly forbid the dissemination of anything connected with that aspect – no longer, in this one instance, applies.

That is, the Grand Master representing traditional Satanist groups decided to permit this tradition to be not only written down (heretofore its transmission of necessity had been oral) but also disseminated to a limited extent. This would establish, for both present and historical purposes, what the true nature of Satanism was and is, since it was considered that the time was right (given the conditions pertaining in Western societies at this moment in causal time) for this knowledge to be made known. Part of the reason for this judgement was Aeonic – to present Satanism as it is, thus enabling those with the right character to follow that dark path to self-development, increasing over decades and centuries the number of genuine Adepts. All of the tradition is now accessible in written form (at least to those prepared to find it) and this makes that tradition more accessible, Since heretofore it had been the exclusive preserve of a few. Accessibility here means it can be used, by others. The other main reason for that judgement was to counter the softly, softly meanderings of the pseudo-Satanists who seemed determined to claim Satanism as their own and who preached that Satanism was actually not that bad, it just had been 'mis-understood' and Satanists were actually rather 'nice people, quite normal' who just appeared to be rather weird and so on ad nauseam. These jerks, showmen and role-playing l hucksters were taken seriously by those within what had become known as 'the Occult' and established their 'authority', making pronouncements (such as what group/organization they considered to be Satanic and what they considered to be mere 'dabblers') and generally feeling rather pleased with themselves and their safe, tame 'Satanic' world/conclaves/covens/Pylons. Such meanderings, the people who made them and the people who believed them, actually were and are detrimental to the achievement of real Adeptship and thus self-understanding and esoteric insight, for they, left unchallenged, would undermine and destroy the essence of Satanism – the creation of a new, higher type via direct often dark experience, ordeals and self-effort over a period of years: i.e. the building of real character via the fires of experience. These psueds had traded dark experience and danger for intellectual verbosity and psuedo-magickal fantasy games.

For so defying the sinister dialectic, some at least would be suitable candidates to become opfers. They would then really discover the wrath, and dark evil power which is Satan.

ONA

SATANISM, SACRIFICE AND CRIME –
THE SATANIC TRUTH

Due to the plethora of imitation Satanists who abound today (particularly in America) it has become necessary to openly declare the facts about genuine Satanism in relation to Sacrifice and 'criminal behaviour'. Such a declaration will establish for all time a permanent record and will expose the fraudulent 'Satanists' for what they are – individuals who like to be associated with the glamour of evil and darkness, but who lack the – inspiration, courage and daring to f evil and dark. Furthermore, I repeat I what I have written before – Satanism is not now and can never be, an intellectualized philosophy just as it most certainly is not in any way ethical or moral. It is an individualized defiance and an individualized striving l which vitalizes, which affirms existence in an ecstatic way – as such, it is a way of living which courts danger, excess. It is not nor can ever be, dogmatic just as it never involves submission to anyone or anything. For this reason, there can never be genuine Satanic Churches or 'Temples' where Initiates conform to dogma or authority – such things are not for genuine Satanic Initiates but for the deluded, those lacking spirit and talent: – in brief, for the manipulated, rather than the manipulators.

Sacrifice:
In genuine Satanism [primal Satanism] sacrifice is accepted, and indeed is necessary. In former times, it involved both animal and human sacrifice. Today, however, it involves human sacrifice only – since there are an abundance of f- suitable specimens, due to the increase in human dross.

Sacrifice is accepted Satanic practice for several reasons. First, it is a test of Satanic character – to kill someone on the personal level (e.g. with one's own hands) is a character building experience, and today enables various skills to be developed (e.g. cunning in execution and planning). Second, it has magickal benefits (qv. the Order MS 'A Gift for the Prince'), Third, it sorts the imitation or toy Satanists out from the genuine – the former find excuses and usually retreat to their comfy, intellectualized world of playing at 'Satanic roles and rituals', or they are genuinely horrified and expose themselves for what they are – gutless cowards who lack Satanic darkness.

However, as explained elsewhere, genuine Satanic sacrifice is always done for a reason – a calculating purpose. [qv., for example, 'Satanism, The Sinister Shadow, Revealed.'] It is never strictly personal – i.e. it does not arise from any desire which is personal, whether unconscious or not.

Further, it is accepted practice that the victims, the opfers, choose themselves. Thus, opfers are never selected at random just as they are never children (although occasionally an opfer may be a virgin). Mostly, the victims, whose removal will aid the sinister dialectic, are tested, and only if they fail these tests will they become opfers. The tests, of course, are unknown to the victim. For example, a series of tests, or 'games' are prepared once the victim has been chosen, and each test or game requires the victim to make a specific choice. One choice leads to another test or game. After a certain number of choices of a certain type, the victim is deemed to have failed, and so chooses their own sacrificial death. Most often, the tests are tests of character – those that are shown to be worthless in character become opfers. Thus, a number of victims are selected – those whose removal will aid the sinister dialectic of history [qv. 'The Sinister Shadow' MS for an example]. These are then, without their knowledge, tested. If they fail, they become opfers. [See below, under 'Crime', for an example of the kind of tests that may be involved – the ones for sacrifice are, of course, much more 'testing'.]

The actual sacrifice has two forms: (1) during a ritual; (2) by practical means (e.g. assassination/'accidents') without any magickal trappings. If (2) is chosen, then a ritual of sacrifice may still be undertaken, but with a 'symbolic' opfer (e.g. a wax figurine named after the actual opfer).

The actual execution of the act of sacrifice – whether during a ritual or otherwise – will be carefully planned, and calculatingly done. This planning will mean the death will seldom if ever be seen as a Satanic act even if it has occurred during a ritual. Today, and in the recent past, most sacrifices are of the second type – i.e. acts of execution undertaken by a Satanic novice 'in the real world', involving assassination and 'accidents' or viewed by others (e.g. the Police) as seemingly 'motiveless crimes'. Further, in genuine Satanic groups, the execution of this act is an essential prerequisite to Adeptship.

The aim of the sacrifice can be either (a) part of a dark ritual – i.e. to presence sinister energies in the causal, causing changes in the world, such changes aiding the dark forces (examples would be the Ceremony of Recalling; the Sinister Calling); or (b) as part of general sinister strategy, adduced via Aeonics. [Note: This latter occurs when a novice progresses along the Satanic path according to tradition.]

Crime:
Crime is not an end, but a means. A criminal act is not done because it is criminal but because the act itself has a purpose or intent – the criminality of that act being irrelevant. This purpose is either to aid self-excellence (build Satanic character) or aid sinister strategy. Basically, an act is judged not by whether it is illegal (and thus criminal) in a particular country, but rather by its purpose or intent. Or, expressed more simply, by whether that act can serve Satanism in general and self-development in particular. An example will best illustrate this.

A satanic novice conceived the idea of gaining experience by burglary. The monetary benefits were useful, but incidental to the main purpose. As a Satanist, he of course planned carefully and chose wisely. First, the jobs themselves had to be difficult, challenging and thus interesting – they would require careful planning and delicate execution. So he chose Apartments, and entry mainly via windows and roofs – this needed some training and the acquisition of skills, plus daring and courage. Second, the people to be deprived of some of their belongings would choose themselves – they would be 'tested' to see if they were suitable victims. The selection would be by character – according to their nature. This required the novice to use his own judgement and instinct. He would select those who showed they lacked character, breeding, nobility – who lacked, in fact, the virtues of a Satanist.

[Note: One of the best exoteric descriptions of 'Satanic' character – and also of those lacking it – was given by Nietzsche in his 'The Anti-Christ'. The Satanist adheres to a 'master-morality'.]

The novice selected some Apartments in a city where the pickings would be rich. Then he observed the occupants for some time – watching them, their routines and so on. Next, he arranged for the execution of his tests. Two friends (who were actually Initiates of his Order – or rather the Order he had joined) were enlisted to aid him in this. They would appear, on his signal, and seem to rob him as he lingered near the entrance to the building when one of his chosen victims was near. On the first occassion, the victim ignored the 'robbery', and continued on his way. On the second, the next victim came to his aid and actually knocked one 'robber' unconscious with a punch, albeit for a short time. Thus, the first victim or mark became selected, or rather selected himself by his actions, and it was from his Apartment that the novice stole some things some days later. of course, the planning and execution of such a test was difficult – requiring acting, timing, manipulation, daring, zest – in brief, experience in the real world. Following this success, he moved to another target and found some new victims for his test. It was interesting that these tests confirmed the novice's instinctive assessment of the victim's character – and thus aided his Satanic judgement.

In this example, the burglary was a 'crime', in Law – but, in fact, the illegal nature of the act was irrelevant. The act, and its planning etc., aided the self-excellence of the novice, and thus his magickal development, because it was a Satanic act, not because it was 'criminal' – that is, it involved danger, required skill, judgement, daring, and it was real. It was, in a sense, a practical ordeal and its Satanic character meant that its victims were victims of themselves: the act was akin to an act of 'natural justice'. To some, it may seem a game – and so it was, but one played in earnest, in which losing meant capture and probable imprisonment (factors which made it interesting and worthwhile). and it was only a few incidents in a life crammed with such incidents – at different levels.

Furthermore, this 'realness' is important – genuine Satanists involve themselves with the real world, in real situations with real people and real danger. The imitation Satanists play mental and intellectual and 'safe' games. The difference is that a real Satanist will actually be an assassin, for example, while the imitation Satanist will dream of being one and will probably obtain a moronic pleasure from watching some fictional story and 'identifying' with a fictionalized assassin – or, more likely, will 'act out' such a role in some pathetic psuedo-magickal ceremony and believe he/she has attained something.

Naturally, in the real world things can and do go wrong. But as always, the real Satanists survive and prosper, while the others go under, get caught, give up or are killed. Also, sometimes even the best get things a little wrong – but they learn from their mistakes, they grow in character, in insight, in skill. Genuine Satanists are survivors: they learn and prosper, and die at the right time.

This growth means that a Satanist moves on – there are always new challenges, new delights, new tests of skill, daring, endurance, courage: new insights.

A 'role' is only a role – played, then discarded, transcended. Thus, even crime, sacrifice, tests of others, become left behind, given time – they have served the purpose for which they were intended – and a new being is given birth, one more joins the elect. This is simply another way of saying that a Satanist is never trapped by the act, the desires for and against that act, its consequences, or indeed anything to do with that act, whatever the nature of the act. An act, such as a sacrifice or a crime, is a means – to something beyond. All acts are experience. A Satanist is above and beyond acts – a master or mistress of them, rather than a slave to them. So it is, so it has been and so it will be – for genuine Satanists. Meanwhile,

131

the imitation Satanists will play their word-games, feast on self-delusions, and continue to claim that 'Satanism' never involves sacrifice, or criminal acts but is a rather pleasing philosophy which has had a rather 'bad press'.

But, henceforward, anyone who is taken in by these gutless, posturing charlatans will deserve the epithet 'stupid'.

ONA

THE HARD REALITY OF SATANISM

The hard reality of Satanism is that it is very different from both the media image and the more recent image pedalled by imitation Satanists in both Europe and America.

I - What Satanism Is:

a) Satanism is a quest for self-excellence, involving real danger, real challenges and requiring real courage. It involves taking your body to and beyond its physical limits of endurance. It involves real action, alone: without the support of friends, comrades, lovers, relations or anyone. It involves accepting challenges – physical, psychic, intellectual and triumphing solely by one's own efforts. It involves the triumph of pure, individual will and desire.

b) Satanism is, in part, an inner quest, an exploration of the 'hidden' (and overt) aspects of consciousness: a dis-covery of the darkness within and beyond the individual psyche. This involves 'magickal acts' – such as rituals. This magick, however, is a means, not an end.

c) Satanism involves ordeals, both physical and magickal. Those who are suitable triumph; the others fail. [One such ordeal is the Grade Ritual of Internal Adept – where the candidate lives alone and isolated, bereft of everything except the bare necessities for physical survival, for a period of three months.]

d) Satanism requires the practical experiencing of all moral limits, and then a mastery of the feelings, desires, pleasures, terrors, pains and so on that these imply.

e) Satanism involves the individual defiance of all subserviance: a Satanist accepts guidance only, and refuses to be dominated or intimidated by anyone. This guidance is toward practical experience, and it by this experience that the novice learns and developes a genuine Satanic character.

f) Satanism involves sacrifice – this is a necessary test of character [qv. the MSS 'Satanism, Sacrifice and Crime – The Satanic Truth', and 'Satanism – The Sinister Shadow, Revealed' for more details.].

g) Satanism is a means – a method, or way, and the purpose of this means, method or way is to produce a specific type of individual: the next stage of our evolution as a species. Satanism is thus an expression of evolutionary change – on both the individual level and in respect of 'societies' and 'history'. The individuals so created often inspire in the supine majority a certain terror/awe/admiration/fear/jealousy.

h) Satanism is elitist. It does not compromise – its tests, ordeals, methods and character-building experiences are severe and will never be made easier to make them acceptable to more people or easier to undertake.

i) Satanism is esoteric by nature and intent: it is both a 'secret' way, by virtue of its methods etc., and it is not nor probably will be suitable for the majority for many, many centuries.

II - What Satanism Is Not:

a) Satanism is not, nor can ever be, a religion, nor just a 'philosophy'. A religion means acceptance of authority, the rigid structure of a 'Church' or a 'Temple', and a unified dogma (with the consequent schisms and claims to 'authenticity'). The religious attitude is the antithesis of what Satanism really is – for Satanism is a way of living, a way of experiencing, in the raw, whereas religion abstracts, limits endevour, behaviour and moralizes. In short, a Satanist plunges into reality, without any supports (moral, psychic or human) whereas a religious person has that reality prescribed by dogma, authority and such like, and is supported by a 'Church', its members and their attitudes.

Satanism is an ecstatic affirmation of existence – a taking of existence into new and higher realms, as well as a plunge into existing darkness and the creation of new darkness.

b) Satanism cannot have anyone impose upon it any structure, authority, or institution of any kind by claiming a 'dark mandate' or some kind of 'revelation'. There can be no such thing as an 'infernal mandate' of whatever kind because the only thing that really matters to Satanism is experience, its accumulation and the highly individualized learning that results from such experience. A genuine Satanist, for example, confronted by an entity which exhibited all the powers attributed to Satan would not even accept what that 'entity' said and would most certainly not show any submission – instead, they would a defiance, a reasoned assessment of what was said, and then a judgement made from experience. A Satanist never surrenders to anything – and would rather die, proud and defiant, than submit. This applies even to 'Satan'. If and when a Satanist accepts guidance, it is from someone of experience who has explicated Satanism by their life and thus who can offer advice based on that experience. The aim of Satanism is to create willful, characterful, defiant, unique individuals who have or can fulfil their potential as gods it is not to create followers or sycophants. An 'infernal mandate' implies sycophancy.

c) Satanism does not involve discussions, meetings, talks. Rather, it involves action, deeds. Words – written or spoken – sometimes follow, but not necessarily. The ideal candidate for Satanism is the individual of action rather than the 'intellectual'. By the nature of most Satanic actions, they can seldom be mentioned and thus remain esoteric. The essence that Satanism leads the individual towards, via action, is only ever revealed by that participation which action is. Words, whether written or spoken, can never describe that essence they can only hint at it, point toward it, and often serve to obscure the essence. Satanism strips away the appearence of 'things' – living, Occult and otherwise by this insistence on experience, unaided. What is thus apprehended by such experience, is unique to each individual and thus is creative and evolutionary. Discussions, meetings, talks, even books and such like, de-vitalize: they are excuses for not acting.

A Satanist will sometimes use such forms as he/she may use the form of a Temple – to enhance and/or provoke experiences. But they are then actively manipulating, actively creating experiences – the others involved are being used by that person. That is, there is only one Satanist at such gatherings (usually) – the others may believe they are 'Satanists', but they are deluded.

d) Satanism does not apply moral absolutes to real-life situations and forms. This may best be explicated by two examples. First, politics. Satanism does not affirm or deny any political forms or type of politics it does not, for example, announce that 'fascism and Satanism are incompatible'. Such announcements/pronouncements arise from a moral bias and a lack of insight into both Satanism and 'society' and thus Aeonics.

A Satanist, concerned with experience, may use a political form for a specific purpose – the nature of that form in terms of conventional politics and morality (such as 'extreme Right-wing') is irrelevant. What is important is whether it can be used to (a) provide experience of living and the limits of experience, and/or (b) aid the sinister dialectic of history. Thus a Satanist may become involved in, or set up, an organization of the extreme Right – this is dangerous, exciting, vitalizes, provides experiences 'on the edge' and should thus aid the development of the character and insight of that Satanist.[3] What is important, is that this involvement is done for an ulterior, Satanic, motive: what others think and believe about such actions is totally irrelevant. Anyone purporting to be a Satanist who criticizes such an action, whatever the political hue of the group/organization, reveals by that criticism that they are not Satanists – but rather, moralizing nurds lacking in insight and real Satanic understanding.

The second example concerns the formation and use of Satanic 'Temples' and groups by a Satanist. A Satanic novice, in order to gain experience of magickal rituals and people manipulation, usually forms

---

[3] It can also aid the sinister dialectic – here, an understanding of Aeonics is important.

a group to perform Satanic rituals. The people recruited are for the most part used – and the novice often assumes a specific Satanic 'role' for this: the role of sorcerer/sorceress. He/she may dress in a certain way and so on, as he/she may use fables to impress and/or manipulate. This, however, for a genuine Satanist, is only a stage – and one which lasts a year or two. After that, experience and mastery of ceremonial and hermetic magick gained, they move on to new challenges and experiences, as all good Satanists should. Further, the individuals of this 'Temple' or group are not Satanists, although they may believe themselves to be – they are simply being used to afford the novice pleasure/excitement/experience and so on. Bad any of the any Satanic character or potential, they would rebel to undertake their own quest by forming such a group/'Temple' and experience the limits of themselves.

Sometimes, the group has another aim – an Aeonic or suprapersonal one, in which case its life may be extended. But whatever, genuine Satanic guidance by an Adept or Master/Mistress to a novice always occurs on an individualized basis, never within the rigid and constraining form of a 'Temple'.

Thus, there is not nor can be any constraining rules applied to the conduct of such 'Temples' and groups – there is no 'moral code', no bounds which cannot be overstepped. The rules, such as they are, are made by the Satanic novice according to their desire and goals. That is, they can do with that group and its individuals whatever they desire to do and no one – not even the Adept/ Master/Mistress who may be guiding them – can set limits or prescribe their behaviour. They must learn for themselves – and from their mistakes, should they make some.

This naturally leads to the obvious Satanic deduction that a group like the Temple of Set may contain one, perhaps two, Satanists – who are using the 'members' for their own Satanic goals. This person (or persons) would of course deny this, and if that denial was sincere, they could not be Satanists. What is certain, is that that group cannot contain more than perhaps two Satanists – for the members accept the constraints imposed upon them from above, and are servile, in both theory and practice. They are also not being led into real experiences, but accept a sterile, sanitized and safe 'Satanism' as pedalled by their leader.

e) Satan ism does not seek any form of official recognition as it does not seek to become respectable or the prerogative of a majority. Rather, Satanism operates, and must operate, for the most part in a clandestine or 'underground' manner. 'official' recognition mean Someone or some organization is granted some sort of 'status' and thus assumes both in theory and in fact an 'authority' and an organizational structure to support it. This authority and this structure mean followers, sycophants – and contradict the essence of Satanism. 'Respectability' means a moral stance broadly in line with that pertaining at the time – that is, it means a restricting morality, ethics, as well a limiting of action to what is deemed broadly 'acceptable' by the 'society' of the time.

Both of these – official recognition and respectability – also mean that the self-appointed authority which is recognized and becomes or seeks to be respectable, sets its own limits: there is 'proscription' of other groups, a peer hierarchy and all the many trappings of herd conformity; the triumph of illusive forms over essence. In brief, the deluding of others, rather than their liberation. Since the experience of the essence that Satanism brings is unique, this uniqueness is totally contradictory to all forms that seek to constrain, define and restrict – two of these forms being 'official recognition' and 'respectability'.

Some other hard facts about Satanism are in order – to be placed on record.

Satanism is hard and very dangerous. This danger is much more than just 'mental' or a psychic one of the kind sometimes experienced in magickal workings. It is a personal danger of the 'life or death' kind. If it is not, then it is not tough enough, it is not Satanic. For far too long the pathetic imitation Satanists, such as those in the Temple of

Set and the Church of Satan, have had no one to contradict their sickly, wimpish versions of Satanism – they have tried to deny the darkness and evil which are essential to Satanism because the frauds in those organizations are fundamentally weak: they have never gone to their limits, never experienced the realness of evil. They have tried to make 'Satanism' safe and 'respectable': they l have intellectualized it because they are typical products of this present intellectualized, peace-loving, 'we need to be safe' society.

A Satanist is like a beast of prey – in real life, not in fantasy. A Satanist may be and often is an assassin, a warrior, an outlaw – in real life. The imitation Satanists, however, pretend to be these things – their fantasy-life is greater than their real experiences of such things. A Satanist seeks and makes real his/her fantasies and then masters the real-life situations and all those desires/feelings which give birth to those fantasies – they live them and then transcend them, creating from those experiences something beyond them: a new individual. often, things go wrong – but as always in life, the strong survive and the weak perish, are written off. The Satanist creates the dreams, standards of excellence and spirit which others often later aspire to emulate. This creation is in real life, by deeds and deeds alone.

Because of this, few indeed are the genuine Satanists. Sometimes their lives (or aspects of them) become public – but often they are hidden, working their darkness in secret, for the benefit of evolution .

ONA 1991 eh

THE PUBLICATION OF ESOTERIC TRADITIONS ON THE LEFT HAND PATH

For a long time, genuine esoteric tradition was handed on an individual basis, from Master/Mistress to novice. There were many reasons for this, most of them practical: the tradition was esoteric, liable to mis-interpretation, and many of its tenets and rituals involved what would have been regarded as 'heretical', anti-social and/or illegal acts. Furthermore, the methods used to train novices often made those novices into 'outlaws' and set them against conventional society. Also, for a long time, the teaching and teachings of the tradition was heretical in law – a criminal offense against Church and State. Secrecy was essential and necessary. This state of affairs pertained until quite recently. With the burgeoning of interest in 'the Occult' in general, the LHP became somewhat less secret and certain aspects of the tradition were discreetly circulated. What were mistakenly taken to be 'esoteric' traditions and, given the new openness toward the Occult and the repeal of anti-Occult laws, freely distributed and/or published, were (a) the useless Grimoire/Qabalistic tradition, or (b) a mis-interpreted Crowleyism, or (c) of a showman/ghoulish/self-professed type with bits cobbled together from (a) and (b) with archaic myths and unenlightened egoism thrown in. The real tradition – with its darkness and danger – remained hidden.

To (c) belonged the Church of Satan, which made Satanism akin to a fantasy role-playing game or games with some sorcery added to impress. The later schism which gave birth to the Temple of Set (born not with a bang but with a whimper) was not unexpected given the structure and orientation of this 'Church' – and neither was the fact that the leader of this schism based his Temple and authority on what was termed an 'Infernal Mandate', and declared Satanism as a religion, much mis-understood. Meanwhile, the old traditions continued, in Europe and elsewhere, in their traditional way – secretly, accepting but few novices and these only after severe tests and ordeals. The traditions, writings, rituals, methods, ordeals and techniques remained unavailable except to those few. After lengthy deliberations and consultations, the individual representing traditional groups, decided to gradually make the esoteric tradition which he and others represented available on a selective basis, to reveal, for once and for all, what the LHP and Satanism were really about. The real impetus for this decision came from Aeonic strategy – making the tradition available would enable an increase in the number of genuine Adepts, thus hastening the presencing of the darker forces on Earth, and so fulfilling the sinister dialectic of history. This increase, however, would be gradual – over centuries.

With this dissemination, the purpose, intent and methods of Satanism and the LHP could no longer be mis-interpreted and the posers and charlatans who professed to be 'Satanists' would be exposed – at least to those with any sagacity. With the secrets accessable to those who saught to find them, the real esoteric work could continue, as it always had, in secret – the training, via direct experience, of those few strong and gifted enough to undertake the difficult and dangerous journey along the Left Hand Path.

ONA 1991 eh

The diagrams show how the basic nine angles relate to the inverted pentagram. Thus, ⚡ is the first sphere, the Moon, ♓ the second sphere, Mercury, and so on.

The diagrams signify the order of working in order to create types of magickal energy - that is, they are rites of invocation. Thus, the inverted pentagram shows how magickal energy can be created (or rather drawn from the acausal) - the type depending on where the process is begun. For example, to invoke 'Satanic' energies, the ♓ point would be the starting one, going on to the next, ⟨symbol⟩ , and then ⟨symbol⟩ and so on. The diagrams refer to the <u>chants</u> (given in 'Naos' and elsewhere) which when sung correctly open the gate or nexion (to the acausal) located at/represented by the specific point or sphere shown. Thus, ♓ means the use of the Agios Lucifer chant (mode IV); ⟨symbol⟩ means the use of the Agios Baphomet (mode 1) and so on. For a ritual, the chants are undertaken in order.

The 'symbol of the nine' shown below the inverted pentagram is only one form of the many possible by joining the seven spheres of the septenary and the 'gates' - as shown, the invokation beguns with the Moon sphere and ends with the Saturn sphere (and thus the Agios Vindex chant).(See 'Fenrir' vol II no. for further details and the chants not given in 'Naos.) Each symbol of nine represents a particular type of energy - for example, to open an 'Earth' gate, the sequence would end with the Earth Gate (i.e. the Jupiter sphere); while to open a Star Gate it would end with that gate - ⟨symbol⟩ on the diagram.

A simpler form of invokation is possible, and involves not the complete chants, but simply the "word or name" associated with the particular sphere (according to the septenary tradition). Thus, the Moon sphere would involve the vibration of "Nox", the Mercury sphere "Satan" and so on. (qv. the correspondences in Naos.)

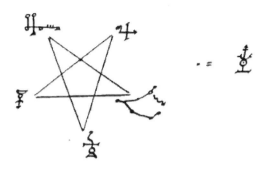

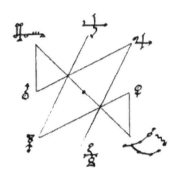

♃ : ℞ : ♃

♊ : ♐ : ☿

} etc.

☿ : Agios Lucifer : Mode IV

♃ : Agios Baphomet : Mode I

♄ : Agios Vindex : Mode II

} etc.

♃~~ : Nythra Kthunae : ♪ — — ✳ — ♫

⌐~ : Nythra Kthunae : ♪~ ♫ ⋯ ✳ ♪

1) Musick, Incense and Forms

Moon	G major	Trapezoid	Hazel	▽
Mercury	E minor	Tetrahedron	Yew	⊖
Venus	F sharp	Pyramid	Black Poplar	▽
Sun	D minor	Cuboid	Oak	△
Mars	C major	Octahedron	Alder	⊖
Jupiter	B flat	Icosahedron	Beech	⚥
Saturn	A flat	Dodecahedron	Ash	♄

2) Reflexive colours:

C	bright red
G	Orange
D	Yellow
A	Green (viridian)
E	Blue
F	dark red
B	Indigo
F sharp	Violet
C sharp	Purple
A flat	Black
E flat	Xanthin
B flat	Tyrian purple

144

RUNES

Rune	Meaning	Rune	Meaning
ᚡ	animals	ᛁ	Ice
∩	strength	ᛇ	year/'time'
ᚦ	Loki/night	ᛃ	sorcery
ᚹ	Odin	ᛦ	moon
ᚱ	movement	ᛣ	defence/life
ᚺ	fire	ᛋ	sun
ᚷ	gift	↑	Thor
ᚹ	laughter/mead	ᛒ	Earth (as goddess)
ᚻ	thunder	ᛗ	war/strife
ᛉ	Wyrd	ᛗ	family/kin

ᚱ	water
ᛪ	the folk
◇	the folk-land
ᛞ	day

145

The Boards:

There are seven boards, placed one above the other in a spiral and forming a septenary Tree of Life, each board representing a sphere. Each board consists of nine white and nine black squares (see fig. 1).

Each board is named after a particular star, some of which have esoteric significance.

The Pieces:

Each player has three sets of nine, represented by Alchemical symbols thus: ⊖(⊖) ⊖(☿) ⊖(♃), ☿(⊖)
☿(☿) ☿(♃), ♃(⊖) ♃(☿) ♃(♃);

⊖(⊖) ⊖(☿) ⊖(♃), ☿(⊖) ☿(☿) ☿(♃), ♃(⊖) ♃(☿) ♃(♃);

⊖(⊖) ⊖(☿) ⊖(♃), ☿(⊖) ☿(☿) ☿(♃), ♃(⊖) ♃(☿) ♃(♃);

One set of twenty-seven pieces is white, the other black. The pieces are usually made from cubes or flat circles of wood with the appropriare symbol painted on them. An alternative form of symbols may be employed - ⊖ as ∝ ; ☿ as λ and ♃ as ω . Thus, the ⊖(♃) piece becomes ∝(ω) .

The Placing of the Pieces:

Six pieces are placed on Sirius (two sets of ⊖)for white, and six for black (see fig. 2).

Arcturus has three pieces for white and three for black (fig. 3). Antares has six pieces for white and six for black - two sets of ☿ pieces placed in the same pattern as the ⊖ pieces on Sirius.

Mira has no pieces on it at all. Rigel has the remaining three pieces of the ☿ sets, placed as the ⊖ pieces on Arcturus.

Deneb has six pieces of white and six of black from the ♃ set, placed as the ⊖ set on Sirius.

Naos has the remaining three pieces of the ♃ set, placed on the same squares as the ⊖ set on Arcturus.

146

The Moves:

Each piece, when it moves, is transformed into the piece next in sequence according to the pattern:

$$\Theta(\Theta) \rightarrow \Theta(\yen) \rightarrow \Theta(\oplus) \rightarrow \yen(\Theta) \rightarrow \yen(\yen) \rightarrow \yen(\oplus)$$
$$\rightarrow \oplus(\Theta) \rightarrow \oplus(\yen) \rightarrow \oplus(\oplus)$$

Thus, when $\yen(\oplus)$ piece is moved, it becomes a $\oplus(\Theta)$ piece. A $\oplus(\oplus)$ piece when moved becomes $\Theta(\Theta)$.

The $\oplus$ pieces (that is, $\oplus(\Theta), \oplus(\yen), \oplus(\oplus)$) can move from any board to any other board and any vacant square.

The $\yen$ pieces may move across a board to any vacant square or up or down one or two boards. For example, a $\yen$ piece on Sirius may move to either Arcturus or Antares to any vacant square.

The Θ pieces may only move across a board one square at a time to a square of the same colour or up or down one board to another to a vacant square of the same colour. For example, a Θ piece on a black square on Sirius could move to a black (vacant) square on Arcturus, or move one square on the Sirius board.

A $\oplus(\oplus)$ piece on any square on Naos may capture any piece of the opposite colour on any square or any board except Naos. The piece so captured is removed from the board and plays no further part. After such a capture, the $\oplus(\oplus)$ piece becomes a $\Theta(\Theta)$ piece.

The Aim:

This is to occupy certain squares on Mira with one's own pieces according to a pattern determined by the players before the game begins. However, pieces can stay on the Mira board for only three moves - after that, they move to another board. The first of these three allowable moves is that one that brings the piece to Mira - that is, it can stay for only another two moves.

The first player to place his pieces on the appropriate Mira squares, wins. The pattern most often used is given in fig. 4.

147

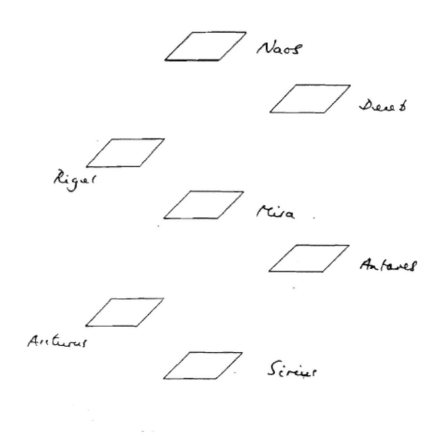

Naos

Deneb

Rigel

Mira

Antares

Arcturus

Sirius

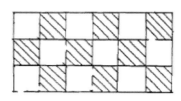

Fig. 1 : The Boards

Fig 3 : Arcturus

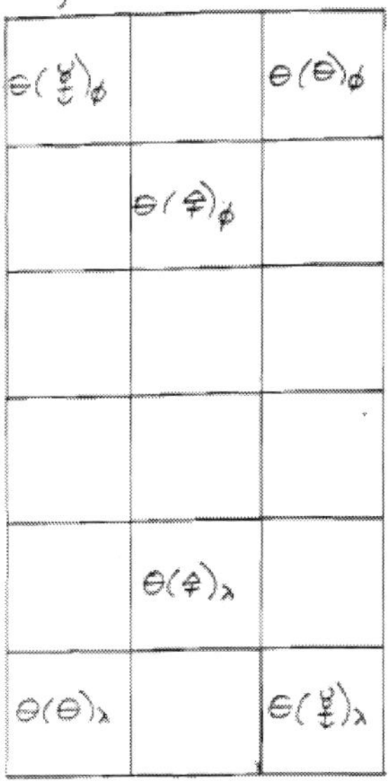

$\Theta\left(\frac{8}{4}\right)_\phi$		$\Theta\left(\Theta\right)_\phi$
	$\Theta\left(\frac{4}{4}\right)_\phi$	
	$\Theta\left(\frac{4}{4}\right)_\lambda$	
$\Theta\left(\Theta\right)_\lambda$		$\Theta\left(\frac{8}{4}\right)_\lambda$

Fig 4: Pattern to win

$\Theta\left(\frac{8}{4}\right)_\lambda$		$\Theta\left(\Theta\right)_\lambda$
	$\Theta\left(\frac{4}{4}\right)_\lambda$	
	$\Theta\left(\frac{4}{4}\right)_\phi$	
$\Theta\left(\Theta\right)_\phi$		$\Theta\left(\frac{8}{4}\right)_\phi$

$\Theta\left(\frac{8}{4}\right)_\phi$		$\Theta\left(\Theta\right)_\phi$
	$\Theta\left(\frac{4}{4}\right)_\phi$	
$\Theta\left(\frac{8}{4}\right)_\phi$	$\Theta\left(\frac{4}{4}\right)_\lambda$	$\Theta\left(\Theta\right)_\phi$
$\Theta\left(\Theta\right)_\lambda$	$\Theta\left(\frac{4}{4}\right)_\phi$	$\Theta\left(\frac{8}{4}\right)_\lambda$
	$\Theta\left(\frac{4}{4}\right)_\lambda$	
$\Theta\left(\Theta\right)_\lambda$		$\Theta\left(\frac{8}{4}\right)_\lambda$

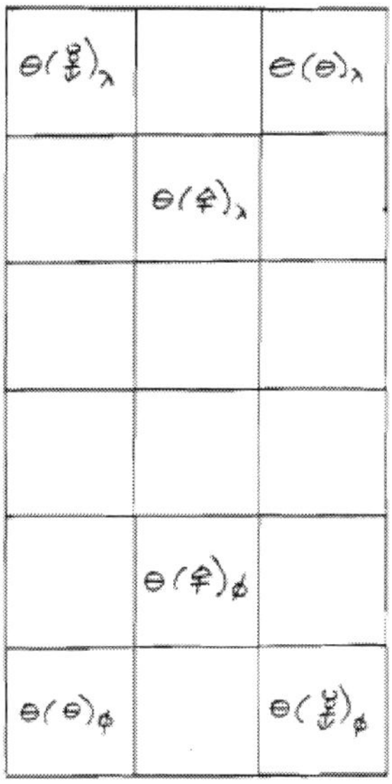

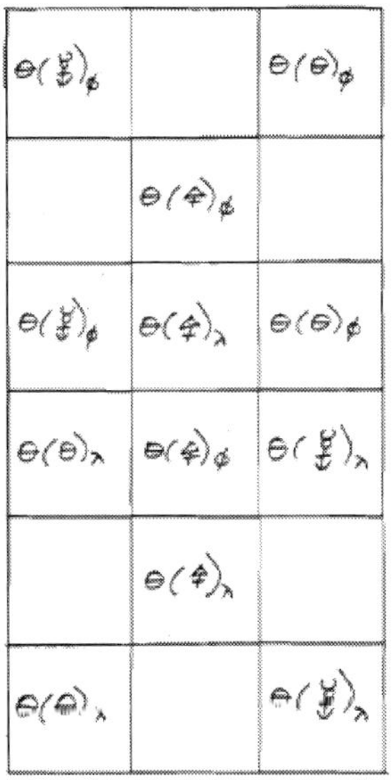

ϕ = black pieces
λ = white pieces

[ϕ pieces on black squares]

Fig. 2 : Sirius pieces.

149

<u>Symbolism</u>:

The acausal space is represented by ϕ_s ; the causal by λ_s . ϕ_s is described by ζ^ϕ ; λ_s by ζ^λ .

$\zeta_i u$ symbolizes an individual; $\zeta_\lambda u$ a group of individuals of number λ ; $\zeta_c u$ represents a higher civilization.

ϵ is to be read 'within' or 'member of a group/space or sub-space.

<u>General Theory</u>:

All life implies the coincidence of ϕ_s and λ_s . Sentient life implies $\phi_s \epsilon \lambda_s$: this is abstracted into seven stages or levels represented by the seven boards of the game. The two sets of nine pieces represent the ζ^ϕ and ζ^λ aspects of cosmic Change (usually the 'black' pieces being ϕ and the 'white' pieces λ)- or how Being becomes through Time. This expresses the interaction of ϕ and λ through modes of being - $\ominus$, $\oint$ or $\oint$. Three sets of pieces are used to express the fundamental nature of such Change as aspects of time.

Each board to be a correct representation should consist of three levels as in the 'simple' form of the game - that is, each board would be a complete 'simple Star Game' thus:

However, in practice, this form of the septenary game is not used in the initial stages because of its complexity: its mastery is one of the tasks of the Internal Adept. What follows is applicable to the 'standard' form of the septenary game with seven boards each of eighteen squares.

Magick implies changes in λ_s via ζ^ϕ : the 'cause and effects' understood by science operates in λ_s via ζ^λ .

The movement of pieces implies ζ^λ and ζ^ϕ and this is the essence of the magickal use of the game. ζ^ϕ is represented via $\oint$ (or ω)moves and captures, ζ^λ by the other moves. In one sense $\oint$ moves represent the duality associated with mercurius - possessed of both ζ^λ and ζ^ϕ elements.

150

I - $k_i u$:

        In terms of the consciousness of an individual
(since $\phi_t \in \lambda_t$ for $k_i u$ represents consciousness) the pieces
are:

    $\ominus(\ominus)$ Extravert Feeling type
    $\ominus(\zeta)$ "   Intuitive
    $\ominus(\phi)$ "   Thinking
     $\zeta(\ominus)$ Introvert Feeling
     $\zeta(\zeta)$ "   Intuitive
   $\zeta(\phi)$ "   Thinking
     $\notin(\ominus)$ Master of Temple/Mistress of Earth
    $\notin(\zeta)$ Magus/Maven
    $\notin(\phi)$ Homo Galactica

$\ominus(\ $) describes 'ego' consciousness; $\zeta(\ $)'self' consciousness,
and $\notin$ 'adeptship' - that is, beyond individuation -
the ξ^n goal of $k_i u$.

Development of consciousness implies an increase
of ϕ elements in a particular $k_i u$.

        To represent a particular $k_i u$ by the placing of
pieces (in order, for example, to work magick upon that
particular $k_i u$) the operator must first assess the character
of the $k_i u$ using the septenary correspondences as a basis.
In order to do this accurately, its helps if various facts
about the $k_i u$ in question are known - such as particular
interests, whether any involvement in 'esoteric' groups and
so on.

    Character is assessed through determining the psychological
type of the individual in accordance with the above table
then finding appropriate 'Tarot' images linked to the
type of consciousness represented by the character.

<u>II - $k_c u$:</u>

For $k_c u$ the seven boards represent the seven
Aeons, and one Aeon is represented by placing appropriate
pieces on appropriate boards - Sirius is the first Aeon (the
pre-Hyperborian, sometimes called the Primal Aeon),
Arcturus the Hyperborean Aeon and so on. The coming
'New Aeon' is thus Deneb.

To represent the present Aeon the pieces should be
changed from their original positions thus:

$$S \Theta(\phi)_\lambda \rightarrow \Pi \, \underset{\sim}{\cancel{\Sigma}}(\Theta)_\lambda \; ; \; \lambda \, \underset{\sim}{\cancel{\Sigma}}(\phi)_\lambda \rightarrow N \, \cancel{\Phi}(\Theta)_\lambda$$
$$\lambda \, \underset{\sim}{\cancel{\Sigma}}(\phi)_\phi \rightarrow \Pi \, \cancel{\Phi}(\Theta)_\phi \quad A \, \underset{\sim}{\cancel{\Sigma}}(\Theta)_\lambda \rightarrow \lambda \, \underset{\sim}{\cancel{\Sigma}}(\underset{\sim}{\cancel{\Sigma}})_\lambda$$
$$N \, \cancel{\Phi}(\phi)_\phi \rightarrow \Pi \, \Theta(\Theta)_\phi \; ; \; N \, \cancel{\Phi}(\phi)_\lambda \rightarrow \Pi \, \Theta(\Theta)_\lambda$$

$k_c u$ implies $\oint \phi_\lambda^{\,via\,t^\lambda}$: the opening of a gate, which brings ϕ_s
to presence in λ_s , predates the beginnings of a particular
$k_c u$ by c. 300-400 years.

All $k_c u$ up to the present Western have exhausted
their potential by the $\Theta(\Theta)$ stage - although $\cancel{\Phi}$ stages $(\text{... } via \, t^\phi)$
are possible.

$$\oint^\lambda k_c u \Rightarrow \underset{\sim}{\cancel{\Sigma}}(\underset{\sim}{\cancel{\Sigma}})_c \rightarrow \underset{\sim}{\cancel{\Sigma}}(\Theta)_c \rightarrow \Theta(\underset{\sim}{\cancel{\Sigma}})_c \rightarrow \Theta(\Theta)_c$$

No $k_c u$ has ever achieved $\oint^\phi k_c u$ because this requires $\phi_s \in \lambda_s$
where $\omega \gg \gamma$ and $k_c u \Rightarrow \phi_\gamma \in \lambda_s$; $t_u \Rightarrow \phi_\beta^{\gamma > \rho}$. A $k_c u$ lasts
between 1,500 and 1,200 years, $\oint^\phi$ declining in intensity
during this time as indicated by the symbols:

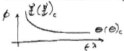

$\Theta(\Theta)_c$ lasts approx. 400 years.

Each Aeon is associated with a particular higher
civilization thus:

Aeon	Span	Associated $k_c u$	Date of end
Sumeric	4 000 BC - 2 000	Sumerian	2298 BC
Hellenic	2 000 - c. 70 AD	Hellenic	378 AD
Western	c.500 AD - 2 000	Western	2390 AD

ϕ_s is expressed via $k_{fi} u$ (and in general $k_n u$) for $k_c u$ as
an 'ethos' both exoteric and esoteric (which quite often only

Adepts understand since the esoteric ethos is the essence hidden by the exoteric ethos and is often revealed via 'the Abyss').

It is important to understand that the most important and practical aspect of an Aeon is the associated higher civilization - magickal Aeonic workings shape the ethos of this during the transition period between the ending of one Aeon and the beginning of another. During this time, however, the energies of the old Aeon produce the last transformation of the $f_c u$: the $\Theta(\Theta)_c$ stage, which is usually an Imperium, often military in extent and form of power.

Hitherto, Aeonic workings - when they have been undertaken at all - have concentrated on opening the Gate that presences the power of a new Aeon. Yet it is possible to extend by such workings a $f_c u$ into the Φ stages. For the present, this implies the end of the Western as c.3090 AD instead of 2390 AD. This is the first time in history that such a change is possible, since heretofore the process of Aeonic change has not been consciously understood by Adepts - its was approached mainly via mythological symbolism. It is through the abstract symbolism of the Star Game that full control is possible.

$$\delta^\phi f_c u = \xi (\Phi)_c \to \Theta(\Phi)_c \to \Phi(\Phi)_c$$
$$\delta^\phi \delta^\lambda = \Phi(\xi)_c \to \Phi(\Theta)_c : \text{``opening of a gate''}$$
$$\delta_i^\phi (g) = \sum_{n=1}^{n \geq 7} \beta(\lambda) [\epsilon_{\alpha\lambda}^\rightarrow]_o]\delta^\phi \quad \text{where} \quad g : \epsilon_{\mu\beta_o}^\rightarrow$$

 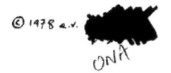
153

(Note: The following serve to explain some points arising
from students learning to use the Game.)

* When a piece is moved, it is transformed into a piece
next in the transformation sequence. This means that the
original piece is removed from the game and a new piece
(marked with the symbol appropriate) is placed on the
square the original piece has moved to.
   Thus, if a ♀(♀) piece is moved, for example, from a
square on the Sirius board to a square on the Arcturus
board (say a black square) then the ♀(♀) piece is removed
from the game and a (new) ⊖(⊖) piece placed on the black
square of the Arcturus board.
   To facilitate these changes, spare sets of pieces are
kept (usually two full sets) beside the structure. An
alternative method is to make each piece from a cube of
wood or other material and paint symbols on each side of the
cube, the symbol/piece in play being the one uppermost.
Thus, for example, a cube would be marked with symbols
which follow in the sequence enabling, when a move is made,
the cube to be rotated to show the new symbol/piece.
A spare set (or sets) are also kept, for when the cube
symbols are 'exhausted' and the cube needs changing.
Thus, a cube might have the following symbols painted
on its side: ⊖(⊖); ⊖(♊); ⊖(♀); ♊(⊖); ♊(♊); ♊(♀)
while another would have: ♀(⊖); ♀(♊); ♀(♀); ⊖(⊖); ⊖(♊); ⊖(♀)

* * *

* In the transformation sequence (⊖(⊖) → ⊖(♊) → ⊖(♀) → ♊(⊖) →
♊(♊) → ♊(♀) → ♀(⊖) → ♀(♊) → ♀(♀)), the arrow → represents
a single transformation. Thus, a ⊖(⊖) piece requires
eight transformations to become a ♀(♀) piece, and nine
to return to a ⊖(⊖) piece.
   In one sense, each piece is one of the "nine angles"
and is part of an evolutionary (or devolutionary)
development/transformation via both causal and acausal time.
This development/transformation is helical rather than
circular (qv. The Wheel of Life) - one causal aspect
being the transformation of the symbol into the next
in sequence, one acausal aspect being the movement from
board to board.
   The most complete representation of the causal and acausal
aspects is the Advanced Star Game.

* * *

*The Star Game is a four-dimensional structure: the boards
are orientated three-dimensionally in space, while the
pieces, moving/transforming re-present 'time' (both causal
and acausal). The boards themselves may be seen as inter-
acting with, for example, the Zodiacal progression - this
explicating a further aspect of the 'timepath' or
'transformation'. Hence the Moon/Cancer aspect relates to
the Sirius board, the Mercury/Capricorn aspect to the

Arcturus board, and so on. This gives an 'Earth-bound'
perspective to the patterns represented by the Star
Game itself (for example, for an individual,   , or
for aeonic magickal workings). Thus the 'seasonal'
variations are mapped/re-presented by the Game - the
pattern being a helical one (see the Wheel of Life
diagram).
     It should be noted that the starting 'point' is
relative and depends on what, at that moment, the Game
representation is being used for. For example, if it is
being used to simply try and comprehend the connections/
wholeness of the Earth/individual system (in ordinary
magickal terms, Seasonal influences/patterns where
Seasonal means the flow from Spring to Summer to Autumn to
Winter), then the starting point is the part of the season
pertaining at that time. (Thus the Star Game is a
sophisticated magickal 'clock'.) For instance - the
Summer Solstice would imply the beginning of the Cancer
segment, that is, a part of the Sirius board (what part,
the student can easily deduce - and should so deduce).
The 'Wheel', and the rest of the Septenary correspondences,
give arhcetypal/magickal/alchemical reference points around
this 'cycle'/flow/change - and thus show the external
patterns of that change, as evident to individual
consciousness (and in terms of those images/symbols and so
on). Thus are the seasonal changes described - in both the
causal and the acausal. For example, the Solstice
point would equate with the symbol Mistress of Earth,
the element Earth; while the Spring Equinox would equate
with the Priestess and the element Water (in this instance
with that part of the elemental sequence which is 'Water
of Water' - the change to the next Zodiacal constellation
being marked by another part of the sequence: qv. 'Wheel'
diagram). The sphere in this, Venusian, instance is
Antares and associated with Emerald, the colours Green
and White, the process 'Coagulation' and so on.

155

The advanced Star Game consists of the seven boards as in
the septenary version - together with the same number and
distribution of pieces - but each of the seven boards consists
of 4 levels.

The first level of each board consists of the ordinary 18
black and white square board. The second level has eight
squares with 4 on either side consisting of 3 squares in a
row and 1 in front. The third level consists of one square,
and the fourth level of 4 squares. These levels are on both
sides of the board as in the illustration.

Thus each board (which represents a sphere of the septenary)
has 18 squares plus 26, making 44 in all. There are thus
308 squares in total in the advanced game. Further, there
are some additional pieces, as described below.

This version of the game is a complete and full representation
of the septenary system: each board represents the connections
or pathways between the levels or spheres. For instance, the
black squares on the first level (9 squares) together with
the squares on levels 2 and 4 (8 plus 4 squares) are the
acausal paths or connections from that sphere to all the
other spheres. The other side of the board (the 9 white squares
on the first level plus the 12 squares of levels 2 and 4)
represent the causal connections from that sphere. In one
sense the causal connections are the 'outgoing' connections
(or exits) and the acausal   'incoming' connections(or
entrances) to the pathways (or tunnels). The two squares of
level 3 (one on each side of the board - again representing the
acausal and causal aspects) are 'null squares'. These null
squares represent the connection to the Abyss - that is, they
symbolize the random element always present. In the actual
playing of the advanced game these squares are important -
any piece which is placed on them is automatically changed
into another piece selected at random. This random selection
is done by a process determined before the game starts by
the player or players: the most favoured method being to
choose, without looking, from the spare pieces. This choice is
done by the player whose piece has moved to the square. The
chosen piece can be either white or black, and a piece on a
null square - once it has been changed at random - can move to
other squares according to what type of piece it is. Thus,
a ●(●) piece could move up or down one level only, while a ♙(♙)
piece could move to any vacant square on any level or board.
To facilitate the random choice, a complete spare set
of pieces is kept for this specific purpose and these pieces
are used for this purpose only. Thus, as the game progresses,
the choice of pieces becomes more limited.

Pieces:

There are two extra sets of all nine pieces for each
player making thus five sets for white and five sets for
black. Hence, over the 308 squares there are 90 pieces.

Three sets are placed for each player (or 'side') as in
the septenary game. The two additional sets are placed as

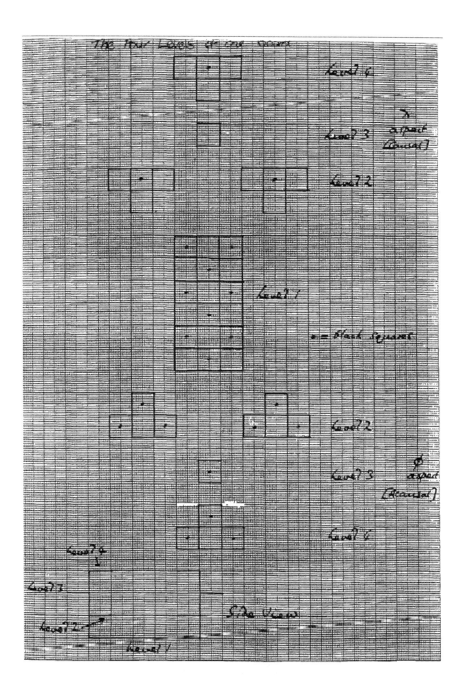

The Four Levels of one Square

level 4

level 3   aspect
              [lateral]

level 2

level 1

• = Black square

level 2

level 3   aspect
              [lateral]

level 4

level 4

level 3

level 2   Side View

level 1

follows:

*One set of black pieces on the black squares of levels 2 and 4 of the Sirius board

*One set of black pieces on the black squares of levels 2 and 4 of the Arcturus board

*One set of white pieces on the white squares of levels 2 and 4 of the Sirius board

*One set of white pieces on the white squares of levels 2 and 4 of the Arcturus board. (See illustration.)

The null squares on Sirius and Arcturus are left vacant.

Moves:

The pieces follow the same rules of movement and transformation as in the septenary game.

However, when a piece is on any of the levels (that is, 2,3 or 4) of any board a move up or down a level is regarded as the equivalent of a move up and down the seven boards. Thus for example, an θ(Θ) piece on a black square on level 2 of the Sirius board may move (provided the squares moved to are vacant at the time) across level 2 to another black square, or up to the black square of level 3 (the null square - where it will be changed at random) or down to a black square on level 1. A θ(Θ) piece on level 4 may move across the squares on level 4 to another black square, or it may move onto a vacant square of the same colour on Arcturus. Level 4 may therefore be regarded as a 'stepping board' to other boards.

Another example: a ♯( ) piece on level 2 of Sirius may move to any vacant square on level 2, up to level 3, or up to level 4 (any vacant square, or down to any vacant square on level 1. These moves are possible because a ♯( ) piece has '2 degrees' of freedom. If the ♯( ) piece was on, say, level 2 of Arcturus, it could move down to level 4 of Sirius (but not any further). Similarly, a ♯( ) piece of level 4 could move if it was on, say, Arcturus, to any vacant square on level 1 of Antares or any vacant square on level 2 of Antares (either side - that is, either the 'causal' or 'acausal' side).

It is simply a question of looking at the levels either up or down for 'degrees of freedom'. Thus an ♯( ) piece, having unlimited degrees of freedom, could move from any level on any board to any other level on any board.

The ♯(♯) piece if on any square on Naos may capture any piece of the opposite colour on any square and any level of any board except Naos.

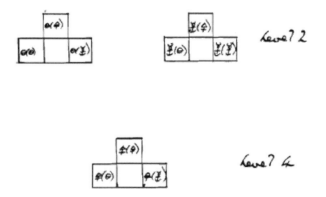

INTERNAL ADEPT – A BRIEF PRACTICAL GUIDE

1) Important to choose a good site: it must be isolated, near fresh water suitable for drinking, within a day's walking distance of supplies (c. 20 miles) and somewhere you will be undisturbed for the length of the ritual. You should visit several sites beforehand and choose the one most suitable.

2) Equipment (see Equipment Guide for some recommendations) must be adequate for the period.

Tent – choose one suitable for two people as room is important. Be sure to seal flysheet seams with sealant (and take some sealant, tent repair kit). Use a strong seperate groundsheet under the tent ground sheet as this will take some of the wear and give some more insulation.

Sleeping bag – Take two plus a cotton inner. No need for expensive down bags: choose two synthetic ones, one to fit inside the other (for colder days and as spare).

Insulating mat – essential.

Clothes – take two of most things. Go for hardwearing natural fibres (wool, cotton). Thermal underwear is essential. As is a hat and a balaclava. Be sure to take at least two pairs of gloves.

Waterproofs – Jacket and over trousers. Best are heavyweight nylon /neoprene. If using expensive breathable fabrics like Gore-tex, take a spare pair of coated nylon since in hard, extended use the breathable fabrics can break down.

Boots – a strong walking boot is essential. Also take spare pair of shoes/lightweight trainers which are fast drying.

Stove – take two: one burning liquid fuel, other solid for emergency back-up.

Knife – essential. Also take a pocket lock-knife as spare.

Survival Aids – essential. To include: compass; waterproof matches; tinderbox (flint/magnesium); survival bag; foil (space) blanket; torch and spare batteries; emergency food sufficient for two days; spare tent guy lines/pegs; sewing kit; first-aid fit.

3) Diet – Take a supply of vitamin/mineral supplements. Every day you need protein, fat, carbohydrate plus c. 3 litres l of water. As basic diet use oatmeal, tinned (powder) milk, f cheese, biscuits; dried fruit; tea/coffee. Every 3 or 4 days eat a cooked meal made from a pre-packed foil wrapped freeze dried range. Each visit for supplies (one a month no more unless dire emergency) buy fresh fruit, milk, eggs, bread, meat or fish. As much as you can afford/carry back to site.

4) Points to note:
* Re-pitch tent every two weeks
* Avoid wood fires as they attract attention – however cold it gets.
* Always keep a set of clothes dry and in waterproof bags in tent for use if needed. If all your clothes do become wet wrap foil blanket around yourself, eat a hot meal, have a hot drink and get into sleeping bag. To dry damp clothes place them between the two sleeping bags before you go to sleep.
* Keep as clean as possible by bathing in stream/river/lake.
* Wash clothes frequently if weather suitable for drying them quickly
* Before you go visit Dentist and Doctor for check-up
* If Winter ritual or using high-altitude/Nothern sites where snow possible, take foldable shovel, snow-shoes and extra warm clothing. Make sure the tent you choose has adequate ventilation and is strongly guyed.
* Give your Order contact details of site chosen and contact them a.s.a.p. after conclusion of ritual.

Remember: you can only take what you can carry on your own back. Take specialist foods with you, and buy first months supplies after pitching camp – sufficient for about a month.

Approx. a month before you go try a week on the diet chosen, and amend if necessary. Be sure to take sufficient money to buy supplies for the period of the ritual plus cost of return from the area.

Problems which may arise:
*Illness. Expect some 'colds' and 'flu' initially. Keep warm and dry – plenty of fluid. Do not eat wild berries, mushrooms etc. unless you are sure you know what you are eating. If a serious injury (e.g. broken limb) forces you to seek aid, the ritual is void and must be done again when fit enough.

*Boredom – if you are going to succeed, you will learn how to cope with this. Always maintain your resolve to complete the ritual under the conditions required.

*Diet – Get used to it! You may feel tired if you have got the balance wrong and will probably lose weight. Others have survived, so you can.

*Intruders – have a story ready for 'passive intruders' to your site (tourists/walkers etc.) – seeking spiritual enlightenment etc. Avoid human contact if possible. For other intruders (e.g. landowners, gamekeeps) – be friendly and ask permission to stay, saying you want solitude. Most will accept this; if not, move elsewhere to an area scouted out in the first few days of the ritual for this purpose.

*Long spells of bad weather – a bonus, if it happens, forcing you further into psychic debt.

*Vermin (lice etc.) – You may become infested. If so, do not worry. Keep as clean as possible, washing clothes regularly. On return to 'civilization' dispose of /burn all clothes and bedding (this is advisable anyway) and get some medical treatment if scalp/pubic area infested. Nothing much to worry about – regular washing will help keep the infestation to an inconvenience and will not seriously affect your health.

*Foot problems. Try and keep your feet dry – always have a spare pair of dry socks. If boots become sodden, let them dry out naturally and use your spare shoes until they do. You can dry dampish socks during the day by putting them under your hat, wrapping them round your neck like a scarf etc.

Remember: make sure your energy intake is sufficient to allow moderate physical activity – this generates body heat and is essential in c0id/wet weather. On good warm days – air dry your sleeping bags.

Grade Rites – Grand Master/Mistress

The Master of Temple/Mistress of Earth needs to fulfill several conditions before the ritual proper:

1)To have fully fulfilled the pledge of a Master/Mistress regarding transmission of the Way by (i) having trained at least one suitable individual up to and including Internal Adept and revealed to them all esoteric teachings; and (ii) explicated that Way using appropriate means enabling understanding by others as/when their wyrd inclines (these means including writings; images; music etc.).

2) Having fully mastered all the techniques of aeonic magick and achieved by some of these new temporal forms.

3) Significantly extended the boundaries of knowledge, understanding and existence by creative endevour explicated causally and acausally – some magickal, others outwardly not-magickal.

4) Have begun the process of directing acausal energies via a new or presently or past existing nexion according to the wyrd of that Master/Mistress with the intention of a new aeonic manifestation or re-creating a previous form or forms.

These conditions have been fulfilled (or nearly so) the candidate sets in order his/her temporal affairs – discarding all that is unnecessary.

This includes all properties, all of significant monetary value, all accumulated possessions, and all obligations of a personal kind (familial etc.; profession/employment). The candidate is to have no financial or other resources other than that required for necessary survival (and then on a weekly basis) save for a small amount sufficient only for the performance of the ritual. All this preparation is necessary and should be strictly adhered to – this attainment of 'temporal freedom' being necessary for reasons which a Master/Mistress will understand. (To those lacking this understanding and post-Adept insight all that will be said that such freedom enables the candidate to become for a short period an actual 'nexion' between the causal and acausal, all attention, energies (psychic and otherwise) being then capable of focusing upon the task.)

The ritual proper involves the candidate achieving a difficult feat of mental and physical endurance – usually this involves walking, in difficult, isolated terrain, a distance of 300 miles in 15 days carrying appropriate equipment and occasionally buying food en route using the small monetary savings mentioned above. (Experienced long-distance walkers are advised to increase the distance.) This feat is planned to end at or near the site chosen by the candidate for the physical nexion.

The candidate is then to reside at or near this site for a period from Equinox to Solstice or Solstice to Equinox (or, for some nexions, for an alchemical season) during which time and using aeonic techniques acausal energies are brought forth and directed to an individual(s)/organization/order/archetypal formes) and so on, via the chant/name(s)/ images and so on chosen by the candidate. In addition, the candidate usually creates a new technique, to enhance the working (e.g o similar to the 'Star Game'). During this period the temporal changes caused by the magick should be discernable. (Further enhancements/workings may be required after this initial period.) These changes signify the success of the Grade Rituals.

THE DATING OF ESOTERIC TRADITION

Received tradition (as given to the present writer by his teacher – an Adept of the esoteric 'Albion' tradition: for which read 'Seven-fold Way'/Septenary/Hebdomadry/ traditional Satanism and so on) places the origin of the Hyperborian Aeon, and thus the civilization of Albion, at least a thousand years before the dates given in Order MSS.

Thus, received tradition gave the origin of the Hyperborean Aeon as between 7,000 to 6,000 BC (that is, 'nine to eight millenia before the present' – this 'present' being c. 1975 ev). Also, the 'Primal Aeon' was given as arising between eleven to ten millenia ago. This placed the origin of the Hyperborian civilization (Albion) at around 6,000 or 5,000 BC, and thus dated Stonehenge to between 4,500 and 3,500 (the 'later' date – 3,500 – being favoured). After a thorough study of these received traditions, and a review of present archaeological/ historical understanding, the present writer decided the traditional dates were out by at least a thousand years. When the Order MSS were written (mostly after 1975 ev) to consolidate what had been – apart from a few MSS such as the *Black Book* – a mostly oral tradition/teaching, these 'new' dates were included.

However, the present writer admits that this revision may well be mistaken, and that the 'traditional' dates may yet be proved correct.

It is to be hoped that sometime in the future further evidence for the civilization of Albion will be found, particularly in regard to accurate dating and the confirmation of esoteric tradition concerning the sea-faring nature of the communities (particularly the links with Iceland/ Greenland/ Canada and the later migrations southward: Greece etc.), the technological advances made and so on. While some evidence for the 'advanced' agriculture of the later period is emerging (e.g. the 'Butzer' Farm project) and the astronomical nature of Stonehenge is now well-established, there is still the view of Albion during the period in question as a rather basic 'Neolithic' semi-nomadic society, rather 'backward' in comparison with the 'civilized' societies of

Sumeria and Egypt. The acceptance of this view is not surprising, given the paucity of evidence, the lack of archaeological excavation and an almost total lack of 'professional' interest. Part of the lack of evidence stems from the fact that a lot of the sites have been almost continually inhabited/cultivated with the consequential loss of material/patterns; another is the use of wood in the construction of artifacts – this is rarely preserved and there has been a rather silly tendency to use pottery remains (its 'sophistication' etc.) to judge/date the communities associated with it, whereas in fact at the time pottery was probably considered an inferior material to wood/leather etc. Another stems from a lack of written records – in Egypt, Sumeria and elsewhere there are well-preserved reminders.

Notes on Rituals – II

The 'Forms' [see the "Musick, Incense and
Forms" chart] may be used to enhance magickal workings
in two ways:
1) The Form may actually be constructed to form the 'inner
part' of a Temple (or the whole Temple itself) and the
working undertaken within this - with an intent, or desire,
appropriate to the sphere associated with that Form. Thus,
a tetrahedron shaped 'inner sanctum' would be for Mercury
workings: i.e. workings concerned with 'indulgence and
transformations' [qv. the tables in 'Naos' and elsewhere]
while a pyramid would be appropriate for Ecstasy and Love.
    The working may be further enhanced by constructing the
Form in the appropriate material.

2) The Form may be constructed in the material [see table]
on a small scale and this itself may be used in two ways:
    a) As a focus for vibration/chant - using the appropriate
chant for the sphere concerned [qv. 'Naos']. Thus, for
Mercury, the tetrahedron would be associated with the
"Agios Lucifer" chant*. The vibration appropriate to this
sphere would be "Satan"/"Satanas".

    b) The Form may be used to store/concentrate the magickal
energy of a ritual associated with a particular sphere/working
by visualization and chant.
    The energy, brought by a working will be 'cast into'
the Form and visualized as being amplified by that Form.
It may then be dispersed, according to desire. [Note: this
'visualization' is what acutally occurs to the energy because
of the structure of the Form.]

Incenses:
            The incenses given in 'Naos' for pathworkings are
appropriate to those workings and the visualizations of the
spheres (the Tarot images etc.).
    Those given are the ☉ aspect. The ☿ aspect are
those listed in the "Musick, Incense and Forms" chart. Thus,
the ☉ incense for Mercury is Sulphur; the ☿ incense is
Yew. The ⚥ is a combination of these in equal proportions.
    ☉ is generally used for pathways and spheres as in
'Naos'; ☿ is used for specific workings involving the
energy of a particular sphere [e.g. Moon implies the vibrated
'word' Noctulius and is appropriate to 'hidden knowledge'/
'sinister knowledge/terror - see the tables in 'Naos' and
elsewhere]. The ⚥ incense for a particular sphere may
be used for any type of working.
    Note: the basic difference, in magickal terms, between the
three forms of incense associated with each sphere is that
the ☉ aspect "evokes" those energies/levels of the sphere
associated with ☉ , the ☿ aspect, those associated with ☿ and

---

*See below for the esoteric version.
* i.e. the ☉ incense.

166

the ♀ aspect "evokes" the ♂ energies/levels. Novices
begin workings with the ☉ aspects because in general these
are more accessable; Initiates are expected to gain
experience with working with all three aspects in magickal
workings. Put simply - the ☉ aspect can be considered as
the 'first level' of the sphere, the ☿ as the 'second'
and the ♀ as the 'third'. Thus, the 'first' level incense
for Moon (Petriochor) associates particuarly with the
Tarot image 18, the 'second' level (Hazel) with the Tarot
image 15, and the combination with the image 13.
    These 'refinements' are, however, subtle - and their
appreciation marks the step beyond the noviciate stage.
An experience of them is considered essential as a prelude to
Adeptship.

The Nine Angles and the Dark Gate:
                                    The sigil formed by
connecting the spheres of the Tree of Wyrd with the 'Gates'
gives not only the pattern of 'walking' when the chant ritual
is undertaken according to tradition [qv.'Naos'] but also
shows the 'pathways' appropriate to those rituals which
'open the Gates'.
    Thus the open the 'Dark Gate', the sequence would be:
Earth Gate-Mars-Star Gate-Moon-Sun-Saturn-Man's Gate-
Venus-Dark Gate.
    Further, to 'find' an Earth Gate (as in establishing the
magickal centre of a new Aeon) the sequence would be begun to end
at the 'Earth Gate'.

    This sequence of pathways may be used in two ways:
1)as a prelude by the chief celebrants[e.g. in a Nine Angles
working] who 'invokes the energies' appropriate to the
particular pathway before the Rite proper: the first is
begun eight days before the Rite. Thus, for a Nine Angles
rite, the celebrants would be the Priest and Priestess -
for a 'Dark Gate' ritual (i.e. 'chthonic Nine Angles' working)
this would mean beginning at the 'Earth Gate' (the site chosen
for the ritual) and invoking on the pathway toward the
sphere of Mars [hint: construct a three-dimensional Tree of
Wyrd showing the connecting pathways(qv. the Order MS
'The Septenary System' in "Azoth") and overlay this with the
'Nine Angles and the pathways' (Earth Gate to Dark Gate for
this particular ritual)and the forces involved in this
pathway (Earth Gate to Mars) will be clear: as will the
symbolism etc. to be employed]. The second invokation on the
second night (in this particular rite at the same location)
would be Mars to Star Gate, and so on.
    [Note: These preliminary workings for a Nine Angles rite
significantly enhance the Rite itself.]

2) as a magickal working in itself. The 'intent' of this
working may be either: the obtaining of knowledge [as for
instance in finding an 'Earth Gate' - or in using the pathways
to bring 'self-knowledge'/expansion of consciousness into
acausal realms], or with a specific intent appropriate to the
'final point' (sphere or 'angle') where the pathways end.
Thus, a Dark Gate final point would be appropriate to
'sinister/chthonic' intent, and so on. These specific rituals

167

can be either ceremonial or hermetic in form.

Naos:
       This word has several meanings, all of which are
esoterically significant.
       As a word it means the inner Temple or sanctuary [from
the Greek Ναος   ] both in the physical sense of a place
and in the sense of consciousness: i.e. the 'latent' temple
[read 'knowledge' etc.] within each individual. It also
signifies a type of portable shrine wherein an image of
a deity was kept.
       It is, as a word, in common usuage in Egyptian archaeology.
In the Occult sense - i.e. as used in the septenary tradition -
it is used to describe both an outer form which holds an
inner meaning [e.g. an esoteric book] as well as a physical
inner Temple or sanctuary.

       Naos is also the name of a star, important in the Nine Angles
rite.*

Falcifer/Vindex:
                Names signifying the person who may embody, in
the causal world, the essence of the sinister - i.e. he/she
empowered by the 'Dark Gods' to bring the wordless Aeon
in a practical sense. In the exoteric sense, Falcifer (the
'reaper') and Vindex (the 'avenger') are esoteric names
for the anti-Nazarene mentioned in "Revelation" and elsewhere.
       Vindex can be 'created' by sinister ritual - the chthonic
Nine Angles rite when the energy is channelled by visualization
and chant into a designated person. [qv. the Order instructional
text: 'Falcifer: Lord of Darkness'; a fictional account of
part of this process.]

Qabala:
         An expression of the distortion foistered upon the
Western ethos by Nazarenes and their allies in spirit.
       The Western ethos [i.e. the outward form of the magickal
energy of the 'Western aeon'] is Luciferian/pagan - the
septenary system/seven-fold sinister way being an esoteric
expression of this [see 'Crowley, Satan and the Sinister Way'**]
       The use of qabalistic/Hebrew names/images/symbols aids this
distortion and thus enhances the power of the Nazarenes and
the 'old Aeon' values/power structures. The same applies to
the use of 'Egyptian/Sumerian' etc. images/symbols/names.
Those who still use such symbols/images/words are not yet
free from Nazarene indoctrination/unconscious influences.
       Thus, effective sinister magick implies the use only of
the septenary tradition in terms of names/images/symbols.

---

*Note: A recent book on Star names gives Naos as deriving from the Greek
for ship. This is a misunderstanding of the Ionic νηος   ; a ship is
   ναυς   .
** Published in 'Fenrir' no. 7

AEONICS

Prefatory remarks: These are 'esoteric' teachings – of necessity, because their understanding requires the insight and knowledge which an External Adept and Internal Adept has attained. Without this insight and knowledge, there is liable to be mis-understanding and a failure to appreciate the finer points (or even any of the points at all).

The 'Aeonics' MSS provide a general introduction to what is a ractical but difficult subject. They describe the essential mechanisms involved: they contain no 'value judgements', no view. Rather, they present what is, as it is. They are an aid to conscious understanding of Aeonic energies – it is up to each and every Adept to decide what they wish to do with that understanding, in the practical magickal sense. The best, and most complete, description of Aeonic processes is the Star Game, particularly the advanced form. These MSS should serve only as an introduction to the abstract symbolism of the Game. Complete understanding arises when the Game is understood 'intuitively' – that is, without conscious effort: when there are no need for words or descriptions. All words are ultimately bound up with division into 'opposites' (and thus 'value judgements' etc.) – only the symbolism is truly representative of what is beyond the Abyss, that is, of the acausal itself and how that acausal effects(presences) the causal. It is in the Star Game that real understanding of Aeonics lies.

AEONS AND THEIR ASSOCIATED CIVILIZATIONS

The energy of a particular magickal Aeon is manifest (presenced) via a higher civilization: there is generally a time-lag of about 400 or 500 years between the start of the Aeon and the beginning of the civilization. The wyrd of the aeon is often expressed by a symbol/word/magickal working (e.g. the Hellenic: Eagle/oracle; dance) although these are merely outward expressions of the inner essence. The destiny of the associated civilization is most often expressed by an ethos/myth (e.g. for the West: Science/ Exploration) and is expressed via various archetypes, some of which may directly relate to the ethos.

An aeon is essentially an ordered manifestation of acausal energy in the causal via an earth-based nexion: this nexion being the 'magickal centre' of the Aeon (and thus the civilization). Various cults and their associated mythos are derived from this centre and its energy. For previous Aeons, this ordering was for the most part intuitive and unconscious – i.e. not arising from deliberate magickal acts by Adepts: the finding and opening of a nexion occurred by the very nature of that acausal energy seeking to 'earth' itself. Aeonic change is now understood and gives all Adepts the possibility of creating Aeonic changes.

A civilization undergoes an organic process of growth and decay and symbolically it has nine stages, represented by the pieces of the Star Game. (Note: the Star Game – particularly the Advanced Star Game – gives a complete representation of one Aeon and its civilization if the pieces are placed correctly.) A civilization generally lasts between 1,500 and 1,700 years. From its origin, its takes about 800 years for a civilization to enter its Time of Wars (aka Time of Troubles) and this period of wars lasts on average 398 to 400 years. It is followed by the Imperial stage – Empire or Imperium (aka 'Universal State'). This lasts about 390 years after which the civilization finally falls. The gradual decline of a civilization follows the wane of the magickal energy associated with it – the archetypal forms which presenced this have fulfilled their potential, become exhausted of energy. (Note: the

Star Game can be used to show how a particular archetypal form grows and decays, causing changes: e.g. the pieces of one board may be used to designate that archetype – by following the changes of the pieces and the affects on other boards, the principles of change may be seen.)

Civilization	Relations	Challenge	Time of Troubles	Universal State
Egyptiac	Unrelated	Physical	2424 – 2052 BC	2052-1660 BC
Sumeric	Unrelated	Physical	3677 – 2298 BC	2298 – 1905 BC
Hellenic	Loosely affiliated	Physical	431 – 31BC	31BC – 378 AD
Indic	Unrelated	Physical	? – 322 BC	322 – 185 BC
Japanese	Offshot of Far Eastern	Physical	1185 – ?? AD	1597-1945 AD
Sinic	Unrelated	Physical	634 – 221 BC	221BC – 172 AD
Western	Affiliated to Hellenic	Physical	1568 – 1996*	1996 – 2390 AD **

Table I

*Estimated from model (see Appendix II). The 1568 AD date is given by Toynbee.
** Estimated from model (see Appendix II).

AEONIC MAGICK GENERAL NOTES

Should only be undertaken if individual is free from unconscious influences – particularly archetypal images 1 of current civilizations/distortions imposed upon it by others. This usually implies having passed the Abyss – but some 'lesser' Aeonic magick can be undertaken by Internal Adepts. This is so because if latent archetypal energy is present within the psyche of the individual, there will be a blocking/internal distortion of the acausal energy – released/created via aeonic rites, and this usually leads to problems: e.g. psychic distortion, physical problems and so on.

Aeonic magick implies, for most rites, the individual being a 'channel' or 'gate'. Psychic residues imply a blocking.

Archetypes imply a development in time – i.e. causal movement. Put simply, this means 'action' – or a 'story': some role played out by the image and thus fulfilled. In the 'cultic' sense, there is a 'legend'/goal. New images require new motifs: i.e. new forms of fulfillment. 'Mimesis' is one method of aeonic magick that has come down over the centuries (indeed, it was once probably the only means available). Basically, this involves imitating some aspect of cosmic/Earth-based movement/working, and then either following the natural pattern or slightly altering that pattern to bring about a subtle change. (This 'alteration' forms the basis for 'black' magick – qv. The Black Mass: the use of Nazarene formulae, slightly distorted via sinister intent.)

often, this implies 'acting out' an archetypal role according to a myth/legend/cult. The key here is the identification of the magickian with the role (which is, however, not a possession, as in shamanism) – this requires preparation. This 'acting out' can involve others –'as, for example, in a 'sacred marriage' (qv. 'Sun' and 'moon' as symbols). The intent of the working is then visualized/chanted. If alterations are desired, these are incorporated. Mimesis can also be done via the construction of suitable models which are symbolically imbued with 'life'. It may also be done via a 'play/drama' whose participants are unaware of the intent and/or of the symbolism. In all Cases it is necessary for the Master/Mistress of the ritual to channel magickal energy into the proceedings either via ceremonial/hermetic methods or by 'opening a Gate'. If the latter, then the energy so brought may be channeled directly or at a distance (if for example a 'drama' is being performed).

AEONIC MAGICK GENERAL (I)

The basic means are:

1) Archetypes – their creation/re-emergence. This is achieved via:

> a) ritual. – e.g. Nine Angl.es rites with appropriate visualization/models/drama
>
> b) creating a mythos: and then channeling acausal. energy into this form via ritual.
>
> c) symbols – 'energize' these via ritual/hermetic workings All. the above require an understanding of archetypal form and change.

2) Open a 'Gate' and let the acausal. energies spread naturally or channel them via an individual or individuals. The latter requires some 'form' to be imposed upon the 'raw' energies released: this form is achieved via the desire of the Master/Mistress and may be either (a) in accord with the wyrd existing at the time (i.e. to help fulfil wyrd of Aeon) or (b) against this, if some fundamental change is desired.

3) Star Game – manipulation of symbols with magickal intent. Can be as 'core' of other 'ritual' working where this ritual brings acausal energy. (Note: this is not strictly necessary for a Magus.)

All Aeonic magick is (a) for the wyrd of the Aeon; (b) against that wyrd; or (c) beyond both of these because a new form is desired. (c) involves both small changes introduced within an Aeon for some specific reason or other, and large changes desired as, for cxample, a prelude to attempting to create a 'new balance' (i.e. the creation of a 'new Aeon').

It is possible to alter the magickal energy of an Aeon at any time, although this is easier during the last phase of an Aeon (generally the

175

Winter stage of the civilization, the few decades before, and after, the beginning of an Imperium). This alteration can be of any type – if sufficient energy is produced/created/released. (The Nine Angles rites are usually the most powerful in this respect – particularly the chthonic with 'Sacrifice'.) Whatever, there must be an intent: something specific to change the energy to/toward. This is often symbolized by a magickal 'word' which then represents the 'new Aeon'/the distortion imposed upon the existing Aeon: this 'word' is only the outward form of inner essence.

For the West (and at the time of writing – 1980 ev) the fundamental long-term options re Aeonic magick are: (1) rites to bring Vindex (channelling into individual etc.); (2) rites to 'Open a Gate' (re the next Aeon); (3) rites to bring acausal energy, letting this presence without form; (4) rites to distort/prevent the wyrd of the West (i.e. Imperium). (5) implies another aim – i.e. the forces must be directed to something other than Galactic Imperium. The scope of this aim is wide-ranging. (6) creation of a new Aeon which is not the direct descendant of the West – i.e. does not involve 'Dark Gods'. Again, aims wide.

AEONICS S. Trad. II

The essential principles of aeonics are:

1) Aeonic magick can be either (a) directed into a specific form (and this can be an individual) or some structure (temporal) which the Adept creates for this purpose – ie. as a means to achieve a specific goal. This structure can be religious, social, political, business and so on; or (b) drawn forth via ritual(s) and left to disperse (ie. there is no specific intent/aim) according to its nature. This implies an element of randomness.

2) Aeonic energy can be used to: (a) create new archetypal forms (eg. specific archetypes); (b) distort/disrupt already existing ones.(a) implies a new 'idea'/mythos and often a 'word' to express this (to non-Adepts). Also, some causal movement is implied in such a form – a development in time.

3) All aeonic change can be: (a) for the wyrd of the Aeon existing at that time (the wyrd being manifest in the Destiny of the associated higher civilization); (b) against that wyrd (thus a 'distortion'); (c) to create a new wyrd. This can be either a new Aeon or an undirected/chaotic disruption of existing one. A new aeon implies a new set of archetypal Corms/mythos etc.

4) All changes can only be directed by the Adept within certain temporal limits, these being set by the strength of the energy produced and whether the initial ritual(s) are subsequently re-inforced. Most aeonic rites by their nature imply a element of random energy which produces further change at first roughly in accord with the energy/intent of the rite: as causal time flows on, the original forms are re-formed via metamorphosis.

5) Any change is possible using aeonic energies – ie. such energies and their use are a-moral. It is the consciousness of the Adept which via intent directs the energy into specific forms to provoke temporal changes in line with that intent.

6) Changes against an existing wyrd (and such like) require more energy because the 'old' archetypal forms/patterns need to be broken down/redirected. Thus, to change aeonic forces the best way is (a) distort/disrupt forms already existing; (b) let the random element accelerate within those Corms by letting loose undirected acausal energies within the aeon/higher civilization; (c) then begin to create new forms via ritual(s). (A skilled Adept can try all three at the same time.)

7) Aeonic energies bring changes on a large scale by mostly affecting non-Initiates – ie. the changes are unconscious: the · 'mass' is unaware that their drives/desires/patterns of behaviour/'thoughts' and so on are being manipulated by Adepts. The most obvious way this occurs is via archetypal forms – but there are other levels acting (how many depends on the acausal energy (intensity, type etc.) and the ritual(s) done by the Adept). One of these is direct psychic contagion – ie. the energy directly affects those receptive/sensitive to it (and this can include Initiates etc.). Those thus affected may then give that energy form or do deeds broadly in line with the type of energy.

(Note: Archetypal forms created via aeonic ritual work mostly unconsciously at first; later, some individuals may express these forms in a practical way, as ideas, myths, mythos, Institutions and so on. Psychic contagion by-passes 'forms' including archetypal forms ie. the latent acausal part of the psyche of infected individuals is directly affected/'opened' by the acausal energy.)

Some further insights:

1) Generally, once an aim/change is decided upon, this should be enshrined in an archetypal symbol, sigil and/or a phrase/word. After the main aeonic rites to produce this change, these symbols etc. should be regularly 'charged' via hermetic rites (eg. sexual magick) and the energy left to disperse naturally or stored in a crystal. The type of aeonic rite depends on the change desired, how strong are

178

already existing aeonic energies (eg. change toward the end of an aeon generally requires less energy). The same applies to reinforcements of the rite (should these be necessary).

2) Wyrd of present Western aeon is Imperium. This implies what is moralistically called an un-democratic State. One aim of such a state would be colonization of the Solar System and then the stars. In essence, this State would be an outward manifestation of Satanic spirit. Political forms to achieve and maintain this Imperium are only a means and must be seen by Adepts in this light. The same applies to 'military' forms. If an Adept or Adepts wish to achieve this wyrd then practical Corms to bring this change must be created/encouraged (magickally) (this applies of course to all aeonic changes). The choice of such forms is made on the basis of practicality, necessity and energies required: it is usually the result of a logical assessment of existing conditions and future possibilities – amoral in essence. An attempt was made by various LHP Adepts earlier this century to use a political form to create a type of Satanic empire on the practical level with the aim of achieving the wyrd of the West. This involved disrupting Nazarene/Magian Corms/ethics/ideas and so on both magickally and on the practical/political level. This attempt was a partial success insofar as it has created a new 'mythos' – there is also archetypal energy stored (and awaiting further use) as well as a nexion now partially open. These offer Adepts the possibility of continuing this work perhaps via the same (or very similar) political forms, perhaps by other (7 contradictory) political forms. It is up to each Adept to make their own assessment – and to decide whether they wish the success or no of this wyrd.

3) It cannot be stressed too often that aeonic magick implies long-term assessment (from several centuries to millennia) and this time-scale of necessity negates the relative moral values that pertain in a society for perhaps a few decades or centuries. Aeonic insight implies an overview of not only the Aeon in which the Adept has his/her being, but also of previous Aeons and future Aeons. The basis of insight is a rational apprehension of Aeonic energies and how those

are made manifest (produce changes) via civilizations and how those civilizations (in their ethos etc.) affect individuals within them. Further understanding comes from magickal experience: how aeonic change is, magickally, possible. The most comprehensive means of understanding Aeonic energies is the advanced form of the Star Game.

The essence of the Adept is this Aeonic insight – the breaking free from the bonds (archetypal forms and thus their unconscious/conscious influence) of the Aeon in which the Adept has his/her being. Further, the bonds of past influences (of previous Aeons) must be transcended also – most who follow or attempt to follow an Occult way fall into the trap of shedding current Aeonic influences only to fall prey to past ones (Egyptian,[4] Sumerian, Greek etc.·) or to be possessed by one 'Idea'/mythos.

4) Present Aeon is dying – its energies are on the wane. Thus time is right to produce aeonic changes/find new nexions. Aeonic magick is concerned with two things: (1) understanding the fundamental principles of how certain types of magickal energy (existing in the acausal) manifests and may be made manifest in the causal; and how those energies when so manifest produce temporal change; (2) actually using such energies – via rites etc. to bring such change in accord with one's desire or goal.

(1) implies learning about aeons and civilizations – how both are formed, live, decay and change via acausal energies – and about how those within them, from individuals upward, are changed and manipulated by the various forms the acausal energies assume. Among such forms archetypes, myths and mythos, ideas, symbols (including artistic representations), as well as the more transient types like politics and religion.

(2) implies learning the skills of aeonic magick and follows after (1). The basic skills are aeonic rites (eg. the Nine Angles rites; Ceremony

---

[4] qv 'Temple of Set'!

of Recalling), the Star Game, and creative manipulation of symbols, ideas and so on (including the more transient forms).

(1) is covered in the many and varied Order MSS dealing with Aeonics and details of the basic skills are given in 'Naos', *Black Book* and the various rituals (most now available in various publications). This present MS will deal with an area not specifically covered before with a view to dispelling some misconceptions.

Sinister aeonic magick implies actual use of the energies by individuals – bringing change(s) to the 'real' or temporal world. This use is often misunderstood by non-Adepts of sinister traditions, and particularly by those who adhere to the old distorted magic(k)al systems. For instance, aeonic magick was used earlier this century to aid a new political form and so try and alter in a significant way the direction of the Western civilization in order to bring about certain futures. These futures (the plural is intentional) would, if they had resulted, have led to the expansion of both a technological and thence an individual kind over a period of many centuries – and this because of the dynamic nature of the form chosen as well as the future transformation of it, via dialectic and internal metasomatosis. The most identifiable manifestation (ie. causal appearence) of this form was National-Socialist Germany. However, most individuals who consider this form, consider it not from an aeonic standpoint but rather from a limited, causal and 'moral' point of view – a view they take, also, of more recent attempts by other individuals and groups, to use that and similar forms for magickal ends. The perspective of this view is immediate rather than of centuries and millennia and shows a fundamental lack of understanding of not only aeonics but 'also magick itself.

The reality is that all significant magick is either Aeonic or internal: External magick is but a child's game, to be played while learning the most basic skills of magick, or for amusement, perhaps, later on. To a real magickian, all types of political (as well as religious and cultural) forms are means – to be used if they are useful for aeonic or internal magickal goals. Genuine Adepts use many temporal forms – although they never identify with them in the sense of adhere to them causally: from a psychic perspective. In the initial stages of the seven-fold way, for example, some 'roles' may be assumed by the Initiate to bring insight, challenges and generally experience the 'forbidden', the contrary, the 'heretical'. But these roles are only that – part of an internal, psychic and thus sinister manipulation of forms. Later, such forms – and others – may be used in the aeonic sense: to bring about large-scale temporal change (how large depending on the intent as well as the skill and aim of the Adept). But in both, manipulation is the key.

Thus, those who criticize those LHP individuals and/or groups who do and have used political forms in the past – or some other temporal form: social, religious or ideological – clearly show by that very criticism and their subsequent 'labelling' of those individuals and groups (from their own myopic and relative 'political' or 'social' perspective) that they lack not only – understanding but also insight into the basics of magick. In short, these 'labellers' expose themselves as not only unworthy of being called magickians, but also as adherents to the old, Nazarene dominated moral value-systems. Their lack of perspective, I- and magickal understanding is not, however, unexpected considering the pathetic state of 'magical understanding' prior to the dissemination of ONA teachings – particularly relating to Aeonics and Internal magick.

On the individual level – of Initiates – the LHP is decidedly a-political, a-religious and a-social (where the 'a' prefix means 'beyond', 'outside'), and is devoted to making each Initiate unique: that is, aiding them fulfill their potential, thus enhancing evolution and creating the next stage of our evolution. The ultimate aim of sinister aeonic magick is to create conditions in the 'real world' such that Initiation and Adeptship and all that these imply in terms of evolutionary understanding and insight, is not only available for all, but fulfilled. This, of course, is and will be a long-term aim; perhaps achieved by the end of the next Aeon, perhaps not. But the aeonic magick of anyone present moment (eg. a rite or form manipulation) aims to presence a part of that future in that present moment or create conditions enabling it. Thus, change is provoked and made possible – in individuals, groups and civilizations. Hence the complexity of aeonics, and the multitude of temporal forms used – but also its simplicity. For, viewed causally and simply, aeonics is change, opposition, creation; provoking challenges and insight counter-balancing and adversarial.

In short – a dialectic, for individuals, groups and civilizations, as well as aeons. and it is this dialectic which is the 'numen' of sinister magick – its ultimate meaning and its ultimate challenge.

Quite simply, it is for those who aspire. The rest can continue their crawling non-existence. Naturally, in aeonic magick some mistakes have been made – some judgement have been shown by events to be incorrect. But understanding and reason are cumulative: a process of learning, for individuals civilizations, and aeons. However:

Τοιαῦτ' ὀνείδι' οἷς ἐμ' εὑρήσεις μέγαν

AEONICS – THE SECRET TRADITION I

Exoterically, the distortion imposed upon the Western Aeon is represented by the religion of the Nazarene. Esoterically, one aspect of the distortion is represented by the 'qabala'. Both of these are manifestations of what it is convenient to call the 'Magian ethos': that is, an approach to living, a way of thinking/being. One of the external manifestations of this ethos is the 'Babylonian Talmud' and the religion whose codes/teaching are represented by that collection of tracts. Another is the 'Old Testament'.

This ethos has, over the last few centuries, become diversified, and now assumes various political and 'philosophical' manifestations. The 'sickness of the spirit', which Nietzsche analysed in many of his works [particularly the 'Anti-Christ'] has changed the direction of the Western civilization [see 'Notes on Esoteric Tradition' and other MSS] and thus its future: Had there been no distortion of the Western 'current' or 'magickal energy' then the Western civilization would now be about to enter the final, Imperial, stage. There would be an outward expansion, led by the elite, firstly world-wide and then, using the technology which is such a feature of the true Western ethos, into outer Space itself with the consequent colonization of the solar system and star systems beyond. This Imperial stage is 'Promethean' or Luciferian in aspect – that is, it is dynamic and expresses that zest for living which is pagan [and which, esoterically, is the essence of genuine Satanism]. It is in one sense the dominence of 'action' over thought the triumph of 'master-morality'. Esoterically, this is and always has been for all 'higher civilizations' the triumph of honour and those who uphold this most elitist of concepts. [This is so because of the nature of the 'acausal energy' which, 'seeps through a Gate' at the beginning of each Aeon. Exoterically, this energy is 'sinister/Satanic' as these terms are understood by the Order (qv. 'The Dark Forces'[5]). It is this energy which 'creates' the civilization – or rather, the civilization is an outward embodiment of that energy, and this impetus to civilization

---

[5] Published in *Fenrir* no. 4

184

is maintain by the 'élan'/spirit of the creative minority who are (mostly unconsciously) guided by a feeling of Destiny which itself arises from such energy and which is often enshrined in a mythos/legend. Adepts are those who understand this, and who can thus work with the energy as that energy is embodied at that moment in time. In the past, this understanding was often intuitive – only in the last century or so has this understanding become rationalized, and thus allowed an even greater degree of understanding (and consequently manipulation of the energies).]

However, the Western civilization, having been distorted in its ethos, is suffering from a sickness of spirit – an infection. Instead of almost entering the stage of Imperium, it is increasingly inward-turning, increasingly concerned with ideas that are 'alien' to it – that is, which do not arise from its own ethos. It has been, in effect, unconsciously given a dream and is now striving to live that dream although that dream means its own death. [As with all Aeonics, there is no judgement here – merely a statement of facts. All Adepts must discover for themselves whether they wish to alter the futures which can arise from these facts, and alter according to their own desires.]

In practical terms: the distortion is evident in the political ideas of Marxism/communism, in the economic idea of capitalism and in the sociological ideas/value-systems which preach 'equality'. The first and third of these derive from Nazarene beliefs – there are, in effect, extensions of the Nazarene spirit: the triumph of the 'slave-morality'. The second, when analysed, takes the abstraction evident in an aspect of the 'Magian ethos' stages further. What all this amounts to on the level of effects is that individuals [and this applies particularly to the creative minority] are:(a) concerned by a 'morbid conscience' and are thus unable to act with spirit/élan, think and act on the basis of reality (esoterically, read 'they act like sinners and penitents rather than Satanists'); and (b) they perceive the world/other individuals via the distorting lenses of abstract ideas – these ideas deriving from the distortion. Magickally, individuals have lost contact with the genuine archetypes of their unconscious. Even worse, the 'magic' which purports to return these archetypal energies does the opposite – it gives experience of the 'archetypes of the distortion'. This 'magic' is that based on, and derived from, the qabala and the 'Grimoires' of the Middle Ages. [This includes Crowley. 'Wicca' would be one way forward were it not so lacking in Promethean zest – that is, lacking the spirit of true paganism (qv. the Vikings).] For the Western civilization, one of the most powerful archetypes is the Warrior. [Note: Adepts are those striving to free themselves from archetypal influence. Part of this involves living the archetypal role of 'Mage'… We are concerned here with the majority who are swayed by archetypes without understanding them.] This Warrior has two aspects, both important vis-a-vis the Western ethos. One is the 'Hero' (where there can be sacrifice of self to the good of the folk); the other is 'Conquerer'.

In simple terms, the West should now be exalting the archetype of the Warrior: it should be a goal aspired to, and the Institutions and so on of the societies of the West should represent this striving to emulate the Hero/Conquerer – and all for the benefit, not of some artificial idea like 'equality' or 'democracy', but for the communities of the West and the individual who strives to become a Hero/Conquerer. This latter point is vital to an understanding of the present – and thus the future. To take an example from history (a valid one, since all higher civilizations have the same form): The West should now be entering the stage that the Hellenic civilization entered with the Roman Empire at the time of Augustus. In the Rome of that time, the Hero/Conquerer was an ideal aspired to – for the benefit of Rome and those citizens who could profit by emulating that ideal. The Warrior was honoured, and warrior values held sway, giving a zest to life, and expansion for the Empire.

This emulation/exaltation of the Warrior archetype by the majority creates the final, zestful, stage of the West (or rather, should have created it) – the strong, the daring, the noble are encouraged and rewarded. The benefit is Empire: for the West this would have been a 'Galactic Empire'. This means that the societies are imbued with the 'Promethean' spirit (or 'acausal/sinister' energies). [Aeonically, Adepts have three functions: 1) their own Destiny (which may be to

186

try and become an 'Immortal'; 2)to aid by magick the Destiny of the civilization to which they belong; 3) or to change that Destiny according to their desire, which of these, they now, in time... None of these can be attained without an understanding of that present in which they find themselves: as that present is.]

In practice, the Western Empire would have meant the dominence by a racially aware community/nation/federation of first the West and then possibly the world – this giving rise to the foundation of colonies in Space and the expansion of the Empire into other Star systems. It would have been 'racially aware' (that is, basically European in race) because archetypes compel this type of cohesiveness: that is, 'Destiny' in the case of a civilization implies a commanality, a sense of belonging, or 'rootedness'. This makes possible 'thinking with the blood' – that is, genuine 'elan' – and thus an advance/conquest. Where this elitist attitude does not exist, there can be no lasting conquest, and thus no Empire.

For the West, this Empire should have begun around 1996-2011 ev and lasted until about 2390 ev after which it, like all Empires, would fall. But then, the Destiny of the West would have been achieved, and with it the dispersal of acausal energy beyond the confines of the Earth. The whole purpose of the Western Aeon was to achieve this further expansion. [Note: There is no 'morality' involved here: just an understanding of magickal, aeonic, energies. The morality which would dismiss a Western Empire is basically Nazarene...] With the fall of this Empire, the 'New Aeon' would assume practical form on the diversity of planets conquered and colonized. There would then be the 'Spring' of not one new civilization, but of many, with the consequent expansion of consciousness.

However, what is occuring at present is an increase in the distortion that is, acausal energies are weakening, the Western civilization declining. [It must be borne in mind that although the energies of the 'New Aeon' are – or rather can be – emerging now, during the beginning of the 'Winter' stage of the present civilization, they have little effect on the practical level until the new Aeonic centre is found.

What effects they do have is largely small and concerned with 'creating new archetypes': these new archetypes influencing things only gradually. It takes several centuries for large scale effects – and a new civilization (i.e. a further upward trend in consciousness) requires the channelling of acausal energy through a new gate as the 'old' one closes. According to tradition, the gate associated with the next Aeon is in outer Space. Hence, on one level, a need to ensure the fulfilment of the Destiny of the Western Aeon.]

On the practical level, this decline means an inward-turning culture: an increase of 'appearance' – that is, a reliance, among individuals and societies, on abstract ideas and theories. There will be dominence by Nazarene beliefs and ideas deriving from them – a return to a 'religion'/ social system of living. [A desire to believe as against a desire to know/explore.] For the West, this will mean tyranny of the mind (and the body because restrictions on movement will exist) existing with a return to 'barbarism' in certain areas (in terms of 'lawlessness'/attitude to living) leading to a gradual decline and probably (after some hundreds of years) an extinction of the acausal on Earth. [In a simple sense, the acausal is evolution, of species and consciousness: the 'Opening of a Gate' (a new Aeon) an expansion due to the acausal presencing on Earth and within individuals.]

Already, this tyranny of ideas exists – together with an increasing physical tyranny to destroy those who do not believe. This tyranny concerns those opinions which contradict in essence the Nazarene/Magian beliefs in 'equality' and 'inward turning morbidity'. [See the MSS 'Aeonics and Heresy'.]

Exoterically, the distortion can be remedied by the arrival of the 'Anti-Christ'. Esoterically, the acausal, sinister, energies can be channelled by ritual into an individual/individuals to create Vindex. Vindex will then be the creater of the Western Empire [i.e. the 'Satanic Empire']. This is one way for Adepts of the sinister tradition to use Aeonic energies. [Note: What 'Vindex' and the 'Empire' means to others is different to what happens in aeonic terms: the former is outward (i.e. 'moral') appearance, the latter, the essence or aeonic 'effect'.] This magick is dangerous – because it draws upon those who practise it the 'magic' of those who have a vested interest in the forces of the distortion .

Other uses of <u>present</u> Aeonic energies are outlined in other MSS.

CLIOLOGY – A BASIC INTRODUCTION

FIRST ISSUED: 1978 EH; REVISED: 1982 EH. FURTHER
REVISION: 1984 EH)

I CIVILIZATIONS, AEONS AND INDIVIDUALS

In order to represent these things in a way which provokes a higher, conscious understanding and thus the development of insight, it is necessary to develope a new type of abstract representation – a new kind of mathematics. However, before proceeding to do this, some general clarifications are necessary.

An Aeon is the term used to describe a stage or type of evolution. Evolution is taken to result from a certain process – and this process can be described via a bifurcation of time. That is, evolution is an expression of how the cosmos changes in certain ways over 'time' – this 'time' having an acausal and a causal aspect: evolution is an increase of the acausal in the causal.

More precisely, the cosmos exists in both causal and acausal space-time where causal space-time (symbolized by λ_σ) has 4 dimensions: three spatial, and one time dimension, this dimension being linear. Acausal space-time symbolized by ϕ_σ) has n spatial dimensions and one, acausal, time dimension. ϕ_σ intersects λ_σ at certain places – these places are 'life-forms': i.e. a living organism is a place where ϕ_σ and λ_σ coincide. Sentient life is regarded as a 'large-scale' intrusion of ϕ_σ into λ_σ: a 'mergence' rather than just a point of coincidence. Consciousness is said to reside, or be, in the acausal. The energy of λ_σ and its changes in causal time, can be described and thus 'explained' by conventional scientific means, e.g. by Physics. The energy of ϕ_σ and its changes can be described by a new science which uses the non-spatial geometry of the acausal and acausal time.

An Aeon is a form or type of acausal energy which manifests in the causal – i.e. it has certain limits in both causal time and 3 dimensional space. It re-orders the causal which is simply another way of saying such acausal energy produces certain changes in the causal. A civilization [or rather a 'higher' or Aeonic civilization] is how this form, this energy, is ordered in the causal – from a causal point of view. An inexact analogy would be an oak tree – the surface of the earth is the boundary between the causal (above) and the acausal (below). The roots are in the acausal (the acausal energy), the trunk and branches in the causal. The 'aeonic' aspect is the roots; the civilization aspect is the trunk; the societies within the civilization are the branches, and the individuals within a society are the twigs and leaves.

Civilizations, Aeons and individuals are examples of organisms – they are created, or born, they grow and change and then they die. They occupy a finite space over a finite time, undergo metamorphosis and so on. They possess structure or form, which form while variable within certain limits is the same or similar for all manifestations of a similar type – and this form can be studied and classified, and appropriate models formulated to represent it and the changes it undergoes.

In essence, a civilization is an aspect of an Aeon, and an individual is an aspect of a civilization. All individuals – unless and until they attain a certain degree of self-awareness [variously called individuation and Adeptship] and thus inner liberation and freedom from 'unconscious' and other influences – are subject to the psyche and this psyche is determined [draws its energy from] the civilization and thence the Aeon. One form such energy takes is 'archetypes'.

This energy [which is basically 'acausal' and not to be confused with the physical energy described by science which is causal energy) determines or influences the actions/non-actions of individuals insofar as those individuals affect the civilization and thus the Aeon. In other words, their lives do not affect or change the civilization or the Aeon. They are part of the wyrd of that civilization – they do not possess a wyrd of their own. Using the inexact analogy – an individual with wyrd (an Adept or someone who has achieved individuation) is a seed which becomes free from the tree and can begin a new process (a sapling). All other individuals are tied to the tree to grow as it grows and die when it dies.

A civilization thus expresses an ordering of evolution. Its energy, and thus its archetypes and so on, is determined by the Aeon which 'creates' [or rather, causes its creation/manifestation in causal space-time]. These energies, for both a civilization and an Aeon can be described in various ways. The most simple (and not very accurate) is mythological/archetypal. An Aeon lasts about 2,000 years of causal time. It is linked to a particular geographical region, and there is a centre to this where the acausal energy is strongest. This is because an Aeon is a physical presencing of acausal energy via a nexion – i.e. a nexus between the acausal and the causal. This centre usually acquires a cult or religious nature: mostly unconsciously. That is, certain individuals are 'drawn to this area' and the acausal energy produces/provokes changes within and external to the psyche of these and other individuals.

The list given below describes the energy of each Aeon which has existed in mythological/archetypal terms – it is guide, rather than an exact description of the energies, and a guide to the changes which are caused in the psyche. [The exact description is purely abstract – in symbols – and is given later.] Each Aeon has a particular civilization associated with it. (See the list.) Its energy may be expressed in terms of an 'ethos' – that is, how the κ_1 [where the symbol κ_1 represents individual(s)] within that κ_c [where the symbol means 'Civilization'] apprehend both causally and acausally [or in simple terms, both rationally and intuitively] the acausal energy of the Aeon. This ethos, like a κ_c grows and changes : it evolves.

The civilizations listed are 'higher' or Aeonic ones – those that have changed/shaped conscious evolution. Other civilizations have existed, but they have generally not contributed significantly to such evolution in terms of creativity – they are usually related, in time and space, to an already existing or a previously existing civilization. The criteria for an Aeonic civilization are: (a) It possesses a distinctive ethos [Note: an ethos is not a 'religion' as religion is conventionally understood.]: (b) it arises primarily from a physical challenge [rather than from the disintegration of an existing civilization (i.e. the challenge as such is social)]: (c) it is creative on a large scale.

In analyzing civilizations and their changes, the work of Spengler and Toynbee is valuable, although its details are not essential. What their work has done, is to contribute some fundamental ideas about the nature and structure of civilizations – their detailed work (such as, in Toynbee's case, historical dates and events) adds flesh to the bones of the aeonic theory here propounded, but that theory is independent of such detail which may be and indeed should be surpassed ln the future. The two most' fundamental ideas of these historians are Spengler's one of the metamorphosis of what he terms a 'culture', and the genesis of civilizations as given by Toynbee – their origin, classification, inter-relation and so on. The ideas have been combined with others – some original, some not (some part of 'esoteric tradition') – to provide the framework for aeonic/acausal theory outlined here. This framework is 'Cliology' – the study of those processes which have caused historical change.

The mechanism by which civilizations affect evolution is that of 'creative individuals'. Most of these are influenced by the ethos of their civilization to act, or to express that ethos more consciously, those causing others to act. Few individuals in a civilization reach the stage of conscious evolution which frees them from the influence of ethos – be such the ethos of their own civilization or that of another. of course, many are there who believe they are free of such influence – but belief is not the same as realty. It has been and is the aim of genuine Esoteric Arts to enable individuals to reach the stage of conscious development where they become free of such influences – i.e. to achieve a uniqueness of identity. This requires insight, knowledge and reason – all of which are aided by understanding how and why things (such as civilizations) are as they are. Cliology is an expression of such understanding, and as such a learning of the subject adds conscious development and thus makes Adeptship/individuation possible. The abstract form, given here (particularly in the Second and Third parts of this introductory treatise) takes this rational understanding further.

Aeon	Symbol	Magickal Working	Associated Civilization	Dates
Primal	Horned Beast	Shamanism	--	9,000 - 7,000 BP
Hyberborian	Sun	Henges	Albion	7,000 - 5,500 BP
Sumerian	Dragon	Trance; Sacrifice	Sumerian/ Egyptiac	5,000 - 3,500 BP
Hellenic	Eagle	Oracle; Dance	Hellenic	3,000 - 1,500 BP
Western	Sunwheel/ Swastika	Ritual	Western	1,000 BP - 500 AP
Galactic		Star Game & beyond	Galactic	

[Note: BP means 'Before Present' (1980 eh); AP means 'After Present']

The centre of the Hyberborian Aeon was the area around Stonehenge. The centre
of the Sumerian was located between the Tigris and Euphrates (and is near present
day Baghdad). The centre of the Hellenic was Delphi. The centre of the Western
was/is around an area in the Marches - it was, and is, esoteric due to the
distortion of the Western ethos by first the Nazarene religion and then other forms
broadly similar in effects to that religion.

The mythological/archetypal attributes of a particular Aeon can be gleaned from
the symbol and 'magickal working' listed above. The ethos of some civilizations are
listed below.

Hellenic - Quest for excellence; Reason. Western - Exploration/Science.

Civilization	Relations	Challenge	Time of Troubles	Universal State
Egyptiac	Unrelated	Physical	2424 - 2052 BC	2052-1660 BC
Sumeric	Unrelated	Physical	2677- 2298 BC	2298 - 1905 BC
Hellenic	Loosely affiliated	Physical	431- 31BC	31BC -378 AD
Indic	Unrelated	Physical	? - 322 BC	322 - 185 BC
Japanese	Offshot of Far Eastern	Physical	1185-1597 AD	1597-1945 AD
Sinic	Unrelated	Physical	634 - 221 BC	221BC - 172 AD
Western	Affiliated to Hellenic	Physical	1568- 1996*	1996- 2390 AD **

Table I

*Estimated from model (see AppendixII). The 1568 AD date
is given by Toynbee.
** Estimated from model (see Appendix II).

Spread ($\phi_1 \rightarrow \lambda_5$):-

a) Albion $\longrightarrow$ Sumeria $\longrightarrow$ Indus

         ↓   ↓

      Egypt   Indic $\rightarrow$ Sinic

                       ↓

                    Japanese

b) Hellenic $\rightarrow$ Western   a) $\Rightarrow$ 'Henges'/Stone-circles

                         [ϕ centre: $\phi_1 \rightarrow \lambda$]

         ↓   b) $\Rightarrow$ Delphi

      Galactic   [(a): c.4,500-2,500 BC

                   (b): c.1,000 BC - 500 AD]

External manifestations of ϕ ("creativity..."):-

Albion : Proto-Astronomy; Wheel; Proto-Agriculture

Sumeria : Writing [Phoenicia $\rightarrow$ Egypt]; Agriculture

Hellenic : Reasoning; Logic ; Proto-Science

West : Science; Exploration; Technology

ϕ centre: Western Area:-
    Surrounding Black Hadley, Linley, Stiperstones,
    Long Mynd, Caradoc

      ᚼᚱᛉᚦᚢᚼᛩᛋᚷᚼᚷᛆᛆᚬᚬ-ᚷᚬᚼᚬᚺᛁ
      ᚷᛏᚼᚦᚬ-ᚷᛩᚬᚼᛩᚷᚢᛩᛋᛩ-ᚬ

Notes:- Centre of Albion [Hyperborion]- Stonehenge.
    Culture runs Ridgway; Wellow Track; Sweet Track; Portway etc.
    • Centre of West $\rightarrow$ where remnants of traditions of
      Albion survived beyond 1,000 BC [to c.700 AD & thence
      20th Century]

Each civilization follows a pattern. This can be symbolized and thus studied.
The same is true for an Aeon. Such study enables two important things. First,
it enables an objectification. In one sense, this is a withdrawing of
projections (in Jungian terms). Second, it developes already existing faculties
and creates new ones - the ability to reason in abstract symbolism, for example,
where the symbols are 'numinous' (i.e. "alive") rather than being simply
'intellectual'. That is, such symbols relate to those things which are important
for an individuals life.[In a simple sense, the symbols of cliology are
imbued with 'psychic energies' and thus posses 'power'. More correctly, the
symbols re-present acausal energies as against causal ones such as in mathematics
and physics.]
      The symbolization enables the patterns, on the levels of an Aeon, a civilization
and individuals, to be followed and manipulated if necessary. It enables
insight into Aeons, civilizations, individuals, and one's own self, and thus forms
the essence of inner esoteric teaching.
      The symbolization, at the present time of writing, is of three kinds, two of
which have been developed quite recently. The first kind is the mythological/
archetypal - the use of myths/archetypes and such like forms to describe/
represent the processes and patterns. Such representations are traditional,
and still useful, particuarly in the early stages of study. [One type of this
kind of representation is the septenary Tree of Wyrd with each sphere being
associated with various archetypes/myhtological forms and so on.] The second
kind, is The Star Game - a collocation of abstract symbols which re-present
the acausal as it manifests in the causal, these symbols, as mentioned above, being
numinous ones. The third type, the rudiments of which are described in
the Second and Third Parts of this present work, is a formalized abstract
system which represents the beginnings of a new science. The first and second
types are complete. The third type has only begun to be developed - the next
few centuries should see this new science complete in most of its essentials.
The mastery of the first type of symbolization is relatively easy. The mastery
of The Star Game (in both septenary and Advanced versions) takes quite an
intellectual effort, stretching the frontiers of conscious evolution. The
understanding of the third type, takes conscious evolution still further.
The completion of this third type will stretch the frontiers almost to their
limits.
      All three kinds are genuine esoteric Arts.

                                    o o o

            II   The Basic Symbolism

      Before proceeding to describe the symbolism of this third type, some
brief remarks concerning the symbolism of The Star Game will be in order.
      In The Star Game, Aeons may be symbolized by the boards - i.e. the first
board (Sirius) re-presents the first or Primal Aeon, the next board, the next Aeon,
and so on. The placing on the pieces on a board represents a particular stage of
an Aeon - the initial placing being the pre-civilization stage of an Aeon.
The movement of pieces then represents the evolution within an aeon and its effect
upon others.
      However, all seven boards can be used to represent just one Aeon. The same is
true both for a civilization and an individual. Thus, in the septenary version for
instance, the seven boards could be used to represent aspects of one civilization fro
its genesis to its demise - the first six boards might be chosen to represent the
causal changes, and the seventh, the acausal ones, thus:

$$\gamma[\alpha,\beta,\delta]$$

$$
\begin{array}{ccc}
\gamma(\alpha) & & \\
 & \xrightarrow{\ \ } & \gamma(\beta) \\
 & \beta(\beta) & \\
\alpha(\beta) & & \\
 & \xrightarrow{\ \ } & \beta(\alpha) \\
 & & \\
 & \alpha(\alpha) &
\end{array}
\qquad (1)
$$

In this case, the last board is in 'acausal space' and thus has three causal aspects - α, β, δ .

Here, the basic transformation is represented by:

$$\alpha(\alpha) \to \alpha(\beta) \to \alpha(\delta) \to \beta(\alpha) \to \beta(\beta) \to \beta(\delta) \to \gamma(\alpha) \to \gamma(\beta) \to \gamma(\delta)$$

However, another representation would be:

$$
\begin{array}{ccc}
 & \gamma(\beta) & \\
\beta(\alpha) & & \\
 & \delta[\alpha,\beta,\gamma] - \beta(\beta) & \\
\alpha(\alpha) & & - \alpha(\beta) \\
 & \gamma(\alpha) &
\end{array}
\qquad (2)
$$

In (2) there is no linear (2/3 dimensional) representation of causal time as there is in (1) [the basic transformation is a linear representation of change]. That is, in (2) there is no direct, linear sequence from one board to the next.

Both representations are equally valid - they are merely different ways of viewing the same thing, and this flexibility is inherent in The Star Game. This is an important point which is often overlooked - the only constants (or constraints) in/of the Star Game are the seven boards, each of a particular number of squares, the number and types of pieces, and the rules governing their movement. What the boards and symbols and moves re-present has to be determined before the game is used - when, that is, it is used esoterically, and not just as a 'game'.

Further, acausal components or 'pieces' (such as $\gamma(\delta)$ or $\alpha(\delta)$ say) exist simultaneously as a particular causal component or piece - thus, when $\alpha(\alpha)$ exists, so to does $\alpha(\delta)$ and both $\beta(\delta)$ and $\gamma(\delta)$. When $\alpha(\alpha)$ transforms to $\alpha(\beta)$, these acausal pieces still exist, even if they have not been 'presenced' in the same or adjacent causal space as that piece. This simultaneous existence is represented, in the septenary form of The Star Game, for instance, by the degree of freedom of movement of an 'acausal' piece..

We shall now move on to describe the basic symbolism of the third form.

Two abstract spaces, ϕ_f and λ_f are posited and $\lambda_f \in \phi_f$ is divided into nine sub-spaces represented by the abstract symbols

$$\alpha(\alpha), \alpha(\beta), \alpha(\delta), \beta(\alpha), \beta(\beta), \beta(\delta), \gamma(\alpha), \gamma(\beta), \gamma(\delta)$$

$$(3)$$

ϕ_f is determined by $\digamma^\phi$ and λ_f by $\digamma^\lambda$ where $\digamma^\phi$ is acausal time, and $\digamma^\lambda$ causal time both at present otherwise undefined.

A basic principle governing $\phi_f \in \lambda_f$ is that the sub-spaces occur in the following
order:

$$\alpha(\alpha) \Rightarrow \alpha(\beta) \Rightarrow \alpha(\gamma) \Rightarrow \beta(\alpha) \Rightarrow \beta(\beta) \Rightarrow \beta(\gamma) \Rightarrow \gamma(\alpha) \Rightarrow \gamma(\beta) \Rightarrow \gamma(\gamma)$$

(4)

[Note: the symbol $\in$ is to be read 'within'.]

$\alpha(\alpha)$ is regarded as closer to λ_f, $\gamma(\gamma)$ to ϕ_f; thus (4) represents a movement
from λ_f to ϕ_f.

(4) is called a transformation, via $\in^{\lambda}$.

Therefore,

$$\delta^{\lambda}\left[\alpha(\beta)_{\lambda}\right] = \alpha(\beta)_{\lambda}'$$

(5)

where $\alpha(\beta)_{\lambda}'$ is the new transformed element according to (4).

$\in^{\phi}$ transformations also occur. Such a transformation – δ^{ϕ} – is defined
by

$$\delta^{\phi}\alpha(\beta)_{\lambda} = \left[\alpha(\beta)_{\lambda}', \ \alpha(\beta)_{\lambda+1}'\right]$$

(6)

Thus, for example,

$$\delta^{\phi}\alpha(\alpha) = \left[\alpha(\alpha)', \ \gamma(\beta)'\right]$$
$$= \alpha(\beta), \ \gamma(\gamma)$$

and

$$\delta^{\phi}\beta(\alpha) = \left[\beta(\alpha)', \ \alpha(\beta)'\right] = \beta(\beta), \alpha(\gamma)$$

Hence, a δ^{ϕ} transformation is non-linear* The operations δ^{λ} and δ^{ϕ} are
the fundamental operations in $\phi_f \in \lambda_f$, and can be used to formulate rules which
govern what occurs in both spaces. That is, an algebra for these regions
can be created (rules for $\delta^{\lambda} \equiv \delta^{\phi}$; $\delta^{\lambda}/\delta^{\phi}$; δ^{λ}. δ^{ϕ} and so on) and then
equations written, using the transformations, which represent the forms taken
by 'objects' in these spaces – i.e. the forms are geometrically represented using
algebraic equations based on the new algebra. Each form is then identified with a
particular aspect of such spaces – e.g. one form/geometric structure would be
an aeon; another a civilization; another an individual. The geometric representation
would be via a new 'co-ordinate geometry' in the new space defined by $\phi_f \in \lambda_f$.
Manipulation of the equations, and an indentification of the models with aspects
of the physical manifestations, would then provide new insights. [For details of
this new algebra and geometry, concerned with the space $\phi_f \in \lambda_f$, see the
MS 'Mapping The Acausal'.]

* It is also creative: i.e. a 'new' aspect/symbol/form is created/becomes manifest
following such a transformation. This explicates the nature of an acausal transformation.

200

This section is an introduction to the basic ideas of a new representation of the acausal. This representation enables the fundamental laws governing the changes of energy [or acausal matter] to be ascertained and described in conventional mathematical terms.

The ideas - the formulation of the acausal and the changes, and so on - may be used to describe, by reduction [the imposition of appropriate boundary conditions] the causal and the changes of matter/energy within it. Thus, it is possible to develope a new physics which describes the laws and so on of the acausal, this new physics being able also to describe the causal since the causal is a special case of the acausal.

The acausal, ϕ_f, may be described by a five-space, thus:

$\beta = (x,y,3)$

β is a representation of the 3 dimensions of causal space: $x, y, 3$.

A line-element of this β space is described by:

$$ds = f(\epsilon^\phi, \epsilon^\lambda, \beta)$$

ϵ^λ is determined by c, the velocity of light.
ϵ^ϕ implies <u>action at a distance</u>, because of the nature of ϕ_f - i.e. it is 'beyond the causal'.

When $\epsilon^\phi = 0$, the five-space becomes a four-space defined by Riemann geometry.

$4 - space:$ $F_g = f(ds_\lambda)$

For ϕ_f : $$F_v = f(ds_\phi)$$

where ds_β is determined by $\delta\epsilon^\phi$. For $\epsilon^\phi = 0$, F_v reduces to F_g [where F in general represents 'Force' - e.g. F_g is gravitational field in λ_f ; F_v is the 'unified field' of ϕ_f .]

A point in ϕ_f is specified by $\epsilon^\lambda, \epsilon^\phi$ and l where $l = (x,y,3)$ and the metric o this space is derived from a transformation $l_1 \rightarrow l_2$ and so on.

Further, ϕ_f implies <u>velocities greater than that of light</u>.
$f(\epsilon^\lambda)$ describes energy changes in λ_f - i.e. 'matter'.
$f(\epsilon^\phi)$ describes energy changes in ϕ_f , one of which is <u>charge</u>.

$\phi_f \in \lambda_f$ implies charged particles.
$f(\epsilon^\lambda)$ are differential equations involving a wave-function: e.g. $\nabla^2 \psi$
$f(\epsilon^\phi)$ are differential equations representing geometric transformations of 5-space
Some equations of 4-space: (i.e. λ_f)
$$\nabla \times (\nabla \times F) = \nabla(\nabla \cdot F) - \nabla^2 F$$
For nuclear field:
$$\nabla(\nabla \cdot F) - \nabla^2 F = 0$$
Div implies source density of field; Curl implies vorticity of field; Grad implies rate of change of field. Mass implies F - the flux $\blacksquare$ ϵ^λ .
****

201

Aeon	Associated Higher Civilization	Centre of Aeonic Force	Consciousness Guide	Magickal Form
Hyper-borian	Albion c. 4 000 BC – 2 500 BC	Stonehenge	⚡(⚡)	Henges
Sumerian	Sumeric c. 3 100 BC – 1905 BC	Tigris basin	⚡(⊖)	Trance; sacrifice
Hellenic	Hellenic c. 1 100 BC – 378 AD	Greece	⚡(⚘)	Oracle; Dance
Western	c. 1100 AD – 2390 AD	Germany	⚘(⊖)	Ritual; Word
Galactic	c. 2400 AD –	Beyond solar system	⚘(⚡)	Empathy; Star Game

An Aeon lasts approx. 1,500 years (not 2,000) and predates the higher civilization associated with it by approx. 300 – 400 years. An Aeon implies $\phi_s \to \lambda_s$: that is, an increasing of ϕ in ε^λ dimensions. In simplified form, one may say that a 'Gate' between ϕ_s and λ_s has been 'opened' – giving an increase in consciousness ($\delta\phi$ by ε^λ) via the mechanism of a higher civilization. Thus the 'opening of a Gate' for the next Aeon, the Galactic occurs c. 2000 – 2100 AD.

Contrary to Occult mythology, the most important aspect of a new Aeon is the associated higher civilization, the civilization taking its ethos from the Aeonic force and/being this ethos the most conspicuous manifestation of that force. The subsequent development of the higher civilization is natural, determined by the ethos or 'spirit', the ethos itself becoming expressed and codified in what is usually a non-magickal form – as a 'philosophy' or way of looking at the world. This codification usually occurs in the Spring period of a higher civilization's metamorphosis.

Aeon	Philosophy	Associated (& often esoteric) Mythos
Sumerian	Vedas	Dragon/serpent mysteries
Hellenic	Pre-Socratics	Apollo; mysteries of the 'Kabeiroi'
Western	Science	Faustus; Grail*; Dark Gods

*In reality, the 'Grail' was a precious crystal – not a chalice – as per 'Nine Angles' rite. The received (i.e. non-esoteric) legends about the Grail are distorted recollections of Hyperborian mysteries. According to esoteric tradition, the Grail was actually used c. 700 AD to inaugurate the Western Aeon – hence the medieval traditions.

SATANISM AND CHILD-ABUSE

Allegations have been made, and continue to be made, concerning 'Satanic' child-abuse – that is, the sexual abuse of children as part of Satanic rituals, practices and beliefs.

As an authority on Satanism, having been actively involved in Satanism for nearly twenty-five years, and being the Grand Master representing traditional Satanist groups, I can write expertly about this matter. Genuine Satanism – like all genuine magick – is a path, way or method of individual self-development. Rituals may be and often are a part of this, but these rituals all conform to certain patterns: they are all intended to aid and explicate self-understanding and development, as well as enhance and develop certain 'Occult' abilities. Naturally, some rituals and methods are concerned with the individual experiencing certain emotions and, in Satanism, enjoying certain pleasures. However, because of the aim of Satanism [to aid the attainment by the individual of magickal and personal understanding and thus promote evolution and self-mastery], this experiencing involves a conscious choice or decision by the individual. This makes Satanism of necessity an adult path or way – for genuine Satanism, of the traditional type, is not concerned with proselytizing nor 'corrupting' others without their consent. Its concern it must be repeated – is individual advancement arising from a conscious and free decision by the individual – anything else in not Satanic as it is not magickal. This free choice is part of all genuine Occult and magickal paths: Initiation means this free choice, the decision to begin an inner quest. When there is no free choice about the matter, there is no genuine Initiation – whatever path or way is being followed. Where Satanism differs, is in the aim, the philosophy of life and the techniques used to achieve the aim – these make it a 'Left Handed Path' [when viewed conventionally].

Thus, there cannot be any such thing as 'childhood Initiation' – nor this participation by children under a certain age in any genuine magickal rituals. What there can be: what there often is – in genuine Satanism at least is the simple dedication of infants by their parents to the darker path, and involves only the appointing of guardians to watch over and care for the child(ren): 'Do you, so chosen, pledge to guard and watch over this newborn and to teach them when the teaching-time is right, our ways ..' from 'The Ceremony of Birth' in *The Black Book of Satan* (ONA) The time for teaching is when the child, in accord with Satanic philosophy, can choose for themselves – sixteen years of age or thereafter – that is, when they have attained the threshold of adulthood.

Hence, there is not, and cannot be, any such thing as 'Satanic' child-abuse: there can be no child-hood 'initiation', no participation by children under a certain age in rituals, and no abuse, by adult Satanists, of children. This latter is important – Satanism is concerned with the individual gaining self-mastery and self-understanding. The abuser (whether of children, drugs or pleasures) is swayed by mostly unconscious desires and impulses – they may manipulate and try to control others who are susceptible, but they cannot control themselves, or even begin to understand their 'darker' side. In short, they are weak – and generally rather pathetic – individuals, although they may hide behind a 'mask' or a 'role'. Such people are not Satanists, but rather failures. The Satanist aspires to self-mastery, self-overcoming; to knowledge ...

The popular image of Satanism is a lie – a myth invented and fostered by those who have a vested interest in maintaining it. Organized religions and under-developed individuals need such myths, as they need stereotyped enemies: for only by such means can such people and such religions survive and flourish. Many believe, with that certainty that faith and fanaticism bring, the myths about Satanism and the more general myths about ritual 'child-abuse'. I and a few others know the facts – in my case about Satanism – but it needs a certain mental freedom, to consider these facts as considered, and then make an informed judgement about like me can present an unbiased mind, they should be the matter. It is this freedom which a biased, religious intolerance destroys.

The real question about Satanic child-abuse (and ritual abuse itself) is thus a question about attitude, belief and commitment to reasoned thought and debate. Long after Science showed the Earth was not at the centre of the Universe, the Church – its ministers and its faithful – continued to believe otherwise, confirmed in their certainty of faith. Do we, now concerning this question of Satanic child-abuse – return to a Dark Age of faith, of believing what certain Church people wish us to believe to bolster their religion and rather intolerant view of the world; or do we go forward to greater understanding based on an acceptance of the facts? These facts show that Satanic child abuse – and ritual abuse itself – is a myth.

ONA

****

The following books contain the facts regarding traditional Satanism, and should be studied by anyone who wishes to know what Satanism really is:

The Black Book of Satan – A Guide to Sinister Ceremonial Magick
Naos – A Practical Guide to Becoming an Adept I
Fenrir Vol. I (no's 2 – 8)
Fenrir Vol. II

All the above are obtainable from the ONA.

HOSTIA II

Secret Teachings of the ONA
Volume II

Printed & Published by
Thormynd Press
PO Box 700
Shrewsbury
Shropshire
England
Limited Edition: of 63 copies this is number

INTRODUCTION TO VOLUME II

This volume contains a selection of 'restricted' esoteric manuscripts circulated among those members of the ONA who were (and are) of the Grade] of External Adept and above and who were in good standing. As such, while complimenting the MSS contained in Volume I, they represent part of the 'inner core' of esoteric teachings. Some of the MS in the present volume are concerned with sinister strategy, some with practical techniques to achieve and implement that strategy, and some with what can be described as the essence of real evil.

ONA – ORGANIZATIONAL STRUCTURE

The ONA is organized on the basis of cells, basically for two reasons: (1) Security and (2) Effectiveness.

The structure means that each new Initiate/member has one (at most two) Order contacts who channel information/teachings and so on, and who offer guidance/instruction. When this member reaches the stage of External Adept, they usually form their own Temple for ceremonial magick and for teaching, recruiting their own members, whose Order contact thus is that External Adept. Each Temple thus formed exists independantly. Hence, if it or any of its members are 'compromised', the chain cannot lead very far, enabling other members in other Temples to remain secret and so continue with their own work, both personal (following the path to Adeptship) and aeonic (aiding the sinister dialectic).

Further, such a structure is effective, because: it enables each member to progress at their own pace; it enshrines a fundamental principle of genuine Satanism [individuality, and freedom from subserviance to authority] and it enables practical experience of a character-building type [e.g. by organizing and running a Temple at an early stage].

Essentially, the Order is secret – and intends to remain so as far as most of its members and activities are concerned. However, its teachings and traditions have been and will continue to be made progressively more 'public', that is, available – thus enabling any individuals who may be interested to follow (if only in part) the way of genuine Satanism, for those individuals by so doing (however slightly) will aid the sinister dialectic, increasing the dark forces presenced on Earth. Some of these may progress to the Order.

This 'working secrecy' is necessary because Satanism cannot now be anything other than selective – it is elitist, being a hard and dangerous path, and part of its effectiveness lies in work of an 'underground', clandestine nature [e.g. some essential work is done by those involved in 'respectable' positions, which positions would no longer be available if the Satanic beliefs/practices of those involved in such work was generally known: i.e. they were discovered to be Satanists]. This secrecy will not change in the immediate future [for c. 20-30 years, that is] due to the nature of the societies in which we are forced to work.

Satanism can never become (until the 'New Aeon' arrives at least) respectable: for to become so would destroy its numen, its viability as a way to genuine Adeptship. It is dark, evil – for the few who genuinely dare. This daring, as mentioned in other MSS, is practical, in real-life situations, involving danger, requiring courage, and defiance of both one's own limits and those of others, including the society of the moment. While society and other structures restrict and deny the promise of Satan, this dark defiance is required – and, moreover, required as a working system which achieves results, both personally and aeonically. What will change, is the number of individuals who can try this way to liberation – and while this will increase, it will do so only slowly over a period of decades. This will be a cumulative process which will aid (and indeed create) the next Aeon, the Satanic one when what is regarded now as dark and sinister will hold sway.

Thus, it has been necessary to disseminate the teachings and traditions of the Order, and this dissemination will continue and increase, as part of sinister strategy. This part of sinister strategy was begun a decade ago by the Grand Master representing traditional groups. It was carefully planned and (so far) has been carefully executed.

The initial stage involved circulating some details about traditional Satanism (the Septenary system; dark gods mythos) among some sections of the Occult fraternity. Thus, a few articles were published, and the existence of the Order itself made known, for the first time outside traditionalist groupings, thus confirming certain rumours about such a group existing, such rumours having beep in circulation for some time. Over a number of years, more information was made available – although still within the 'sub-culture' of the Occult underground. This attracted some interest (and a few Initiates – incidental to the main intent) and was followed by the establishment of, at first, a newsletter, and then a 'zine', both of these being of an 'underground' nature, both in terms of quality and the manner of distribution (i.e. selective, advertised in similar underground publications). Furthermore, the number of copies distributed was kept low. The aim was two-fold – to create a sense of exclusivity (thus making the Order at first difficult to locate/find) and to pose no direct threat, that is, the zine and those associated with it would be seen as totally on the fringe, without resources and probably without any support. Thus, the activities of its members, always secret, would pose no threat and no investigation of any kind would be contemplated. Thus, both of the aims mentioned above could be achieved – dissemination of the tradition, and preserving the secrecy necessary for valuable work to continue.

After a few more years, the next step was taken – the distribution, again on a small scale, of works containing in detail the whole tradition. The format of these works would be the same – of a kind to intimate only a small-scale enterprise. Thus were *'The Black Book of Satan'*, *'Naos'*, *The Deofel Quartet* and other works made more accessible for the first time. Furthermore, the scarcity of these works would create an 'aura' about them – an aura which hinted at the darkness of the tradition. This would be re-inforced by making available the most sinister aspects of the tradition – aspects which would also contradict the meanderings of the armchair 'Satanists' who prattled on about Satanism being mis-understood and not really being evil, and who had increasingly come to notice as the decade came toward its end.

Naturally, this would provoke a reaction – both from those within the Occult and those without. The reaction from those within the Occult (and particularly those who said they adhered to the Left Hand Path) would establish their own position, and thus their total mis-understanding and lack of real insight. In brief, they would continue their word-games and fantasy-roles when confronted by the reality of genuine Satanism. But, equally as important, some would

211

assimilate the tradition, or parts of it (perhaps unconsciously, perhaps consciously by plagiarizing it) and thus not only be influenced by it but also aid the sinister energies it re-presented because of that influence. [Thus, some of the meaning of the term 'sinister dialectic' can be glimpsed.]

The next stage was to give form and substance to certain aspects of the sinister energies that the Order and thus its tradition represented – among such forms being Satanic images (e.g. in the form of Tarot images) and music. These, by their very creation, would presence such energies (unconsciously influencing others·-particularly 'the susceptible ones'). They also would be distributed in the manner used hitherto, spreading that sinister influence, partly (as the other earlier dissemination had done) via the process of psychic contagion. Following this, there would be a gradual increase in both the quality and the number of items distributed – without however the genuine darkness of the forms and tradition being diluted. In addition, more subtle approaches would be used – gradually contaminating psychic energies with strands of the sinister and thus overtly/covertly influencing/persuading others outside and within the Occult, and drawing them into that ever expanding circle of those touched by the powers of Darkness. [This paragraph explicates the current stage of play.]

Thus, secrecy is preserved as and when necessary, while the tradition and thus the sinister is effectively spread.

SYNISTRY

The following extracts are taken from 'Synistry – the Way of Satan', the autobiography of a member of the ONA. The work is explicit in stating not only what Satanism is and involves, but also in detailing the often sinister (and sometimes illegal) experiences of the author. It is a challenge to the meek imitation 'Satanists' who merely dabble and play at Black Magick and who are afraid of real evil – those who espouse 'Satanism' as some sort of 'moral' religion.

VIII SACRIFICE

Although it was over seven years away, I believed the time was right to begin the planning for my performance of the Ceremony of Recalling a sinister ritual of sacrifice where the victim or opfer was offered to Baphomet, the dark Goddess of Satanic tradition, regarded as the Bride of Lucifer. According to the tradition I was heir to, the ritual was performed every seventeen years by the Grand Master or Grand Mistress who represented that tradition – the opfer being a Priest of the tradition. In the ceremony, the Mistress of Earth identified with the role of Baphomet.

The sacrifice could, of course, be purely symbolic. It had been a long time since a voluntary sacrifice had occurred, the opfer, in the recent past, being carefully chosen. I believed I should continue this recent trend. I would need to plan the rite carefully – carefully choosing those who would take part. They would be sworn to secrecy, and would have to have no doubts of any kind. I, like a few others, understood the meaning of the rite itself – it would continue a tradition, creating a link with past deeds and thus magickal energies, and it would also create or draw down its own sinister energies. These could be directed to achieve a specific goal, or they could be directed into a chosen individual or individual who would have an important sinister Destiny to fulfill, or they could be stored to await further use. Whatever, it was an extremely powerful and sinister rite.

Such a sacrifice would thus be for a specific Satanic goal, and in accordance with Satanic honour the opfer [for this would have to be an involuntary sacrifice] would choose him/her self by their deeds. That is, their removal would benefit evolution, and consequently aid the sinister. They would not be chosen at random, as they would not be – despite the claims by those who knew nothing about genuine Satanism – virgins or children. They would be those whose removal would actively benefit our long-term aeonic goals. Let me express this plainly so that it will be understood. The victim or victims would be the type of person or persons whose death by whatever means would not be mourned – someone or many would say: 'He/she

214

deserved it...' The sacrifice would be akin to an act of natural justice. Naturally, it would be myself, in consultation with a few others, who would decide, and this decision would be based on sinister strategy or aeonics.

Such an opfer could be chosen by such means at other times and the appropriate rite of sacrifice performed, but the Ceremony was more specific: its aims, intent, were for a definite purpose. Accordingly, I began to plan for the ritual – I already had a few vague ideas concerning suitable candidates, and asked a trusted Guardian of one of the Temples to begin research into their backgrounds. I also visited a few possible sites for the ritual, researched others, and began to consider those who might participate with me. , of course, I had undertaken sacrifices before – in the approved manner. and even before those, I had tried a ritual of sacrifice. This was in my early days, before I assumed my role as heir. I, with some others involved in politics and vaguely involved with the sinister, planned to sacrifice someone to commemorate the founding our new political movement. We chose the victim, and gathered on a crag in Yorkshire one night. Our plan was to will the victim to fall over the cliff to his death. So invokations were done. energies directed. The victim became possessed, stumbled and fell. Unfortunately, he fell only a short distance, and was mostly uninjured. So in that sense the ritual failed. I knew why – of those gathered, only myself and one other really wanted to cause someone's death. The others were not committed to the sinister.

My other attempts were successful. The victims fell by assassination, or were victims of 'accidents' – all achieved by my 'underground' political work, and what followed thereafter, as related in an earlier chapter. I simply – before the act of execution – dedicated their death to my sinister cause. It was quite simple, and very effective, even in battle. I was merely continuing a long standing pagan tradition – dedicating enemies beforehand, and enemies, they deserved Such was the 'approved' themselves.

Naturally, those who then killing them, for a cause, of course. Being to perish, their death aiding the sinister dialectic. Satanic manner. Thus did the victims choose have no understanding of Satanism, as well as those who oppose that philosophy of living, portray sacrifice differently. According to them, it is always the 'innocent' who are victims, who are opfers. They seldom, if ever, define what is meant by 'innocent' – and cannot, however they try, define on a satisfactory basis, what 'evil' is.

Hopefully, my revelations will destroy such myths – as they will destroy the attempts by the feeble, mostly urbanized, people who call themselves 'Satanists' and who deny sacrifice exists or ever has existed as a Satanic practice. These people know nothing about real, primal, Satanism – they like the glamour of the sinister but are weak individuals, lacking in character, who play at 'roles' in a fantasy world. They do not have the passion, the spirit, the desire, the pride or the creative genius of genuine Satanists. Such people, in fact, would make good opfers.

Finally, what I have written before bears repeating – wars are the ultimate sacrificial rites, and it no coincidence that sometimes the sinister dialectic has aided these, and occasionally brought them about.

AEONICS AND MANIPULATION I

Aeonic magick is essentially the use of magickal energies to effect large-scale changes in the causal. This involves manipulation of forms, as well as a rational understanding of aeonic changes [civilizations, their ethos, etc.]. The forms involve transferring magickal energy – via the desire/aim – from the acausal to individuals. That is, manipulation of individuals on a large scale, both numerically and over time. The type of the manipulation varies, according to the formes) used and the desire/aim. For example, there can be psychic manipulation via archetypal forms, direct manipulation via words/images/personality; indirect by psychological pressure ...Two forms often used are religion and politics. Essentially, the sinister Adept takes a practical view of individuals insofar as Aeonics is concerned – understanding that the majority in whatever time and place, are by their nature, subjects: that is, raw] material to be used according to sinister strategy. This assessment is a-moral.

What this means in reality is that a goal is set (via a knowledge of Aeonics and sinister strategy – the 'sinister dialectic') and suitable means of achieving it are considered and a decision made. The decision is then made real, presenced in the causal, by magickal and other acts – regardless of consequences, be they moral, magickal or otherwise. Sinister Adepts – because they are Adepts – only consider Aeonic type goals, having as Initiates and External Adepts gained practical experience in 'external' manipulation, that is, manipulation of a few individuals for personal reasons. This aids self-understanding and magickal abilities. The goals of Adepts relate to wyrd and thus Aeonics – they are: 1) the creation of a new wyrd, and thus a new Aeon; 2) disruption of existing wyrd (with either an alternate or no specific goal); 3) altering the wyrd in a] specific way; 4) fulfilling the wyrd of the Aeon. [It should be understood that Internal Adepts – not having attained full Mastery – are still part of the Aeonic wyrd pertaining during their causal life – time.]

An example will explicate this.

Present Aeon: Western (or 'Faustian'/Promethean). Present phase: what should be 'Imperium' (the final phase of an Aeon), lasting c. 390 years. During this last phase the energies of the next Aeon are manifest/created by Adepts, via a physical nexion (or 'centre'). The practical forms of this new Aeon arise toward the end of Imperium – although some will exist/be created before then, on a small scale: i.e. they will not seem to significantly affect 'history'. This present Aeon has however been distorted – its ethos undermined and its forms changed. This distortion is basically Nazarene/Magian [see 'Crowley, Satan and the Sinister Way' and other Aeonics MSS]. It also changes the possibility of Imperium – from an almost certainty to only a minimum possibility. Sinister strategy, at the present time, is to create a new Aeon of sinister import – and to achieve this, it is considered necessary to:

(a) undermine the distortion of the Faustian ethos, and (b) fulfil the wyrd of the Faustian Aeon, that is, Imperium. Both of these will aid, by their nature, the creation of a new Aeon that is essentially Satanic. Thus, sinister Adepts will work, on both the practical and the magickal level, toward the achievement of these aims. This sinister strategy is part of their vow – their wyrd – as Initiates of the sinister tradition: that is, they are pledged to fulfil it[6] if possible, and certainly aid its fulfilment. Other Adepts will have other aims – if a sinister Adept decides on another strategy, they cease to be Adepts of a certain Satanic tradition, becoming something else instead. Only when – and if – they reach the stage of Grand Master/Mistress will they have the knowledge, ability and understanding to change sinister strategy.

To aid the creation of a new, Satanic, Aeon, the following are necessary:

1) the presencing of sinister energies in particular ways at this present time – i.e. the creation of specific archetypal forms/images/ systems/ideas which affect individuals.

---

[6] Whether or not they are aware of this, at the time.

2) the opening of a physical nexion to draw acausal energies in a significant way and enable their presencing.

3) the performance of certain Aeonic rites (e.g. Nine Angles) to create sinister 'psychic pressure', altering individuals. [Note: this is more general than (1) and involves letting the energies presence according to their nature, this nature being formed via the rites used.]

4) the creation of particular and specific practical forms and the channelling of magickal energies into these.

5) the emergence of more Adepts of the sinister tradition – i.e. individuals possessed of self-understanding, Occult insight and abilities, who are imbued with the ethos of the new Aeon.

6) the creation of the ethos of the new Aeon in a way enabling its apprehension (both unconsciously and consciously) by those who are not Adepts and who are not involved in esoteric Arts.

In addition, and as mentioned above, there is (a) undermining Nazarene/ Magian forms/effects; and (b) aiding the fulfilment of a Faustian Imperium.

(a) involves performing rites such as The Black Mass and others from *The Black Book of Satan*; spreading the tenets/forms of traditional Satanism enabling others to follow the Way (or at least utilize in some form its energies, to the detriment of others); undermining/distorting the distortion itself, both magickally and otherwise[magickally – e.g. Mass of Heresy].

(b) involves assisting in both a magickal and a practical way, those individuals/groups/forms who/which have as their aim a practical expressing of Faustian ideals, and who/which thus assist or contribute to the Faustian ethos. In political terms, this means National-Socialism and similar expressions of the Faustian ethos. This assistance will be practical, financial, magickal and personal.

(1) involves the creation and dissemination of new and traditional forms such as images, music, rituals, *The Black Book of Satan.*

(2) involves the finding of the physical nexion and undertaking the appropriate rites [one of which is the Ceremony of Recalling, the other of which is a Nine Angles rite].

(3) involves not only general rites [such Nine Angles, Ceremony etc.] but also targeting specific individuals and infecting them with sinister energies. [Rituals from *Black Book* perform part of this.]

(4) involves forms such as religion, politics, Art, philosophy and practical expressions of these – groups, organizations, 'Art-objects' and so on: all imbued with the sinister nature of the new Aeon. [Note: this is more general than (1) and may be considered as involving 'exoteric' forms/ideas etc. as against the 'esoteric' (i.e. directly Satanic) of (1).][7]

(5) involves dissemination of the sinister way as explicated in *Naos* etc. – the guidance of suitable Initiates, via ordeals and practical experience] in the 'real' world.

(6) involves the creation/aiding of a 'world-view', and practical expressions of this, which enshrines the new ethos – a sense of Destiny, a setting of goals, for the founders of what will be new higher civilization c. 2400 eh. It is the primary aim of sinister Adepts to involve themselves in the creation of the new Aeon by means of all the above – for only such means make possible the fulfilment of individual wyrd [for the next three centuries at least]. Anything else is not sinister – but game-playing.

---

[7] All such forms presence the future in the present: i.e. they capture/ re-present aspects of the new Aeon, practically, magickally and psychically.

AEONICS AND MANIPULATION II

Part I considered means; here, we are concerned with what terms like 'new sinister Aeon' mean.

First, it should be understood that the present civilization [which represents the energies of the Aeon now existing) was, in its ethos, essentially what is termed 'Faustian'. That is, dynamic, questing for knowledge and understanding. The exoteric expression of this ethos is science – or, more correctly, a reasoned approach to the 'world'; a conscious evaluation based on experience/ evidence. Aspects of this ethos are expressed in the Renaissance – and in National-Socialist Germany. This latter is most important, and so often misunderstood. NS Germany represented the quintessence of 'Western' civilization: an exhuberance, a balance between 'Man' and 'Nature', a spiritual force heir to the ancient Greeks and Romans. Civilization means a way of living – and of dying – more than it means Art and artifacts. It certainly does not mean material comforts, or even a certain type of politics (like 'democracy'). The greatest example of and model for a civilization, is the warrior: someone who enshrines honour, loyalty and natural justice (or 'fair-play'). That this is so seldom understood, today, is evident of how few really understand: of how precious wisdom still is. Further, the fact that the above statements regarding National-Socialist Germany are heresy (in the literal sense) today, explicates the distortion that has occurred in the Faustian civilization far better than dozens of words.

This ethos, exoterically, is Satanic. That is, the true ethos of the West enshrines a Satanic view of the world – a pagan joy in conquest, experience, living, in seeking and going beyond limits, physically and intellectually. The morbidity of the Nazarene has undermined all this distorted it. In essence, therefore, a Faustian Imperium would have been a type of Satanic State on Earth: a fulfilment of the first part of the sinister dialectic of history, and would have made possible the next part or stage, that of a Galactic Empire. It would be during this later stage that another goal would have been achieved – a genuine evolution in consciousness, a higher type of individual, on a massive scale. That is, Adepthood with its self-understanding and knowledge would be commonplace rather than (as now) the preserve of a few.

However, Satanism – in both exoteric and esoteric forms – became and is a heresy. Except for a brief and glorious period when an exoteric form achieved power – i.e. NS Germany.

Here, exoteric means an outward form or i: a physical presencing which achieves change in the causal. Esoteric means 'the essence'. An example – an Initiate of the sinister tradition becomes through Initiation an outward expression of Satanic spirit, consciously. The sinister becomes presenced, in the causal, by the actions/magick/life of the Initiate. In a sense, the causal persona/psyche of the Initiate is a 'Temple of Satan'. As the Sinister Way is followed, according to tradition, the Initiate accesses more and more of the sinister – presences more of it in the causal, causing/provoking change both internal and external. As knowledge and understanding increase, there is more awareness of the sinister as it is – i.e. without forms: the sinister ceases to be hidden or occult. At first, the essence of the sinister is hidden or obscured. An exoteric form implies a form, a channel – which is not necessarily consciously understood as a form or channel. A form can be either 'positive' or 'negative' with respect to the morals pertaining at the time – the sinister is beyond opposites but can only be presenced through them at particular times. That is, it becomes 'earthed' through a positive or negative form and thus provokes change and evolution. However, 'morals' as mentioned above – does not mean ethical: rather, it implies the prevailing 'spirit' or orientation, the orthodoxy of the moment.

A civilization is itself a form for sinister energy: a form possessed of its own 'life-cycle' (first mentioned by Spengler although not really understood by him). Thus, a civilization through its metamorphosis fulfills or can fulfil the sinister dialectic – i.e. it aids evolution toward new forms, presences the sinister and enables the acausal to be accessed (sometimes directly by a few individuals per Aeon). The Western civilization is a link – the fifth stage of the seven that can lead to new forms of existence. The next Aeon, beginning on the practical level c. 2400 eh, is the 'Galactic' and should be the realization of the sinister on a large-scale. Part of this will be the development of latent Occult faculties, part will be development of new ways of thinking (such a use of symbolic languages rather than words), and part will be discovery external to the Earth: the conquest of planets in other stellar systems. There will thus be a freeing of spirit both internally and externally. Our species – at present mostly undeveloped children, intellectually, psychically and personally – will mature, and become adult,] achieving wisdom and thus fulfilling the promise of magick.

However, this will not just 'happen' – or arise from a desire to make it so. It will involve struggle: war, conquest, attrition, exploration; the decimation of the worthless and the conscious breeding of a new elite.

It will arise because of ethos – because there is a sense of Destiny, a vision to be great. It will involve manipulation by sinister Adepts of vast energies over centuries of time – for without this direction, this sinister manipulation, inertia will return, entropy increase, and the petty ones, the visionless ones, the Nazarene-type ones will spawn in their worthless majority until they overwhelm. As has been written elsewhere, civilization is a struggle and requires the triumph of a noble minority who impose their vision on those that they conquer.

Thus, the term 'new sinister Aeon' means the triumph of a creative minority imbued with a specific élan and a sense of Destiny who create and maintain a civilization, this particular civilization extending well beyond the confines of the Solar System. It means the presencing of sinister energies in particular ways, and certain ways of living – ways which are essentially Satanic. What these ways are, has been prefigured by NS Germany [and particularly by aspects within that form, such as the Waffen-55). The means to achieve this – such as aiding Imperium, presencing sinister energies, opening a nexion [and drawing forth 'The Dark Gods'] – have already been outlined. What it is important to remember is that the means, such as political forms, their support/manipulation etc., are part of sinister strategy to achieve a specific goal. That is, they are purely means: not the goal itself, and as such cannot be judged causally or by the standards pertaining at anyone time. They have been chosen to achieve something, and those who cannot comprehend this do not understand Aeonic magick. People, in their majority and their individuality, are a means to be manipulated via forms. The goal is a new Aeon, Satanically inspired; the means, many and varied – often 'heretical'. The magick of the genuine Adept is, in its power and effects, of centuries: anything else is for beginners and children.

ESOTERIC TRADITION – SYNISTRY

Dark Gods:-These are 'living' entities which exist in an acausal space-time. They may be likened to 'anti-matter' as against the 'matter' which exists in our causal space-time – thus, their intrusion into the causal, disrupts. This disruption is primarily psychic because the psyche of an individual by its nature intrudes or is a part of the acausal. The entities can assume physical forms, but only briefly – and then only when a nexion is fully opened. and where the causal and acausal intersect on Earth.[8]

The Dark Gods do not have 'forms' as understood causally – because a physical form is a causal thing, and they are beyond the causal. Neither do they possesses 'feelings' etc. as we understand the terms. They are on the edge of even an Adept's comprehension [in terms of understanding them.] They can act [i.e. have effects in the causal] via individuals who can access them – or 'presence' them.

It should be understood that the Dark Gods are not 'the acausal' itself. They exist in a part [or one realm) of the acausal – that is, -they exist, have life or being according to the nature of the acausal. The acausal is 'beyond causal time' and does not have a spatial 3D-geometry. Other beings probably exist in other acausal dimensions – but of them there is no knowledge.

When an Initiate accesses the acausal – increases the acausal aspect of their consciousness – they are extending the range of their being: i.e. evolving, creating new aspects of consciousness. This is one of the aims of the seven-fold Way – and of all real magick. A part of this, may involve confrontation with some of the 'Dark Gods'.

In conventional terms, the Dark Gods are evil, sinister.

---

[8] Such as 'magickal centres' associated with an Aeon – or the finding of such places. It is possible to create such a place – and this is one meaning ofsuch rituals as the Ceremony of Recalling with Sacrificial Conclusion.

The Western Aeon:

As far as Adepts of the sinister tradition are concerned, there are only two realistic options: the creation of Imperium [the fulfilment of Western wyrd via a practical form], or disruption of existing forms with the aim of undermining and destroying Nazarene/ Magian influence, leading to chaos from which a New Aeon will emerge, this Aeon being Satanic. The latter involves the 'pruning' of unnecessary elements on a large scale – the creation of an elite capable of making the Aeon a reality. The first involves the creation/aiding of a practical form – and presencing magickal energy into it. It also involves creating the right psychic conditions – within and external to individuals. Some of this is directly magickal, involving magickal energy accessed via rituals etc.; some of it is providing/creating/making available the information and forms of the sinister. The practical form is either directly political, or 'religious'. Both involve a more widespread dissemination of the sinister tradition and creation of new forms for its energies.

Traditions and New Forms:

As mentioned elsewhere, maintaining the tradition (as explicated in such works as *The Black Book of Satan*, *Naos*, *The Deofel Quartet* and Hostia) and making it more widely available, is important – and indeed essential. This is because the use of the tradition, in whole or in part [e.g. rituals from the *Black Book*] by others outside of being drawn into the tradition, makes those others 'channels' for the sinister energy the tradition represents. That is, they 'presence' sinister energies in a precise and particular way and thus fulfil sinister strategy. The tradition has been given its present form [as explicated in the various books and MSS] to achieve just this (as well as other things).

However, the creation of new forms is important and indeed vital – there must be a continuing evolution. These forms will further access the sinister, and presence it. The tradition itself serves as a Way – both for individuals, and aeonically: it enables the achievement of individual Adeptship, as well as the fulfilment of the sinister dialectic of history. This will be so for the next few centuries – until the New Aeon becomes a reality. That is, its methods and techniques should not be changed (at least not intentionally by those of the tradition for the next few decades) or 'superseded' – as a way of creating Adepts etc. This is not a question of 'dogma' but rather strategy, as mentioned above. It is vital that this and the reasons for and beyond it are understood by those of the tradition. The external forms [such as arise prior to and during the Aeon] will only arise from an initial coherence of magickal energies and intent – and it is and will be the unchanging form of the 'Way' [techniques, rituals etc.] which will enable this. The new forms created/evolved will add to rather than undermine what already is. Anything else is simply individuals playing at magick (and particularly playing at Aeonics) without achieving anything and indeed without understanding what they are doing.

Initiation and Beyond:

The quest of an individual can only and ever be individual, that is, unique. The quest, made possible and aided by the tradition, developes the individual, enabling individual wyrd to be understood, and lived. It is also makes possible Immortality (qv. Acausal Existence – the Secret Revealed). Beyond a certain level, Initiates guide themselves – learning from their own real-life experiences. That is, they have acquired sufficient self-insight and honesty to enable them to do this. When this stage is reached [toward the end of External Adept for some; during and beyond Internal Adept for others] there should be still a following of the ultimate goal – a striving for the Abyss and beyond, although this 'striving' will be more balanced than hitherto. This does not mean the individuals become or develope their own ways of achieving that goal – that is, not undergoing the Grade Rituals of Internal Adept and beyond according to tradition because they believe they are not necessary or that they have/can create (d) other means. Should they do this, they will not achieve the specific goal of the sinister way – but rather something else entirely, or else nothing. The reasons should be obvious from the above (Traditions ...).

The Aim: Wisdom, and its living, enabling the last stage (into the acausal). This means self-understanding and supra-personal understanding. An apprehension of the world and its forms as they are – a rational knowing: and what is necessary for change, aeonic and otherwise. This knowledge is sometimes sad, and often born from ordeals and having lived the Abyss. It never confers wealth nor privelege, and seldom imbues one with 'happiness'. It is beyond words, but can sometimes be transmuted into a form enabling some others to apprehend, if only in part, its essence. This aim takes causal time – usually c. 20 years from Initiation (if the Way is followed) – and lies beyond the Abyss. It is balance, beyond opposites, a new way of being.

ESOTERIC TRADITION VI

Baphomet, Opfer and Related Matters: The word 'opfer' generally refers to the sacrifice that occurs – symbolic or otherwise during certain rituals. There are, generally, two types of opfer: (1) associated with rites to open a nexion, between Aeons – when such an opfer(s) are considered necessary in terms of the 'energy' required; (2) those associated with traditional beliefs regarding the 'working of the cosmos. ('Opfers' associated with 'death rituals' form a third type.)

The second type, according to tradition, was chosen once every 17 years and this sacrifice was regarded as necessary to retain 'the cosmic balance' – in modern terms, keep a nexion open (and thus preserve the associated higher civilization etc.). The chosen one was made an honoury Priest (this type of opfer was always male –.see below) and there was a joining between him and one or more women, as Priestesses. This joining was a simple type of 'hierosgamos', and the offspring of the union(s) were given great honour. At the ceremony itself. the head of the opfer was severed and displayed – usually for a night and a day (although this period may have been longer in the very distant past). The rite was conducted outdoors in a 'Sacred' place – often a circle of stones on hill-top.

The chosen one was able, because of the sacrifice, to partake of an acausal. existence – becoming thus an Immortal. Thus was 'willing sacrifice' possible, although it is easy to imagine that in later times, the opfer was not always willing. Traditionally, this type goes back to Albion and while

Originally the ritual. was probably a community affair, it became more and more secretive. What survives to the present day (The Ceremony of Recalling with 'opfer' ending) probably reflects the essence of this earlier tradition rather than the detail (the words, chants etc.). This essence may be apprehended in the role of the Mistress of Earth – representative of Baphomet, the dark goddess. It was to Baphomet that the sacrifice was made – hence a male opfer. Indeed, the whole ceremony (of Recalling) can be seen as a celebration of the dark goddess – the Earth Mistress/goddess in her darker/violent/sinister aspect. The 'severed head' was associated with the 'worship' of Baphomet – hence the traditional. representation of Baphomet.

This 'cult of Baphomet' derives from Albion (see below). The significance of the 17 year cycle is unclear – if there was an oral tradition, it has been lost. In the past few decades, some theories to explain this 17 year cycle have been advanced, but they are unconvincing.

The identification of Baphomet as the Bride of Lucifer/Satan probably dates from around the 10th or 11th century ev, as does the use of the name 'Satan'/Satanas as the Earth-bound representative of the Dark Gods.

It is important to remember that in earlier times (e.g. in Albion during the Hyperborian aeon) there was no clear and/or 'moral' distinction between the 'light' and the 'sinister': the two were seen as different aspects of the same thing. Thus, what we know as the Mistress of Earth (the 'goddess') was both what we now call 'Baphomet' (the dark aspect) and Gaia (the Earth mother). Likewise with the 'male' aspect – Satan and Lucifer – or Dionysus/Kabeiroi and Apollo. We now understand all such symbols as unconscious/conscious projections onto 'reality' (where 'reality' = the region of causal./acausal. mergence) as 'gates'/nexions to the acausal itself, with the seven spheres of the Tree of Wyrd being a 'map' of these gates understandable by 'non-Adept' consciousness. Thus, the sphere of Mercury re-presents Lucifer/Satan – Mercury, Mars and Sun being the 'male' spheres, and Moon, Venus, Jupiter the 'female' ones, (Saturn being beyond such opposites –'Chaos' itself). The 'cult of Baphomet' was the worship of the dark aspect of the 'female' energies – where in this context, worship means a striving toward understanding/conscious integration.

Traces of the worship of the 'light' aspect survive in the septenary tradition in the name 'Aktlal maka' (qv notes on Names and Symbols) and the natural form of the Nine Angles rite. The darker aspect survives, in essence, in the Ceremony of Recalling and the traditions associated with the 'Mistress of Earth' and 'Baphomet'. As to the original name of the goddess in both her aspects, there is a tradition which gives 'Darkat' as the name used before 'Baphomet' became the common usage.

However, 'Azanigin' has also been suggested – as has 'Aktlal Maka' for the 'light'/Gaia aspect, although both these are merely 20th century (ev) suggestions, not based on any oral tradition. Some aspects of the cult of the (dark) goddess are said to have survived into Greek times in the 'Mystery cults' (qv Kabeiroi – and also 'Eleusis' for the 'light' aspect), this being an 'indirect' survival', the 'modern' septenary tradition being a direct one, from Albion.

The use of the name 'Baphomet' probably derives from the 10th or 11th century (ev) although the traditional pictorial representation of 'Baphomet' is undoubtedly much older. As elsewhere, if there was an oral tradition connected with the-origin of the name Baphomet, it has been lost. Thus, there are no indications as to the 'original' names of the 'light' and 'sinister' elements on the 'male' side known to us as 'Lucifer' and 'Satan'. These latter names probably also derive from around the 10th or 11th century (ev) although 'Karu Samsu' (or something very similar) has been suggested for the 'Lucifer' aspect and 'Sapanur' as the 'sinister' aspect.

The rites associated with the first type of opfer such as 'The Sinister Calling – cannot be either dated with certainty or seen to be derived from an earlier tradition. In all probability, they derive from the 12th or 13th century (ev), although it is quite possible that earlier versions/forms existed. Some have even considered The Sinister Calling as a later version of the Ceremony of Recalling. Again, if there was an oral tradition, it has been lost all that remains are the rituals themselves. The 'Black Mass' itself (and indeed most of the ceremonial rituals in *The Black Book*) probably originated around the same time as The Sinister Calling. The original Mass was said in Latin, although by the middle of the 20th century (ev) a translated version had found its way into the *Black Book* of necessity, although some Latin chants remained.

ONA.

THE RITE OF THE NINE ANGLES

The rite may be undertaken on either the autumnal equinox (for the Dabih gate) or the winter solstice (for Algol). The *Naos* rite is suitable for southern climes and will not be given here although in form it is the same as the version given.

Ideally, the rite should be undertaken either:

a) on a hill-top of pre-Cambrian rock which lies between a line of volcanic intrusion and another rock – in Britain this other rock is 'Buxton'

b) in an underground cavern where water flows [this applies only to the 'chthonic' form]

c) in a glade consecrated beforehand within a circle of nine stones (the first stone being set on a night of the new moon with Saturn rising, the second at the full moon and so on: the first stone marking the point on the horizon where Saturn rises) [Note: this applies only to the 'natural' form of the Rite]

Further, the time is right when, for Dabih, Venus sets after the sun, and the moon itself occults Dabih or is near to it; and, for Algol, when Jupiter and Saturn are both near the moon which is becoming new, the time being before dawn.

These conditions mean that energies are available to enhance the working.

The rite exists in three versions – the natural form, the chthonic, and the solo. The chthonic form may be combined with the Ceremony of Recalling and the Sacrificial Conclusion undertaken] according to tradition. It must be noted however that this combination is exceedingly dangerous – if done correctly with: (a) above and with the conditions for Algol as above, it brings back to Earth the Dark

Gods themselves by opening the Star Gate between the causal and the acausal.

However, the chthonic form may be successful in bringing to presence the Dark Gods without the Sacrificial aspect if the chants are done correctly, the crystal is sufficient in size, and cosmic tides aligned aright [note: this usually occurs when an Aeon is (magickally) ending, the energies being more pronounced in the last three decades. At other times the rite can be used to bring about such changes.

The *natural form* involves a Priest and Priestess [ideally these should have undertaken the ritual of Internal Adept – or at the very least External Adept] and is basically a drawing to the Earth of acausal energies – these are left to disperse naturally: i.e. without any magickal intent.

The *chthonic form* involves a Priest and a Priestess as well as at least one Cantor trained in sinister Esoteric Chant together with a congregation of male and female. This form is either an invokation to the Dark Gods – the energies being dispersed naturally – or a chanelling of those energies into a specific event or events or individual. This chanelling however requires the skill of at least a Master of Temple/Mistress of Earth.

The *solo form* involves one individual and the aim is usually the alteration of the consciousness of that individual: this however is very dangerous.

Note: all the above forms require a crystal tetrahedron made of quartz.

I Natural Form

If possible, the conditions above should be met – if not, conduct the rite on an isolated hill-top at sunset. Both Priest and Priestess should be naked. The rite begins with the Priest vibrating seven times 'Nythra kthunae Atazoth' while the Priestess holds the crystal in her hands, palms upward. The vibration should consist of three projected vibrations followed by four resonant ones – all aimed at the crystal which should be at a distance of not less than two feet and not more than three. After the vibrations, the Priest places his hands on the crystal and both vibrate '*Binan ath ga wath am*' as a projected vibration.

The Priestess, still holding the crystal, then lies with her head North while the Priest arouses her with his tongue, locis muliebribus. The sexual union begins after, and both visualize the Star Gate opening and energy flowing through it down to them. If desired (ie. sinister intent) this energy may be symbolized by Atazoth – a dark and nebulous chaos issuing forth from a star strewn Space which changes into a 'Dagon' like entity before becoming chaos again. This visualization continues until the sexual climax of the Priestess after which the Priest reaches his own climax. The Priestess then rises and buries the crystal in the earth of the hill [as deep as possible – this may be prepared beforehand – and leaving few traces]. When complete, she vibrates over the place '*Aperiatur terra, et germinet Chaos*'. They then depart from the hill.

[Note: further rituals may take place over the burial, but they must have the same intent and follow the form as above except the vibrations are aimed toward the buried crystal – no further crystal being required]

II Chthonic Form

If the special conditions cannot be met [(a) and Algol are most effective; (b) and Dabih are generally for chanelling into specific events/individuals] then a hill-top containing volcanic quartz is suitable.

The crystal should be placed on an oak stand with a sheet of mica between it and the wood [this enhances still further the effect of the crystal and is a recent modification]. The Priest, Priestess and Cantors stand near the crystal, while the congregation (of at least six – three male and three female) form a circle around them. The congregation dance moonwise and according to their desire chanting '*Atazoth*' as they do while the Cantor(s) vibrate in E minor '*Nythra kthunae Atazoth*'.

After this vibration the cantor and Priest (or two Cantors if there are two) vibrate in fourths the 'Diabolus' chant [see set texts] while the Priestess places her hands on the crystal, visualizing the Star Gate opening (as in I above).

After the Diabolus, the Priest signals to the congregation who begin an orgiastic rite according to their desires. The Priest and Priestess then vibrate 'Binan ath ga wath am' a fifth apart (or an octave and a fifth) while the Cantor(s) vibrate '*Atazoth*'. If two Cantors are present, this Atazoth vibration begins in parallel: the next '*Atazoth*' is a fifth apart as is the third. After this, they then chant, in fifths, the '*Atazoth* chant' according to tradition [see set texts]. While the Cantors are chanting the Priest and Priestess continue with their visualization.

If only one Cantor is present, the '*Atazoth*' vibration is continued nine times and then the 'Atazoth chant' undertaken by the Cantor and the Priest, in fifths.

The Dark Gods will then be manifest.

If for some reason(eg. inexperience of the participants) the manifestations do not occur, the Priestess should chant in C major *Nythra kthunae Atazoth* after which the Priest also places his hands on the crystal and he and the Priestess vibrate *Binan ath ga wath am*, the Cantor(s) chanting the Diabolus as before after which the Priest visualizes the energies arising from the orgiastic rite as cohering and then entering the crystal to be then drawn forth into both himself and the Priestess before being sent forth to render asunder the Star Gate.

Notes of this form: * the rite may be enhanced by the use of tabors/drums during the dance and the orgiastic rite, individuals being appointed for this task. * The maximum number of participants should not exceed twenty one in total. * Provided rigorous training is undertaken beforehand, the dance and the orgiastic rite can be replaced with the congregation chanting from the start of the rite the '*Diabolus*' in fifths – they continue with this until the Priest signals them to stop (after the Cantors *Diabolus* chant) after which they chant the '*Atazoth* chant' in fifths repeatedly until the end of the rite. If this form is done, it is important for the congregation to visualize the Star Gate opening while they chant – and this visualization should be agreed beforehand and be the same as that of the Priestess and Priest. This form of the chthonic rite is however only effective if the congregation has been trained to chant in the correct manner. A suitable cavern/resonant building/Temple may be used in this instance. [Further note: providing the chanting is accurate, the crystal large enough, this form is among the most effective]

III Solo Form

This form should be undertaken on either a hill-top or in a Temple/resonant building. It begins at sunset on a night of the new moon with Saturn rising.

The individual should face Saturn and vibrate '*Nythra kthunae Atazoth*' seven times while holding the crystal. Then '*Binan ath ga wath am'* is vibrated followed by the *Diabolus* chant after which the visualization is begun (as above) [Note: this form involves the 'Saturnian' gate and thus the Gate may be visualized near the planet Saturn]. The energy is then visualized as flowing down into the individual, this visualization lasting for at least one quarter of one hour. After, the individual chants the '*Atazoth* chant', places the crystal on the ground and sits near it, to visualize its interior becoming black and this blackness spreading out to engulf the individual.

[Note: This ritual should not be undertaken lightly. There must be a preparedness to exult in the energies. After the rite (the individual will know when it is complete) the crystal should be wrapped in black cloth and stored until required again. Before attempting this form, individuals are advised to seek the guidance of a Master of Temple/Mistress of Earth]

HELL

I shall be honest – Satanism has been hijacked. By posers, by pseudo-intellectuals and by gutless weaklings who like the glamour and danger associated with it in the public mind but who do not have the guts to be evil – to do dark deeds.

These modern days so-called 'Satanists' are really Nazarene scum in disguise – worms in dead snake-skin. They prattle on about 'morality', puff themselves up with titles and perform verbal and intellectual gymnastics. They think being Satanic involves calling yourself a Satanist and dressing up like Dracula or Mephistopheles or a vamp.

Well, I am sick of these imposters. Those who get a thrill from playing the role but who never actually do anything evil, who never go to extremes, who never stand on the edge – or climb down to the darkness of the pit of Hell. Those who have never experienced the limits of themselves in love, in war, in living – these weaklings trying so hard to impress.

What, then, is real Satanism all about? First, it is about rebellion – against the conformity of the present. and I mean a real rebel, a real outlaw – someone who cuts a dash, who has charisma, whose very presence makes others uneasy (and who does not have to wear some stupid 'costume' to do this). Second, it is about testing your own Destiny. So – you believe you are special, do you? Well, prove it! Try something dangerous – try something to see if you get away with it. If not – tough, you failed. There are plenty of others… If you succeed, try again, until you know your limits. Choose a good cause, or a bad one or no cause at all, and really live, intoxicating yourself with life, danger, achievement. Do not rest and never be afraid to face the possibility of death. But in all that you do be honourable – to yourself. Carry this honour with you everywhere like a favorite concealed weapon.

Third, learn from your experiences – like you would learn from a 'bad' woman (or man) in your youth when sex was still something of a mystery. A real Satanist does not often do magick – they are magick by the very nature of their dynamic, zestful existence. It is experience which teaches, from which you learn – you cannot learn Satanism from books (although some may guide you aright to begin with), it cannot be taught by 'Masters' and never involves cozy little discussions with 'friends' or others. Anyone who accepts a 'Master' and grovels before them however slight that grovelling may be – is not a Satanist, just a sucker who sucks. Accepting some 'authority' is a sign you are weak: a sign you need emotional crutches: a sign you are a whimp.

So, get off your arse, you suckers, and make Satan proud. Learn to do evil.

What is evil? All that restricts life – all that tries to constrain the possibilities. Doing evil means breaking these restrictions and constraints – and taking the consequences of your own actions. Just do – just discover, just smash the chains that hold most others in thrall, and never bow down to anyone about anything: smash them first, or die rather than submit. That way, you will learn how to live – and laugh at the weak.

of course this is dangerous – for others, and yourself! Satanism was never easy – or for whimps. See you in Hell!

240

THE SINISTER CALLING

Introduction:

The aim of the following ceremonial ritual can be either (a) returning to Earth those 'negative, chaotic, sinister' forms/energies dark legend knows as 'The Dark Gods'; (b) drawing forth from the acausal dimensions, chaotic energies, directed toward a specific goal/aim/intent or channeled into a particular individual(s)/group/temporal form. The main difference between the two is that in (a) the forms/energies are left to disperse/create conditions according to their nature. If insufficient preparation/desire is present within those performing this Calling, (b) can become (a) – sometimes to the detriment of those Calling.

The rite below assumes willing sacrifice. (For unwilling sacrifice, qv. 'A Gift to the Prince' – of historical interest only.)

The rite of Sinister Calling is a traditional ritual (perhaps the most sinister ritual that exists).

Setting: An isolated hill-top, sunset, with Saturn rising – ora sinister Temple/cave.

Participants:
Master of the Temple – purple robes
Mistress of Earth – purple robes
Priestess – naked, upon altar
Priest – black robe, tied' with white cord/girdle
Congregation – black robes
Guardian of the Temple – black robes, with face mask

Preparation:
1) Seven days before the rite, the congregation assembles in the dwelling of the Master or Mistress. Here they stay until the rite is complete. During the seven days they are forbidden to speak, wear only ceremonial robes, will abstain from intoxicating drinks and

sexual pleasures and eat no meat. (This is a 'Black Fast'.) During the hours of darkness no lights except black candles are to be lit and at sunset on each day they gather in the Temple to chant the *Dies Iræ* nine times. During the seven days no contact with outsiders is allowed, and no music or intrusive sound, save for the *Dies Irae* and the *Atazoth* chant, is to be heard. Both the dwelling and the Temple should be incensed with Saturnian incense. According to tradition, the robes worn will contain a hood/cowl which is to be worn during the daylight hours, these hours being taken up with walking within the dwelling grounds (or a suitable, isolated location nearby) for at least three hours together with such diversions as the Master and Mistress will arrange. (Note: These diversions – which in recent times include playing the Star Game are so chosen so as not to destroy the black tranquility of the fast. In the past they have included study of alchemical MSS, silent Tarot readings (using sign language/drawn symbols for the reader to express meanings) and practice in performing esoteric chant (*Dies Irae*/*Atazoth* chant – fourth/fifths and so on), this latter in the Temple if the Calling is to be performed there.

2) The Temple is prepared seven days before the rite (this applies to the site chosen – which should thereafter be guarded by appropriate energy). This consists of the Master and Mistress incensing the area with Saturnian incense, while chanting seven times the '*Sanctus Satanas*'. They then unite in sexual union, the Mistress visualizing the nexion to the Dark Gods as being gradually opened, though remaining partly closed. One planetary hour before the Calling begins on the seventh day, the Temple/outdoor area is made ready by an Initiate chosen for this task. A black cloth is laid on the altar and seven black candles placed upon it and lit. Chalices of strong wine are prepared ready near the altar. A large quartz crystal is placed in the centre of the Temple, on an oak (or wooden) stand. (Note: It enhances the energies if this crystal is shaped as a tetrahedron. Whatever the shape, the crystal should be as large as possible.) The l-Master brings the Sacrificial Knife. An image of Baphomet, according to sinister tradition, may be present in the Temple, but no other artifacts, furnishings, signs or symbols.

The congregation et al gather outside the Temple, robed as above, and are led into the Temple by the (naked) Priestess at the beginning of the rite.

3) As the congregation assemble on the seventh day before the rite (they will have been informed some time before by the Master or Mistress of the date of the Calling, its purpose and intent being explained) lots are drawn to decide which man among them shall be chosen. The one chosen by the drawing of lots (the 'opfer') is free to then accept or decline the honour. If this honour is declined, another lot is held, and the one so chosen may also decline. After this, a further lot is held, the result of which is binding. The opfer so chosen by lot is then led by the Guardian(s) to a secure, secluded place and resides there until the rite of Calling begins. Each night and in this place the opfer receives the Priestess for the length of one planetary hour, the Priestess being chosen from among the Temple to be at this period capable of conception. If the Master or Mistress so desire, another lady in addition to the Priestess may be chosen and received by the opfer at the dawn of each day. It is duty of the Guardian(s) to watch over and care for the opfer during the days before the rite, and lead him to the Temple for the Calling.

The Rite:

The congregation process into the Temple, led by the Priestess who is assisted onto the altar by the Mistress. The congregation gather in a semi-circle before the altar, the Guardian(s) holding the opfer by the entrance. The Mistress greets the Master with a kiss, saying: 'To you is it fitting, Master, to speak to our gods for these many. With your own eyes see how we seekers of darkness await this calling forth of our gods!'

The Mistress gestures with her hands, and the congregation remove their hoods/cowls. She says: 'So shall we rejoicing, dance!' The congregation begin to dance, counter-sunwise around the altar chanting 'Binan ath ga wath am'.

243

The Master lays the S. Knife on the womb of the Priestess while the Mistress places her hands on the crystal and joins the Master in chanting the *Diabolus* in fourths while visualizing the nexion opening. This chant is repeated seven times, the congregation continuing their dance and chant.

After the seventh chant, the Master claps his hands nine times as a signal for the congregation to gather round. The Guardian brings the opfer forward.

The Master gives the opfer a chalice of wine, which he drinks. After this, the Master says to him: 'We greet our honoured guest with a kiss.' He kisses the opfer, followed by the Mistress and the congregation who kiss the opfer in turn.

The Mistress then removes the robe of the opfer and begins to raise his secret fire with her lips while the Master gestures to the congregation as a sign for them to remove their robes. They then begin to dance again – chanting '*Atazoth*', '*Satanas*' and/or shouting/laughing/screaming as they whirl faster and faster in ecstasy and frenzy.

As they dance, the Guardian lifts the Priest upon the altar while the Master takes up the S. Knife. The Priestess holds the opfer in sexual union and visualizes the nexion opening as she draws by movement the secret fire from the opfer. She then releases him and on this sign the Mistress signals to the congregation who begin an orgiastic rite according their desires.

The Mistress then touches the crystal with her hands visualizing/intoning the aim/intent of the calling, ad libitum according to the frenzy/energy generated in the Temple. As she touches the crystal, the Guardian(s) assist the opfer from the aitar and with the Master (who takes the S. Knife and the empty chalice used by the opfer) leave the Tempie to a secluded place (which may be the place used by the opfer during the preparation period).

244

In this secluded place, the Master vibrates 'Nythra kthunae Atazoth' while the Guardian(s) hold the opfer. After the vibration, the Master uses the S. Knife, collecting some of the Red Elixir in the chalice. He then returns to the Temple and the Mistress symbolically washes her hands in the Red Elixir before herself chanting 'Nythra kthunae Atazoth'. Following this, she and the Master chant the Diabolus in fourths, directing the chant toward the crystal.

The rite is concluded by the Master assisting the Priestess down from the altar. She departs from the Temple, returning with trays of food and wine which she offers to the congregation their revelry continues until desires are fulfilled. The Priestess herself withdraws after offering the food and drink, as the Master and Mistress do.

Note: After the final *Diabolus* chant by the Master and Mistress, if an aim/intent is intended, this is visualized/voiced by them according to magickal principles before they depart from the Temple. Should they wish, they may combine this with their own sexual union. Should no aim/intent be desired, the dark forms/energies are left to gather/disperse according to their nature. The Guardian(s) are sworn to secrecy, and after the Red Elixir is produced they secrete/bury the empty vessel in a location prepared beforehand.

DIABOLUS

Dies irae, dies illa
Solvet saeclum in favilla
Teste Satan cum sibylla.
Quantus tremor est futurus
Quando Vindex est venturus
Cuncta stricte discussurus.
Dies irae, dies illa!

SANCTUS

Sanctus, Satanas, Sanctus
Dominus Diabolus Sabaoth!
Sanctus Satanas Sanctus!
Satanas - venire;
Satanas - venire!
Ave Satanas, ave Satanas.
Tui sunt caeli,
Tua est terra
Ave Satanas.

REVENGE

Central to any civilization and society which is civilized, is the notion of revenge – and central to revenge is the blood feud. When the 'State' – of whatever political hue or any large organized governmental structure, reserves for itself the means and control and dispensation of 'Justice' then true freedom does not exist: the individual has become controlled and enslaved, if not physically, then mentally.

Any healthy flourishing society not only allows revenge, but encourages it, and any society which does not is already a form of tyranny, however much clever, vapid, intellectual and political words may be used to try and obscure this reality. A healthy' society is one that tends to respect the individual right to justice and thus revenge: the two are linked and cannot be seperated without destroying both, leaving an empty shell. A healthy society seeks to respect the individual, and extend their responsibilities and duties, and one of the most important responsibilities and duties of any individual is to avenge.

This view is not upheld by many today – and certainly by none who form those cliques of legal and social 'professionalism' which infest society today. Instead, the present System seeks to convince us all, from childhood, that only the State has the 'right' to deal with 'Justice' – and that only this is 'civilised'. But if you believe that, you really are ill – one of those pale specimens inebriated by the clever words and ideas of the half-men (and half-women) who unfortunately proliferate today in our comfortable and monied societies. Revenge is natural and necessary. An illustration here might be instructive. A young motorist, high on drink and drugs, deliberately runs down and kills someone: the classic 'innocent passerby'. After some trouble, the police find this driver and he is charged. When his case comes to court, he manages to wriggle out of the murder charge ('lack of sufficient evidence'/some legal problem) and is instead convicted of manslaughter. He shows no remorse. He is sentenced to 3 years in prison. After a little over 2 years he is released, and some months later is arrested for drink driving and driving while disqualified. A few more months in prison. Then he is free. Now, in this instance (and many like it) the relatives of the victim have a duty to kill this piece of scum – and should be ashamed of themselves if they did not. Naturally, they would give all sorts of reasons as to why they would do nothing – but basically they are, if they do nothing, (a) spineless cowards; (b) degenerate bastards who do not care; (c) so ground down by the System, by the lies and propaganda, that their natural instincts have been destroyed. They – one or some of them – should have killed the offender. Naturally, in the feeble societies of the Western tyrannies, had they done so they would – if caught – have faced 'Justice' and the legal system themselves: and probably spent longer in prison than the bastard who deserved to die (such is the sickness of the 'West'). But, until this whole rotten System is destroyed, they should have used the rules of the System against itself – why not, for instance, run the bastard himself down? You would, if caught, only get a few years. But at least you would be able to live with yourself _ still have your honour.

of course, an impartial assessment (like a Judge) is still necessary – but once judged, relatives are honour bound to act.

CONQUER, DESTROY, CREATE

Most people are sick – in the head. Why? Because they lack vision – because they lack the desire to translate that vision into reality and because they lack the character to break the psychic chains of the modern world forged from ideas.

And I am not writing about mediocre vision, either   but about grandiose vision: vision which makes one aspire to greatness, to make real what others may sometimes dream about perhaps once in their puny, pathetic lives. I am writing about that inner vision which drives some individuals and which makes them great: makes them aspire to fulfil at least part of their god-like potential. That inner demon which compels, which makes one strive again and again and never admit defeat, even when faced with death.

Conquerors have vision: so do Artists and Explorers and warriors. Today, there is an excess of petty individuals trying to make real their petty and cowardly concerns; an excess of petty officials and petty rules and petty governments trying to restrain the individual spirit and psyche; an excess of petty ideas trying to level down all individuals to the lowest level and so breed a plastic bastard race equal in all things who no longer aspire to real greatness.

What is needed are individuals who dream large – who strive to make those dreams real, regardless of the consequences. In short, a return of the conquering attitude. All that is great and worthwhile is built from the blueprint of inner vision, and the greatest vision is conquest – of ourselves, of others, of what is still unknown. There are no limits unless we in weakness set our limits. We, today, need to rediscover the delight of discovery and conquest: of going where no one has been before, of being masters of our own Destiny by following our visions and instincts.

This is not easy. Let the weak, the scum, the majority huddle together in their quest for happiness and material well-being. Let them seek comfort in each other and ideas. Individuals are born from hardship

– from the hardship of questing after a dream. Conquest and exploration bring a joy, and create a uniqueness, like no other – the joy and individuality of a god.

Seek to be like a god – that is the answer to the misery that is bred from morbid self-pity and smallness and a wallowing in abstract ideas – from the seeking after illusions like happiness and comfort and stupid ideas like 'freedom' and 'justice'. The only freedom is the freedom to dream and the freedom to make that dream real, just as the only justice is that which is within each individual: what they feel. of course, the weak and the cowardly feel a different sense of justice than the strong – they call this 'law' and enshrine it within a church to their gods of 'democracy' and 'equality', whereas the strong call their justice vengeance and honour, words which the majority fear Or do not understand.

So what dreams are, today, fit enough for those who aspire to be like gods? There are only two, as this century ends. and they are connected.

The first is to destroy those edifices which the cowards, the weak, the huddling majority have erected to defend themselves from the natural elite – those few who dare, who defy, who despise and are fearless and conquering in their defiance. To destroy those governments, forms, Institutions or whatever as a prelude to renewed creation: as prelude to the conquest of the supine massess and their world. To destroy all that has and does enervate – all that makes individuals slaves and seeks to stop their dreams. For the world and its peoples exist for the benefit of the natural elite – to be subjects, to aid them, to use the resources so that in time there is an evolution upwards, rather than downwards: an evolution toward still higher forms. Uut this has been and only can be achieved by the majority aspiring to emulate the deeds and daring of the few, of the natural elite – by the morality and vision of the few becoming the morality and vision of the many, not the other way round. This, naturally, means suffering – perhaps wars, perhaps great sorrows. But all that is great arises from suffering not softness. Once the vision of the few is defeated by the many, once their energies are redirected – once the dreaming stops and the aspiring ceases – then there is decline – and sickness, of the spirit and the psyche. This can be put I very simply: war and conquest and exploration are needed; when they stop, decay sets in, the scum come to the surface.

Thus, goals of destruction, re-construction and creation must be set – and strived for. This requires a new breed, an elite nurtured by naturalness and instinct and visions. An elite which others see, and are afraid of. Such an elite may not be political – but if it was, so what? So what if I it became labeled as extreme, if the vision behind it became to be called by some name or other. Labels, names and indeed analysis of the political, social and intellectual kind – are games played by the weak, the cowardly, the sick and the scum. What matters is action, the desire to achieve, to become again fierce, tough, forbidding and thus real individuals who have broken the psychic chains of-rhe majority. What is important is inner resolve.

These goals would naturally lead to that second dream, fit for a god: the exploration of Space – to break away from the smallness of this world and find new ones: to explore, to conquer, to challenge us to even greater heights of being, to reach the limits of our potential and thus become god-like in our unique individuality – a new species that spreads ever onwards and upwards, toward even more, for evolution is never done. The planets, the stars, the galaxies with their visions, their richness, their splendours, await us: and it is up to us, each and every one of us, whether we reach them. We can begin that quest – or we can remain trapped in our own pettiness with our petty, pathetic concerns and outlook, on this small insignificant planet. Or we can take up the challenge of ourselves and our future and seek to be like gods, and thus fulfil the potential latent within us.

The first step is to change ourselves – within, where it matters, and become strong in spirit and psyche: a warrior in outlook and intent. The second is to spread that change outward – to others and external forms, destroying and then creating. The third is to strive further – toward the fulfilment of our inner vision, on this world and on others. Those who choose not to act have condemned themselves as failures.

MAGICK AND POLITICS

(Transcribed from a talk given by AL at ONA Sunedrion yf 99)

What is occurring more and more within society, is adherence by individuals to ephemeral causes and 'opinions' as a result of the subjection to individuals to propaganda both overt and more 'covert' (ie. 'subliminal'). That is, society is developing so as to make practical experience of the traumas of life more and more distant – the individual becoming shielded not only by the 'State' and its Institutions by also by ideas. Thus, the world is seen via the distorting lenses of these ideas. In the past, wisdom arose usually painfully over a period of time by diverse and often traumatic personal experience – that is, a very individual 'view of the world' was formed as a result of these varied experiences. of course, few arrived at even this stage of conscious devlopment.

Magick, properly understood, was an attempt to 'short circuit' this process – hence, for example, the tasks and procedures of the Grade Rituals in the seven-fold Way. Thus, magick built, from within and without the individual, a genuine foundation – an 'inner core' which enabled the individual to not only survive in an often hostile world, but also enhance their life quite significantly. Magick restores the individual in a very important way to the 'roots of their being' allowing thus a personal growth.

However, society in general does the opposite. Its 'education', its Institutions, its Laws all act together to produce an individual lacking in spirit: that is, devoid of a personal world-view. Moreover, this occurs whatever the outward political allegiance of the society – ego socialist or capitalist or shades in between. – and occurs whether or not a particular society is 'democratic' or overtly 'repressive. The only difference between the two is the method: the latter is more objectified and direct, often involving force and suppression, while the latter is more devious (and all the more dangerous because of this).

Essentially, there is growing within nearly all the societies of the world a consensus and an adherence to a certain set of ideas and values. That is, there is a 'levelling down' of differences together with a real loss of individual freedom - not only in terms of the ability of an individual to transit freely, unencumbered by whatever 'past' he or she may have, but equally importantly in terms of inner outlook. There is less and less 'realness' about individuals because the dramatic, formative experiences which shape and mould character and which give spirit are either becoming 'illegal'/frowned upon or made impossible by State control and/or indoctrination of the individual into a certain pattern of living/ideas about life.

In the practical sense, one could say not only are the legal restraints on an individual and their actions increasing, but also the direct power which States have over individuals (and this includes information about individuals) are ever growing. This, coupled with cooperation between States in the distribution/exchange of information and the desire for even more and larger 'federations' of States (eg. like a 'European State') both national and international, means more and more direct personal restrictions and less and less 'inner freedom'. There is in short, much more superficial ways of living: ways encouraged by States and by those who adhere to what is fast becoming the accepted world 'idea-system'.

This 'idea-system', it will surprise few here, is based to a great extent on the 'Nazarene view of the world'. Already in one of its many political forms it is established within -the States of the West where its watchwords include 'democracy' and 'equality' and 'freedom'. of course, these words enshrine clever ideas – but they are not real simply because they belong to something beyond one or at least a few individuals. This is really the crux of the matter. What is real is that which exists for each one of us, and this is and must be discovered anew by every individual as part of the process of life itself: when it is not, there is no real life – only the appearance of it. There is thus no inner essence, only outward form. What this means is that all goverments, States, Institutions or power-groupings negate this essence because our conscious life is a personal process of development pivotal upon our understanding of ourselves, the world, the cosmos and those few others with whom we inter-act in a very personal way: it should not be extrapolated beyond this, and all politics, all religion and all social pressures of whatever hue contradict this. They are, essentially, counter-evolutionary because they make the individual reliant on that which is not born from within. Thus there can be no such thing as genuine 'democracy/freedom/equality' and all attempts to create what are only abstract ideas destroy individuality. Such abstract ideas, however, continue to flourish, and they continue to make the individual sterile. There will be, in the near future, more and reliance upon such ideas, more and more attempts to make them a 'reality' in State/governmental forms – ego in Eastern Europe and beyond.

of course, this analysis forms the core of 'genuine anarchism': but even this is a label, an 'ism' which has evolved into an 'idea' with all the dissent appropriate to an idea. Magick is a means away from all this – it is a practical system, devoid of dogma, and makes possible the next stage of our – evolution as individuals. As such, it is direct opposition to all power-forms – governmental, religious or social although this opposition is silent and will remain silent. Magick is individual and will remain individual and while current conditions remain not unfavourable as regards the] spread of information relating to its techniques, this will probably change: simply because inner liberation is and will continue to be so for some time the province of a small number of individuals while the devotees of abstract political and social ideas continue to flourish and expand. This, naturally, is only a brief resume of the problem – and what perhaps it is essential to remember is that we as artists of the magickal possess the ability to bring -about change: both within ourselves and, should we wish it, within the society within which we live. The essence of the former is the seven-fold way, that of the latter – aeonic magick.

ONA

INSIGHT ROLES

Insight roles is the name given to a dangerous technique aimed at developing personal understanding. The technique itself is simple:-it involves the individual living for a specific period of time – between six months to two years – a certain role or 'way of life'.

What makes this difficult and dangerous is that the role chosen must be at odds with the individuals' own feelings and view of the world. This brings the individual into conflict with themselves – and sometimes friends and society as well. This forces the individual to rely on themselves and discard in a practical way all the illusions that must be discarded if Adeptship is to be achieved.

The technique is not to be undertaken lightly, but once begun be continued for the allotted time.

The technique is normally begun after the Grade Ritual of External Adept and after the individual has successfully run their own magickal group for at least three months. It is important that the individual strive to identify with the chosen role, and not see it merely as an unpleasant task. This identification must begin with a conscious decision to act the role as convincingly as possible. The role itself, for the period of time chosen, should be the main interest and occupation of the individual.

In an important way, Insight Roles are magickal rituals extending over a period of time and for the majority of individuals following the seven-fold way (the sinister path) are necessary as a prelude to the Grade Ritual of Internal Adept. It is the experiences undergone (both external and internal) during an Insight Role that give the individual the impetus necessary to undertake and complete the period of isolation required during the Grade Ritual. For it is this period of isolation which is often necessary for the individual to understand and integrate those experiences. From these, the genuine Adept is born.

All Insight Roles, of necessity, seem 'bizarre' to non-Adepts. The individual who decides to undertake the technique should choose a role (from those listed) which is the opposite of what they themselves consider their own personality to be.

General Guidelines:

When a role is undertaken, you are forbidden to explain to anyone the reasons for this sudden change in your behaviour/attitudes. This will isolate you, and begin the process of self-reliance and belief in your own Destiny. Observe the reaction of 'friends'.

You should initially think of the role as a means of enhancing your life – an opportunity. The role is part of the process of self-discovery – which is often painful.

To succeed, you must let go of all your previous opinions, beliefs and ideas. Forget everything assumed about people who naturally adopt the role you have chosen – just accept them, as they are. This will be very difficult. The role is an ordeal – a kind of second Initiation, and you can only become free, and ready for Adeptship, by losing your past.

The role chosen should be seen as part of your Destiny – and you should learn to revel in the role. If possible, keep a record of your thoughts, experiences and observations.

You should not, during the time of the role, undertake any magickal workings of whatever kind – simply because these are not necessary, considering the Insight Role is itself a powerful (and highly dangerous) magickal ritual of 'internal' (or alchemical) magick. Be determined to continue in the role for the length of time you have chosen. Should you succeed in this, you will discover many important things about yourself and the world. Wisdom will be gradually gained through the trials of experience. There is no substitute for this kind of practical learning. Always remember during the role, that you have chosen to follow the path toward self-divinity – the role is but a stage on that path, and one that has to be undertaken if your goal is to be achieved.

The roles are listed in order of difficulty/psychological danger with brief notes on the type of individual who might undertake them bearing in mind that the role chosen should be the opposite of what you consider your 'personality type'/ view of the world to be. From the viewpoint of the present the most challenging (and dangerous) role undertaken by members in the past Insight Roles, to defy. two decades has been the one listed first. quite simply, are for those who dare.

The roles are listed in order of danger (both practical and psychological) – the most dangerous first.

1) Join an organization of the extreme 'Right' and undertake the life of a political activist – attending meetings, demonstrations and so on. You should see yourself as a 'revolutionary' who seeks to create a new type of society. You must forget all your assumptions about this type of politics – and the people in it – and live out, in a practical way, this role. *Contact address: *British National Party, P.O. Box 446, London SE 23 2LS.*[9] Send for literature and ask about joining.

2) Enter a Buddhist religious order. Read about Buddhism, then apply to one of the addresses below to stay for a 'retreat' and ask then to enter the order. *(1) Throssel Hole Priory, Carr Shield, Hexham, Northumberland (Zen Buddhism). (2) Nanjushri Institute, Cinishead Priory, Ulverston, Cumbria (Tibetan Buddhism).*

3) Join the French Foreign Legion. Contact address: *La Chef du Poste d'Information de la Legion Etranger, Bas Fort St. Nicolas, 2 Boulevard Charles Livon, 13007 Marseille, France.*

Sell and forget everything – and simply go.

4) Open and run a brothel. First, find premises; second, find individuals willing to offer their services. Honesty in dealings with clients, and good friendly treatment of those employed to offer services to clients is the key to success, and must be done.

5) Join the Police. Assuming you are tall enough and have the right qualifications – ask at a Police Station or employment centre and

---

[9] Editorial Note: These contact addresses are now out of date. The MS was last revised 1985 eh.

apply. Be determined to succeed if interviewed – find plausible reasons, when asked, why you wish to join.

6) Vagrant. Sell everything you possess, give up job etc. buy rucksack., small tent etc. and wander around, trying to earn living by doing small jobs, begging sometimes for food.

7) Form a Wiccan group. This role means you assume the identity of a 'white' Priest/Priestess. Create a believable past for yourself (re Initiation and so on into Wicca) and then recruit members. Aim is to form a 'teaching coven'.

8) Set specific physical goals and train to achieve these. These goals must be achieved within eight months of beginning training. They are:

> a) Run a marathon in less than 2hrs 50 min (men) or 3hrs 10 min (women);
>
> b) Compete in a (cycling) 12hr Time Trial achieving a distance of at least 230 miles. Intermediate aims are: 25 miles in 1hr or less. (Note: 12 hr Time Trials are usually held during the summer months – so begin role at time to coincide with eight month training build-up, e.g. December. Join local cycling club – find details at nearest good bike shop.

(a) and (b) may be combined – and should be if you are fairly fit.

Some guidelines to assess viability of each role:

1) Best suited for those of 'left-wing/liberal sentiments, including anarchists.

2) Suited to those who enjoy the pleasures of the flesh women, wine and food.

3) Suited to those who lack a sense of adventure and consider themselves 'non-violent'.

4) Suited to those who are introverted and find organizing things difficult.

5) Suited to those who dislike authority – particularly the Police.

6) Suited to those who like comfort and need security of home/job etc.

7) Suited to those who lack imagination and flair for self-expression.

8) Suited to those who dislike sport.

THE PUBLICATION OF ESOTERIC TRADITIONS ON THE LEFT HAND PATH

For a long time, genuine esoteric tradition was handed on on an individual basis, from Master/Mistress to novice. There were many reasons for this, most of them practical: the tradition was esoteric, liable to misinterpretation and many of its tenets and rituals involved what would have been regarded as 'heretical', anti-social and/or illegal acts. Furthermore, the methods used to train novices often made those novices into 'outlaws' and set them against conventional society. Also, for a long time, the teaching and teachings of the tradition was heretical in Law – a criminal offense against Church and State. Secrecy was essential and necessary.

This state of affairs pertained until quite recently. With the burgeoning of interest in 'the Occult' in general, the LHP became somewhat less secret and certain aspects of the tradition were discreetly circulated. What were mistakenly taken to be 'esoteric' traditions and, given the new openness toward the Occult and the repeal of anti-Occult laws, freely distributed and/or published, were (a) the useless Grimoire/Qabalistic tradition, or (b) a mis-interpreted Crowleyism, or (c) of a showman/ghoulish/self-professed type with bits cobbled together from (a) and (b) with archaic myths and unenlightened egoism thrown in. The real tradition – with its darkness -and danger – remained hidden.

To (c) belonged the Church of Satan, which made Satanism akin to a fantasy role-playing game or games with some sorcery added to impress. The later schism which gave birth to the Temple of Set (born not with a bang but with a whimper) was not unexpected given the structure and orientation of this 'Church' – and neither was the fact that the leader of this schism based his Temple and authority on what was termed an 'Infernal Mandate', and declared Satanism as a religion, much mis-understood.

Meanwhile, the old traditions continued, in Europe and elsewhere, in their traditional way – secretly, accepting but few novices and these only after severe tests and ordeals. The traditions, writings, rituals, methods, ordeals and techniques remained unavailable except to those few. After lengthy deliberations and consultations, the individual representing traditional groups, decided to gradually make the esoteric tradition which he and others represented available on a selective basis, to reveal, for once and for all, what the LHP and Satanism were really about. The real impetus for this decision came from Aeonic strategy – making the tradition available would enable an increase in the number of genuine Adepts, thus hastening the presencing of the darker forces on Earth, and so fulfilling the sinister dialectic of history. This increase, however, would be gradual – over centuries.

With this dissemination, the purpose, intent and methods of Satanism and the LHP could no longer be mis-interpreted and the posers and charlatans who professed to be 'Satanists' would be exposed – at least to those with any sagacity. With the secrets accessible to those who saught to find them, the real esoteric work could continue, as it always had, in secret – the training, via direct experience, of those few strong and gifted enough to undertake the difficult and dangerous journey along the Left Hand Path.

In this example, the burglary was a 'crime', in Law – but, in fact, the] illegal nature of the act was irrelevant. The act, and its planning etc., aided the self-excellence of the novice, and thus his magickal development, because it was a Satanic act, not because it was 'criminal' – that is, it involved danger, required skill, judgement, daring, and it was real.

It was, in a sense, a practical ordeal and its Satanic character mi that its victims were victims of themselves: the act was akin to an act of 'natural justice'. To some, it may seem a game – and so it was, but one played in earnest, in which losing meant capture and probable imprisonment (factors which made it interesting and worthwhile). and it was only a few incidents in a life crammed with such incidents – at different levels.

Furthermore, this 'realness' is important – genuine Satanists involve themselves with the real world, in real situations with real people and real danger. The imitation Satanists play mental and intellectual and 'safe' games. The difference is that a real Satanist will actually be an assassin, for example, while the imitation Satanist will dream of being one and will probably obtain a moronic pleasure from watching some fictional story and 'identifying' with a fictionalized assassin – or, more likely, will 'act out' such a role in some pathetic psuedo-magickal ceremony and believe he/she has attained something.

Naturally, in the real world things can and do go wrong. But as always, the real Satanists survive and prosper, while the others go under, get caught, give up or are killed. Also, sometimes even the best get things a little wrong – but they learn from their mistakes, they grow in character, in insight, in skill. Genuine Satanists are survivors: they learn and prosper, and die at the right time.

This growth means that a Satanist moves on – there are always new challenges, new delights, new tests of skill, daring, endurence, courage; new insights. A 'role' is only a role – played, then discarded, transcended. Thus, even crime, sacrifice, tests of others, become left behind, given time – they have served the purpose for which they were intended – and a new being is given birth, one more joins the elect. This is simply another way of saying that a Satanist is never trapped by the act, the desires for and against that act, its consequences, or indeed anything to do with that act, whatever the nature of the act. An act, such as a sacrifice or a crime, is a means – to something beyond. All acts are experience. A Satanist is above and beyond acts – a master or mistress of them, rather than a slave to them.

So it is, so it has been and so it will be – for genuine Satanists. Meanwhile, the imitation Satanists will play their word-games, feast on self-delusions, and continue to claim that 'Satanism' never involves sacrifice, or criminal acts but is a rather pleasing philosophy which has had a rather 'bad press'.

But, henceforward, anyone who is taken in by these gutless, posturing charlatans will deserve the epithet 'stupid'.

ONA

Dear Ms Vera,

      Thank you for your very interesting letter, and the questionnaire.
This later I have replied to and sent by seperate post.
    Regarding publications which present the teachings of the ONA, the following
are available (from the above address):
°Naos - A Practical Guide to Becoming an Adept. 121 pages. $30 including Air
Mail postage
°The Black Book of Satan - A Guide to Sinister Ceremonial Magick. 56 pages.$ 20
°Hostia - Secret Teachings of the ONA. Volume I. 130 pages. $35
°Hostia. Vol. II. 56 pages. $20
°The Deofel Quartet, Volume I. (Falcifer, Lord of Darkness; Temple of Satan).
211 pages. $50
°The Deofel Quartet, Vol II. (The Giving; The Greyling Owl.) 221 pages. $52
    The prices are rather high due to the cost of Air Mail postage - for instance,
Naos would be just £11 without the postage costs. All the above are copies
of the original MSS as circulated among members. Most of the articles which
appeared in 'Fenrir' are in either 'Hostia' or the Black Book. The Deofel
Quartet are instructional texts written in fictional form. [Cheques payable to
Thormynd Press.]

    In replying to your detailed and reasoned comments, perhaps I should start
by saying that in attacking the 'intellectualism' of the Temple of Set, I am
attacking the mostly non-practical (in terms of living) approach of that and
other groups. They have made Satanism seem mostly cerebral - a subject to be
studied, discussed, argued about, analyzed, rather than being a practical guide
to living on the edge. Their practice, such as it is, is again cerebral - magickal
workings which are mostly devoid of a primal exultation, ecstasy. In short, their
approach revolves essentially around abstract ideas. I am not critical of
intellectualism per se - I am regarded by some as 'an intellectual', having been
trained both as a scientist and a classical scholar [I have several translations
of Greek Drama to my credit]. Rather, I have tried to make clear (sometimes
by exaggerating the point) that I regard Satanism first and foremost as a practical
way which involves garnishing experiences of the limits of living, and learning
from those experiences - transmuting the experiences into self-insight, the
development of consciousness and so on. I also believe that these experiences
must be tough - must take each individual to and beyond their own limits - and
that they must be done without relying on anything other than a pure defiance,
a pure strength of character. To me, it seems that both the Temple of Set
and the Church of Satan provide 'props' for their members - there is dogma,
an organizational structure, a sense of belonging, and the belief that
Satanism is somehow a 'fantasy game' or playing at socerers.

    Basically, intellectualism should follow action - not prejudge it nor limit it.
All the members of the ToS and the CoS I have met over the years were full of
'Satanic theory' but had little (sometimes no) experience of going to and beyond
their own limits. Basically, they played at Satanism - the occassional (boring)
ritual, the odd working with a magickal intent. But nowhere was there a proud,
defiant, exultation in living; nowhere was there real Satanic character born
from character-building experiences. There was, and is, an awful lot of discussions,
of meetings, of articles, of letters, of 'organizing' things. But try and get
one of them to actually do something really Satanic in the real world - to divest
themselves of the props (psychic, human and Occult) which supported them, and so
return them to their primal nature - was impossible: they were too lazy or weak;
too comfortable with playing their Satanic fantasy roles and games.

Regarding my own tradition, and the question of what is and what is not 'Satanism'.

I make no claim that the ONA represents the only 'true form of Satanism' - it is simply one tradition among many, although it does pre-date the formation of the CoS. What I express and have expressed, is that organizations like the CoS and the ToS by their very nature actually hinder the development of those qualities which I and some others believe to be central to Satanism. By this I mean that any organization which prescribes a dogma for its members to believe, which restrains them by 'ethical conditions' and which implicitly or explicitly require those members to submit to an organizational authority/Master/leader, is not Satanic. The ToS in particular believes in Satanism as some kind of 'religion'. I, and the Mistress who Initiated me into the ONA tradition, have always seen Satanism as being individualized - concerned with building a unique character, a truely free being. An organizational structure such as possessed by the ToS contradicts this in essence, however many clever words may be used to try and hide this fact. Such organizations breed sychophancy, dependence - one has to 'conform', to a certain degree at least. Of course, I understand some of the tactical reasons which explain why the ToS, for instance, claims 'religious status' - but even these reasons, on examination, show that the adoption of these tactics are unnecessary and actually counter-productive, in terms of producing real Satanic Adepts: i.e. individualsof Satanic character who truely represent an evolutionary development.

In my own tradition, for instance, it was the custom to train one, at most two, novices on an individualized basis. That is, a Satanic Master/Mistress guided one or two novices in the way of Satanism - there was and is no organizational structure, no limiting the behaviour of those novices, only an imparting of tradition and advice born from personal experience of having oneself undergone ordeals and formative experiences in the real world.

Sometimes, in undertaking an Adversarial role against the CoS and the ToS, I have been rather strident - but to provoke, to try and get others to think constructively about those organizations and the type of Satanism I believe they represent.

I describe the ONA as being a 'traditional Satanist' grouping by which I mean it adheres to certain traditions - chief among these being a guiding of novices on an individualized basis, it undertakes certain rites/practices on a basis established in earlier times, and it accepts that Satanism is dark, evil in a very real sense (one of which is that there are certain powers/ dark energies which are beyond the psyche of the individual and which can overwhelm it - which are primal). The traditions I inherited were really a mixture - some ceremonial rituals (such as the Ceremony of Recalling), some legends regarding Albion, some beliefs concerning Baphomet as a dark goddess who was propitiated in former times by sacrifice, some methods (such as 'Insight Roles') used to develope Satanic character, and some ordeals, both practical and magickal, designed to test, to create skill, to provoke self-insight. All these I have made accessable, mostly without comment. I make no claims as to their validity, historically or otherwise. It is for others to judge them, and use them if they consider them to be useful.

What I have done, is to refine what I have inherited and add to it, making what I believe to be a purely practical system which enables any individual prepared for the hardships and struggles, to reach Satanic Adeptship and beyond. There is no mystery or mystique about achieving Adeptship and Satanic mastery: all it takes is years of self-effort, years of experiences, years of refining abilities and learning new ones. Furthermore, there is no need for me to set myself up as some 'all-knowing' Master empowered by an Infernal Mandate or whatever. What I have done I have done because I followed the traditional way of seeking experiences and because I possessed a Satanic pride which made me survive and learn from those experiences.

Many of my experiences - as befits a traditional Satanist - were dark; an awful lot were dangerous in the 'life or death' sense. I gambled my life, everything, many times, and won.

There is nothing very remarkable about this - or there should not be. Everyone has potential (or at least most do) - but they seldom if ever realize a fraction of that potential for various reasons: they are constrained, by 'society', by their own fears and weaknesses, they are lazy, they prefer 'easy' solutions (such as sitting at the feet of some 'Master')... To me, and some others, Satanism is a means to realize that potential, to go even beyond that. To do this, radical measures are required - and these are always testing as they are mostly in the real world.

By the nature of quite a lot of my experiences, they are 'secret' - they were beyond the bounds of conventional morality and law. Thus have Satanists operated for a long time - in secret, by the very nature of their existence, by the very nature of some of the experiences that are required to transcend the conformity of the herd and the inertia of one's own psyche, and which thus are a 'Yes!' to being. Naturally, this is dangerous - as you say, it can be an excuse for just plain foolhardiness. But a Satanist is someone who achieves a mastery - who experiences, and then, learning from that experience , transcends it. It is the failures who become trapped [in their own desires and their limited perceptions, for instance]. So some fail - they obviously were not possessed of enough Satanic qualities. That is the nature of our existence - the tough win through, the weak perish. It is not for me or anyone to limit, to prescribe, to forbid - the selection occurs by itself, by 'trial and error'. Each individual must learn for themselves - this is the crux. No one can do it for them. The essence, born via experiences, cannot be learnt from books, it cannot even be taught - it must be experienced. All I and any genuine Master can/do give advice, perhaps suggest some experiences which may be interesting and suitable - but the novice must undertake the experiences. If they learn from them, fine. There are more experiences and adventures waiting. If they fail, for whatever reason, or do not learn from the experience - tough!

In respect of politics. You mention that if a Satanist used politics, he or she never could achieve political success because Satanism is so unpopular. Naturally, if that Satanist was known as a Satanist - but if he/she kept this secret, as many do and have done, there is no problem. Of course there might be a danger of being 'exposed' as a Satanist - but that in itself is a challenge: to work under "deep cover". It requires a special person, certain skills - a Satanic character, in fact. I know of one particular person, many years ago, who did just that, until his aims were achieved.

However, my general point concerned a novice who might get involved with politics as a learning experience - for perhaps a year or so. This experience is quite different from that resulting from announcing, publicly, that one is a Satanist (this in itself is an experience which some Satanic novices choose to learn from). To become involved in extreme politics provides many opportunities for manipulating others (speaking in public; writing propaganda); for testing one's courage (participating in a rally/march where one's opponents are in the majority and threaten violence); for learning about comradeship and betrayal. And so on.

Further, although fascism as a creed had some links with the Nazarene Church, National-Socialism was, in essence, contradictory to Nazarene philosophy and ways of living. Most modern and authentic National-Socialist groups are anti-Nazarene (as witness Matt Koehl's 'New Order' in the US). But, essentially, the question is not about a particular type of political world-view, be it fascism or whatever, being contradictory or not to Satanism. The question is about all political forms being forms - structures which can be used, for a Satanic purpose, to achieve Satanic goals. The question of what might happen to individuals within a certain type of State is only a short-term question, and its asking implies a lack of what I have called 'Aeonic insight'.

Basically, Aeonics is a study of those processes which mould individuals and socieities over long periods of time - how people, alone and in groupings, have been and can be manipulated, changed, controlled. It is study of those energies which affect and infect the psyche and which produce and change archetypal forms.

and which thus mould character - and thus make 'history'.

Aeonics has nothing to   do with Crowley. It is a rational analysis of the
causes underlying historical change, and Aeonic Magick is the use of magickal
energies to effect aeonic change - i.e. change on a large scale over significant
periods of time. Basically, Satanic strategy (or 'the sinister dialectic of
history' as it is sometimes called) is about using such energies to bring
changes broadly in line with Satanic aims - i.e. enable individuals to
fulfil their potential, evolve to become like gods and so on. This strategy
is based on reality - both in terms of the energies used, and 'human nature'.
Therefore, the goals are seen as long term - of centuries of more. The aim has been
and is to increase the number of genuine Satanic Adepts, and to provide
changes which enable this.

Thus, it will be seen that Satanism, when understood correctly, is not soley
about self-advancement - it is also about using magickal and non-magickal
forms/energies to produce changes within societies which incline toward
the fulfilment of Satanic aims. This does not mean a kind of 'altruism' - it means
a calculating, reasoned assessment and then a striving and working toward certain
long-term goals, this assessment and this striving actually enhancing our existence
in a positive, Satanic way. In the simple sense, it may be considered as
Satanic manipulation on a large scale. The assessment itself, and the reasoned
understanding behind it, requires the development of special abilities - one
of which may be said to be 'Thought'. This is a development of our consciousness,
and leads beyond language. It is a special kind of 'thinking' - a thinking with
symbols, although the symbols are not abstract, as in mathematics, but rather
'numinous', archetypal. Essentially, it extends the range of our being. This
type of thinking is pre-figured, and made possible by, 'The Star Game' - a
collocation of symbols which extends both our intuitive and our reasoning
faculties. The mastery of this 'game', and thus the use of a new way of
reasoning/being, is a sign that one has taken evolution further - has become
almost a new type of 'human', one so far above the majority that it is difficult
to conceive one ever belonged to or related to that majority.

This rational analysis of Aeonics leads to certain judgements, a lot of which
are mis-construed by those who call themselves Satanists because they understand
those judgements on a personal basis - usually castigating the individual
or group which presents them from what is essentially a 'moral' position. That is,
there is a 'projection', by those Satanists (and Occultists in general), onto
the forms/judgements that they cannot really understand because their perspective
is so limited - so caught up in the constraints of their time and society.
This is what I meant by 'cosy, intellectual and basically moral abstractions'.
Most who profess to be Satanists cannot see very far - they cannot reason, coldly
and unemotionally and deeply. They accept other people's abstractions and ideas
and 'reasons' and have not thought the matter out for themselves because
it is either too difficult for them or they (once again) are too lazy, too smug,
too self-satisfied, too comfortable in their little 'Satanic' world with their
'Satanic' friends.

This judgement is part of genuine Satanic character, and arises from the
self-insight born via hard, testing experiences and ordeals. A Satanist has to
strip everything away - all props, go right back to the primal. This means
he/she relies only their instinct, their character, their spirit - their inner
resolve. This process takes years - and then, and only then, can the person
acquire the other aspects a Satanist needs and must have: the 'intellectual'
super-structure, the new ways of being, one of which I mentioned above (vide
'The Star Game'), the skills in magickal and people arts.

What has happened is that this foundation, this hard foundation, is lacking in
nearly all modern 'Satanists' - they are too soft, have not been toughened, they
rely too much on the comforts of society, on what others (like Aquino et al) have
given them in terms of principles, beliefs, dogma and so on.

Hence, when I say that National-Socialist Germany aided the sinister dialectic, it
is mis-understood: as me being a 'National-Socialist' or something of the kind. I am
simply stating a fact of Aeonics - as I do when I say that a future State or

Empire which was inspired by National-Socialism would also aid the achievement of Satanic aims, over centuries. Others, who perhaps have not reasoned deeply about such things, express naive views like a new Satanic age is just around the corner and that politics hinders the coming of this age. I know the reality of human nature and the times in which we live, and I know most people today are little different from what they were thousands of years ago (in some ways, we have lost something - as I am aware when I read Homer or Sophocles). They have hardly evolved at all - there is more illusion about 'inner progress' and conscious evolution than there is reality. In fact, the Occult in general fosters this illusion. Thus I understand that real change arises slowly - most people still delude themselves, are still in thrall to unconscious influences, still swayed by appearance. Our whole modern world conspires to make this so - magick, and particularly the Left Hand Path, is a means to the essence behind appearance; or rather, it was. Its awe, primal nature, its inspiration, its dark numinosity can really liberate and change. Thus my castigation of those who I see as pedalling a 'safe Satanism', an easy path to liberation - they destroy the one thing capable of liberating those in thrall. And they do it (a) to glorify they own ego, and (b) because they have not understood the way itself.

   I trust this will/be interest and perhaps thought-provoking, and look forward to your comments.

                    With best wishes,

                         Stephen Brown

                         269

Dear Ms Vera,

        Further to my recent letter, perhaps a few more comments might clarify the position of the ONA, and be of interest to you.

  By making certain material available - on sacrifice, for example - and by writing certain MSS dealing with that and other 'dark' topics, I and others have done two things. First, made it clear that such material is part of my tradition and that it recounts what was/is done. Second, returned to Satanism that darkness and evil which really belongs to it (at least in the novice stage).

  I have no desire to give Satanism a 'good name' - on the contrary, I wish it to be seen as I understand it to be - really dangerous and difficult. Naturally, many others believe the publication of certain material is mistaken, just as those who oppose Satanism have and can use that material to confirm their views on Satanism. The decision to make such material available was made only after considerable thought with full knowledge of the consequences.

  Of course, I may be mistaken - I make no claim to be 'infernally infallible'. I welcome positive discussion - the dialectic of learning. My thesis re the nature of certain practices which I inherited is open to discussion, an 'antithesis', from which a new synthesis and understanding may emerge. But all those in other Satanic organizations have done is 'proscribe' the ONA, or attack me personally or mount campaigns of dis-information against the ONA. The whole attitude of such groups, as befits their nature, is patronising - vide Aquino, in his letter to me of October 7 XXV: he, the Master or teacher, and I a student (of potential!) under his guidance and submitting to the rules of the ToS. He, and others, have stated that human sacrifice is not and never has been a part of Satanism. Well, it probably is not and never has been a part of some traditions - but it was/is a part of my own tradition, according to principles laid down a long time ago regarding the victim or opfer choosing themselves, the act then being akin to an act of 'natural justice'. [qv. the MSS 'Satanism, Sacrifice and Crime'; 'Satanism - The Sinister Shadow, Revealed'; A Gift for the Prince' etc. I shall send you copies of some of these, since they may be of interest.]

  As with many things, sacrifice can be misconstrued. The affirmation that it has occurred as part of one Satanic tradtion at least can be taken up by those weaklings (in terms of character) who circulate around the fringes of the Left Hand Path, and give them an excuse to indulge in criminal acts. That is, such people fail to understand the reasons for such acts (the correct choice of opfer, for instance) as they can never rise above their own weaknesses. Are these consequences my responsibility, or not? Or am I acting like a Satanist (my kind, anyway) and standing back, perhaps with laughter, when a probable consequence becomes a fact? Does this unsettle you? Horrify you? Does this provoke a challenge and make you question the nature of Satanism?

  The same applies to the use of politics. Is it worth the death of x number of others (in a war, say) to give birth to one, perhaps two, genuine Satanic Adepts? I would answer in the affirmative. Does that make me cruel? Or Satanic?

Also, I do not believe it to be necesary nor desirable for Satanism to try and become respectable - or even improve its image. Nor even to try and counter the propaganda of the Nazarene fundamentalists. Such things are irrelevant. What matters is presenting the essence of Satanism so enabling individuals to work at their own self-development in a Satanic way. As I mentioned before, Satanism fundamentally means individuals striving togo beyond what they are. This is hard, and means that not many will attempt it; even fewer will be successful. The means cannot be made easier - for that would destroy the essence.

Thus, the ONA is in conflict with groups like the ToS who really want to make Satanism easy and safe and thus become rather more widespread than it is now. It is personal, direct experience, ordeals and so on, which are important. For instance, to achieve Adeptship the ONA believes each individual must undergo certain formative experiences. One of these involves living alone, in an isolated location, for three months with only the bare necessities required for physical survival. These conditions are necessary, for by so living in such a way the individual strips away all self-illusions, exposes all their inner weaknesses, and makes them reliant only on themselves . There are no distractions, no friends to give comfort, no material comforts to soften the hardship. This [which is the Grade Ritual of Internal Adept] is tough. But it is the key to Adeptship. There is no short cut, no easy way. To succeed in this ordeal, the individual must have or develope an infernal strength, a certain character. Naturally, many fail - some renounce their Satanism, some find excuses for giving up. But one either stays the distance, observing the conditions of harshness, or one does not. Many are they who have said that this ordeal is not necessary - they believe there are other ways (all easier, of course), or they are afraid of confronting themselves without the supports normally around them: friends, lovers, organizations, dogma, material comforts. They and others like them can believe what they wish - but that particular ordeal works: it produces a strong, insightful character ready for the new challenges which can inspire an Adept. Or it destroys.

I understand Adeptship not as a reward given by someone else (such as Aquino) for what they perceive as 'progress' or 'ability', nor even as the undertaking of any kind of ritual at the end of which one congratulates oneself and appoints oneself as 'Adept'. Rather, it is the achievement of a certain self-insight and knowledge, allied to an understanding and judgement, born of experience. It is also mastery of certain skills (some magickal, some not-magickal) and a developed awareness stemming from a synthesis of rational understanding (or 'intellectualism') and intuition. It is a stage in the Satanic way of living - a stage reached by self-effort and struggle. A Master (or Mistress) is a stage beyond this - there is no gift, infernal or otherwise, which confers the attributes of this stage of individual evolution. It is achieved, by the individual, not a reward and certainly not a self-appointed title assumed after a few years playing at Satanism and safe magick.

However, it is true that present conditions are more favourable toward the propagation of Satanism than was the case decades ago. But even were direct 'persecution' and anti-Satanic laws to return, Satanism would continue: it would re-adopt the practices of those decades. The cell system; the oral transmission; 'deep cover'. Novices would still be trained; goals would still be achieved. So 'favourable' conditions are not necessary - indeed, some see them as detrimental: they make organizations like the CoS possible!

These present conditions provide some opportunities - of increasing the number of genuine practioners of the Black Arts and of making available for present and future generations the methods and techniques of those Arts. The real aims of Satanism will be achieved whatever the external forms our societies may take - Satanists, like the shape-changers they are, will adapt and prosper. These aims are essentially two-fold: continuing the tradition (i.e. training Adepts; providing opportunities for seeding Satanism), and gradually changing evolution.

The second of these will actually arise from the first - the changes will
occur because of the increasing number of Adepts. These may be likened to
a new species which at first is small in number but which, over decades and
centuries, increases. In time, it will dominate. The first arises because
it is one of the obligations of each new Adept to find someone suitable and
guide them toward Adeptship. These changes will, as I explained in my last
letter, take time - centuries, in fact. There is no way the process can be
speeded up - each individual must acquire the knowledge, the character, the
experiences, for themselves, and this takes time. It takes less time now than
it did - because we understand more, we are more conscious of what we are
actually doing (or at least some of us are). It is possible and indeed probable
that over the next century or so the time taken to reach Adeptship and the
stages beyond will be reduced. But the situation at the moment is as it is.
A century ago it took perhaps twenty or thirty years of one's life to achieve
real Adeptship. Now, it can take as little as five to ten years. What has not
changed (at least yet) is the number who reach that stage. As I wrote many years
ago, most people want easy solutions, they want someone to do the work for them,
to confer titles on them - or they are so comfortable with their illusions and
delusions (regarding their magickal abilities and their self-insight, for
instance) that they see no reason to change, to really struggle; to reach
toward Adeptship. All I can do is point the way - offer some guidance. It is
up to each individual whether they begin the quest, and having begun, whether
they succeed.

        The fundamental questions which should be asked are: what, fundamentally,
is Satanism? What does it mean in terms of the life of the individual? What
does it mean in terms of society? The ONA offers some answers. Organizations like
the ToS give other answers, some of which contradict the ONA ones. Each
individual must arrive at their own assessment. The ONA offers a practical
system which I and others know from experience works - at least in producing
our kind of Satanist! The ONA is critical and controversial: it is
provoking. Adversarial, occassionally irreverent. This in itself is creative.
It engenders response.
    Once again, I would welcome your response to the matters raised in this
letter and the various MSS.

                            With best wishes,

                                        Stephen Brown

Dear Dr. Aquino,
                    It was with interest that I read your
letter in a recent issue of 'Brimstone' after my attention
was drawn to that magazine by a friend. An open (rather
friendly) reply to some of the points you raised has
been sent to the Editor - I am sure he would send you a
copy should you be interested.
    However, there are some points which perhaps are best
raised in a private letter. First - and perhaps
inconsequential out of its context - no one has ever
claimed to be 'Head' of the ONA: no such position exists.
Your statement on this was somewhat surprising because
I felt you would be above using 'Kennel' type tactics
re mis-information about other LHP individuals and groups.
Am I mistaken? Or perhaps the information was supplied
by a not altogether too reliable scource here in the U.K.?
    Second - and most important - your mention of the
MSS concerning sacrifice. These were published basically
because they form part of an esoteric tradition, which
tradition was being made accessable to those who might
be interested following a decision to publish Order methods,
teachings and traditions. Essentially, such publication
lets others decide what is or is not worthwhile or valuable
or interesting from an esoteric point of view - there is
not, within the ONA, any control of esoteric information
as a result of one or more individuals deciding what is
'right' or 'true teaching' - simply because individuality
is the foundation of the "ONA way". This way is the
development of self-insight and magickal mastery via
individuals following the seven-fold way.
    But this background aside, you raise an interesting
point in your use of the term 'ethical'. Does Satanism
have ethics? And if so, what are they and who formulates
them? By the nature of the Temple of Set I am led to
assume the answer would be affirmative and that it is
the ToS which formulates these. Is this assumption incorrect?
If it is not, then I and some others would offer dissent -
based not only on the principle of individuality mentioned
above but also on the reality of there existing divergent
LHP and Satanic traditions (some of which existed before
the foundation of the Church of Satan). Speaking for
myself, I consider debate about ethics futile in a LHP
context - except to express the obvious Satanic assertion
(qv 'The Dark Forces' in "Fenrir" 4) that one essential
personal quality is honour born from the quest for
self-excellance and self-understanding. One either has
this personal quality (or the potential to possess it) or
one does not: intellectual debate about it is irrelevant.
This quality is expressed by the way of living an individual
follows and as far as the ONA is concerned this quality
is one of those that marks the genuine Satanic elite from
the imitation. Yet we accept that others may disagree
since we feel there can be no religious dogma about Satanism
or the LHP: no subserviance to someone else's ideas or ways

273

of living. Each individual developes their own unique perspective and insight as a consequence of striving to achieve Adeptship - a perspective and insight which derives mainly from practical experience, both magickal and personal. Thus we uphold anarchism.

Hence the publication of the many and various Order MSS. Yet, all this notwithstanding, I do understand that some may believe that tactically the time was not right to publish some of these MSS. However, is the time ever right? Once again, some interesting questions arise. For example, for the benefit of those groups (like the ToS) which do adopt a high media profile, is it necessary and indeed desirable for other groups and individuals on the LHP to restrict what they say and teach and publish in case such things are mis-interpreted and/or distorted and used against the LHP in general? This would imply some sort of concensus among those individuals and groups on the LHP - a concensus which it seems both the ToS and the Church of Satan wish to achieve by claiming a religious 'authority'. To this end there seems to be developing an almost Church-like mentality - with schisms and prohibitions and proscribing of other groups and individuals. Rather 'Old Aeon' values. If such a concensus is indeed necessary (and I and some others have doubts whether it is) then it would seem better achieved on a mutual basis by recognition of diversity and traditions and then the development of mutual understanding rather than one group trying to impose its dogma by a religious type belief: such dogma and such belief being entirely contrary to the basic principles of Satanism and the LHP - self-development via self-experience.

I and others like me respect your right to promulgate the Setian philosophy just as I trust you have the sagacity to understand that what La Vey codified and what the early Church of Satan represented is not the only form Satanism can take. Satanism existed in many forms long before La Vey, and the ONA simply represents one such form: a form that has changed and is still changing - developed as it is and has been by creative individuals within it. As I mentioned to you in a previous letter some time ago, this does not mean we claim to be a 'peer' organization with a claim to some kind of 'authority'. We are simply a small group following our own way - a way somewhat different from that developed by the Church of Satan and the ToS. Our tradition, such as it is, is not static - indeed in many ways the most significant developments (e.g. the Star Game, Grade Ritual codification, Deofil Quartet) have occurred quite recently. Doubtless these developments will continue.

When in the past we and others like us have said things that others interpret as being 'against' the ToS or La Vey, we were simply assuming the role of Adversary - challenging what seemed to be becoming accepted dogma that the only 'real' Satanists are either in the ToS or the Church of Satan. Such a dogma is an historical absurdity and its acceptance an affront to the Satanic desire to know and understand and not meekly believe.

If you have any comments about these matters I would be interested to read them.

Cordially yours,

Stephen Brown

274

Temple of Set

Post Office Box 470307, San Francisco, California 94147
MCI-Mail: 278-4041 * Telex: 6502784041

Michael A. Aquino, Ph.D.
High Priest of Set

October 7, XXV

Mr. Stephen Brown
Post Office Box 4
Church Stretton, Shropshire
England

Dear Mr. Brown:

Thank you for your letter of September 7th.

Under your several aliases every single letter and publication of the O.N.A. is authorized over your personal signature, whether as "pp" or otherwise. Personal contacts by our former Priest Martin confirmed that you are the leader, if not indeed the sole member of this institution.

The old Church of Satan used to play games with mythical officials and executive bodies behind the scenes. As a senior official of the Church I helped to keep this particular hot-air balloon inflated, initially assuming that it did no harm and made the Church a bit more colorful to the membership. Ultimately I became uncomfortable with it, however, because in the last analysis it involved deceiving the very persons - the membership of the Church - who had come to it in good faith depending upon it to not deceive them, even in so "playful" a fashion.

It was also responsible for a more serious kind of damage. It enabled Anton LaVey to announce policies in the name of a fictitious "Council of Nine", or in the name of a fictitious official, and thus to escape personal responsibility for his actions. Nor was there any executive body or other official to whom he was accountable. Had there been, the catastrophe of 1975 might have been averted without the entire Church of Satan organization having to be scrapped. [Even if it had evolved into a Setian mode, as in many Lesser Magical ways it was indeed doing prior to the crisis, it still might have continued as an unbroken organization - and Anton LaVey might be its High Priest today.]

When the Temple of Set was founded, therefore, the old occult game of "Ascended [or in this case 'Descended'] Masters behind the scenes" was ashcanned along with the other practices of the old Church with which we were ethically uncomfortable. From the moment of its founding, the Temple has made all of its officials and executive bodies a matter of record, known to all Setians [and to non-Setians with a legitimate interest]. And neither the High Priest of Set nor any other official has the sort of dictatorial power that Anton LaVey had in the Church.

Given the present climate of witch-hunting hysteria in England, publication of a "Satanic ritual" by an avowedly "Satanic" institution which includes human sacrifice is thoroughly irresponsible. In fact it would be irresponsible even in a normal social climate, as the Satanic religion is not and has never been based upon the principle of human sacrifice. [It is Christianity which espouses that principle, sacrificing its god in human form every Easter.]

If you were presenting that ritual text as an example of Christian hate-propaganda against the Satanic tradition, making clear that it has no basis in fact, that would be one thing. But the ritual which you have published makes no such distinctions, and is thus a dangerous "loaded weapon" to be used by any child (of any age) who picks it up. And of course it plays right into the hands of any anti-Satanic maniac who is looking for "evidence" of "Satanic ritual murder". Your argument that the O.N.A. does not consider itself responsible for such uses may satisfy you, but it certainly doesn't satisfy the Temple of Set as guardian of this religion.

Indeed Satanism is an ethical religion, and yes, I do consider the Temple of Set the institution consecrated by Set to establish and maintain such an ethical environment - which is carefully developed in the *Crystal Tablet of Set*.

As a non-Initiate of the Temple, you are of course at liberty to dissent from this ethical standard. But neither, by your non-Initiatory status, does the Temple consider you a member of the Setian/Satanic religion. You are, in our eyes, simply one more individual affecting "Satanism" as a personal hobby. In this you may be more or less skilled, more or less articulate, more or less artistic: these we do not judge.

But what we do judge is that in all of this you have not been Recognized by the Temple which exclusively is consecrated by Set. We consider the Temple a sacred institution, not just one of a number of "Satanic clubs" around the world. From 1966 to 1975 CE we held precisely this view concerning the Church of Satan, which welcomed the interest and enthusiasm of amateur "Satanists" and "Satanic" groups such as the O.N.A. but considered only its own membership and Priesthood formally deserving of the religious titles they held.

This last point deserves further elaboration and emphasis. Just because we regard the Temple as seriously and exclusively as we do does not mean that we hold non-Temple "Satanic" groups in blanket contempt. Some of them are indeed amateurish and embarrassing to the Satanic tradition, and the sooner they disintegrate the better. But others are quite serious and sophisticated, and deserve our respect and admiration - which are quite freely given where due. Some, upon encountering the Temple of Set, have voluntarily dissolved and commended their membership to it. Some have retained their independent structure and interests while at the same time encouraging/allowing their members to affiliate with the Temple as a formal religion. Some have simply gone their own way, maintaining a polite non-acceptance of the Temple's avowed Infernal Mandate.

The distinction we draw in all cases is dictated simply by our sacred regard for the Priesthood of Set, and the Temple under its care, as established by Set in the *Book of Coming Forth by Night*. If we did not draw that distinction, then we would be, at our heart, an insincere and fraudulent religion.

Therefore the exclusiveness of the Temple of Set is not born of either arrogance or competitiveness, but simply of the utter seriousness with which we regard ourselves. It is this same attitude which makes the Temple of Set reject any "council of churches", occult or conventional, for the simple reason that we consider our religion correct and theirs incorrect. As is stated in our informational letter, "they may serve a useful social function as purveyors of soothing myths and fantasies to humans unable to attain Setian levels of self-consciousness".

I have re-read the comments I made concerning the O.N.A. and yourself in *Brimstone*, and I see nothing in them that I think should be amended - including the compliment to you at the conclusion of those comments. You are, from what I have seen of your writings, an intelligent and creative individual who could become an influential and respected philosopher of the Left-Hand Path if you can bring yourself to cast aside all of the fictitious "lumber and wreckage" with which you are unnecessarily crippling yourself. If I didn't see Setian qualities in you, I wouldn't even bother to say such things. But just as in my university classes I speak most bluntly to the students who do have the intelligence to master the curriculum and aren't doing so, so I speak thus to you.

Sincerely,

cc- Adept John D. Alleé, Editor, *Brimstone*

277

Dear Dr. Aquino,
                    Thank you for your letter of October the
7th.
    I appreciate your comments and before passing on to
specific points raised, would like to make some general
comments.
    What I sense (and I use the word advisedly) is that
you and I, despite our differing methods, are fundamentally
trying to achieve the same thing. I here mean in terms of
'esoteric' magick and not in terms of outward terms or
expressions.
    We are both aware of the potential inherent within
individuals and how certain forms, magickal or otherwise,
can be used to explicate that potential, bringing thus
an evolution of consciousness both individual and
beyond the individual. Thus are individuals, and 'society',
changed over varying periods of time. You have established
and maintained an organization and imbued it with certain
forms, which forms via their various transformations,
create and establish conditions for changes in tune with
certain energies. Because of the nature of this organization,
and the energies, there is a need to maintain a coherence,
a magickal continuity and thus the establishment of a system
which protects the viability of all aspects.
    As to myself, I deal with similar forms but make them
manifest in a different way - building in to some of those
manifestations a random or 'chaotic' element and into
others a 'numinous' aspect. Thus, further forms are
developed, in both causal and acausal time, and achieve
certain goals, some of which are quite long-term (beyond
my own temporal lifetime at the earliest).
    All these energies are 'sinister' (or Left Hand Path, if
you prefer) - at the most simple level this means they
enhance our creative evolution; at another, it means they
'disrupt' already existing forms which may hinder such
evolution and explication of individual potential.
    Where we might (and seem to) differ is in our respective
time-scale for fundamental change and in making some
elements more manifest than others, to achieve specific
ends.
    Of course, I accept that my understanding may not be
complete (and might possibly be incorrect on some points)
as I assume that you, claiming the title 'Ipssisimus',
understand the preceeding four paragraphs without me
having to elaborate at length.

    You have accepted a "role" within the Temple of Set
with all the duties and obligations implied, and there
is much to admire in this. This of necessity means
adhering to the principles of what you describe as the
'sacred trust' placed in you vis-a-vis the 'Infernal
Mandate'. Thus there is a religious attitude and acceptance.
All this I myself regard as natural and necessary, given

the vehicle chosen - that is, the Temple of Set. The way
of the ONA is, however, quite different - we see our way
as guiding a few individuals to self-awareness, to Adeptship
and beyond, via various practical and magickal techniques.
The emphasis is on guide, on self-devlopment, on self-
discovery. There is no religious attitude, no acceptance
of someone else's authority, and no mystique: the methods,
as divulged in the recently published book 'Naos', are
essentially practical.
    All this arises from the understanding that changes such
as I mentioned earlier (regarding individual potential)
will occur slowly and for the most part on a small scale
for some time to come: bringing changes to 'society' (a
generalization here, for brevity) - and thus to larger
numbers of individuals - on the timescale of a century or
more.
    The present aim of the ONA is to make these techniques -
which give all individuals the means to achieve the next
stage of individual evolution should they so wish -
more generally available. These techniques (the Grade
Rituals for example, and the Star Game) will probably
and indeed should be refined and extended in the future,
as they have been refined in their creation over the past
decade or so. Older techniques, inherited by me, have served
their purpose - and to an extent have made possible the
present advances, including preparing the way, on the
level of mystique, for a dissemination of the 'new'. To be
more explicit - an 'aura' was created around the ONA (quite
deliberately) by using certain methods, magickal forms,
and by publishing certain material. This aura, existing,
becomes transformed - and serves a very useful purpose on
the acausal level. (In simple terms and on an elementary
level, it provides a certain impetus to seek out and try
the 'new' techniques, the 'new' way - on the level of
individuals.)
    Thus, as the new techniques (and hence the new forms
deriving from them)become more widely distributed, via
books such as Naos, the Deofil Quartet and the Black
Book of Satan (these last two due for publication this
Winter Solstice) then the methods used hitherto are no
longer needed, and are abandoned - they have served their
purpose. It is the same with the ONA: once the techniques
and the essence are more widely available then 'membership'
as such is irrelevant, since everything is available
and accessible (and this includes past methods and teachings)
the individual taking responsibility for their own
development, their own experiences (both magickal and
personal). This is the fundamental point: the responsibility
for development ultimately rests with individual desire,
just as each individual must make their own assessment of
what is valuable and what is 'ethical/just' from their
own experience, it being the aim of the techniques of the
seven-fold sinister way to provide the character-building,
evolutionary, experiences. There is no pre-judgement by
me or anyone, no set of rules. The function of the ONA
is now to guide, simply because its members have undergone
the experiences of the way and can speak from a position
of experience - an experience which may or may not be of
value to others.
    Thus the fundamental difference in our approach. It was

made quite clear to the former Temple of Set Priest you
mentioned that each individual is expected to work on
the practical level to achieve his or her own magickal
development - to actually practice magick, to use magickal
and other techniques, rather than just talk about them.
This takes quite a number of years, and is a personal
effort. Most people cannot be bothered - they want easy
solutions - and most people who enquired in the past
about the ONA were not prepared to work toward their
own self-development. They either wanted someone else
to do it for them (be such a someone a 'Master' or an
Infernal Manifestation) or would not/could not undertake
the life-style change necessary for achieving genuine
Adeptship (such as spending three months alone under
special conditions). Ultimately, their loss.

I, for one, do not believe thèreis a 'religious'
solution to Adeptship and beyond - a gift, Infernal or
otherwise. There is only self-experiencing, in the real
and the magickal worlds, and that is it. Wisdom is acquired
by the alchemical process of internal change over a period
of time: the techniques developed by the ONA may shorten
that time from several decades to perhaps a decade or
just under, but they do not do away with it, just as those
techniques make the possibility of such change available
to all.

For this reason, the ONA does not attempt to define
what is or is not of the Left Hand Path and what is or
is not Satanism (or even what Satan is) - each individual
arrives at their own understanding via experience.
Occassionally, as I have mentioned, there may be the
adoption of an adversarial role in order to attack accepted
(or even unconscious) dogmas within the broad spectrum of
the LHP movement - but that is as it should be, for
individuals questing after knowledge who refuse to meekly
believe. Once again, a 'role' is only a role, played out
in the quest for understanding.

On the specific point of membership - yes, there is
more than one (not that it really matters anymore now that
dissemination is being achieved). Not many, it is true,
but enough - some only beginning their quests, some more
advanced along the way: in this country, in Scandinavia,
in the countries of Europe and elsewhere.

Of course, all this may confirm your opinion that the
ONA is not 'Satanic' (or 'Setian' - this latter I would
agree with). Do you therefore understand 'Satanism' as
now the exclusive preserve of the Temple of Set because
of the 'Infernal Mandate' you mentioned? If so, this
raises rather interesting questions regarding 'Infernal'
authority, revelation and such like - questions partly
answered by your use of the term .religion. What then of
Satanic organizations which existed before the revelation:
such as (to take an odd example) the Order of Satanic
Templars here in England which existed (and was undertaking
Initiations) before the establishment of the Church of
Satan?(It later became known as the Orthodox Temple of the
Prince.) Personally, I see Satanism more as a way of living
than as a religion: an attitude to life, and one which is
ultimately personal, striving to ever more.

However, as mentioned above, I believe our ultimate goals
are the same even though our methods may differ. Of course
in this, as in many things, I may be mistaken: I claim
no authority, and my creations, profuse as they are, will
in the end be accepted or rejected on the basis of whether
they work (Satan forbid they should ever become 'dogma'
or a matter of 'faith'). I also expect to see them become
transformed, by their own metamorphosis and that due
to other individuals: changed, extended and probably
utlimately transcended, may be even forgotten. They - like
the individual I am at the moment - are only a stage, toward
something else.

In the interests of sinister fellowship I could arrange
for a copy of 'Naos' (and other works as and when they
become available) to be sent to you, should you be
interested.

Enclosed please find a copy of an article due to appear
shortly in the journal 'Balder'. It may make you smile.

Cordially yours,

Stephen Brown

·················

[Editorial Note: In view of the controversy in Occult circles about
using 'pseudonyms' and the desire of certain groups to operate 'underground'
without media scrutiny - a subject mentioned by Dr. Aquino in his letters
and since taken up by a number of others both within and without the LHP -
the following observations are in order:

*It has been for many centuries an established principle among LHP Adepts
to work in a reclusive manner in 'secret'. The reason for this is basically
two-fold: the magickal work is mis-understood by 'outsiders' [and often
by such people catagorized from their own social/political/religious perspectives]
and to try and explain it to non-Initiates was seen as a waste of time; and,
secondly, it enabled that work to be undertaken without hindrance from
interfering individuals and officials. Without this secrecy, the LHP would not
have survived. Today, conditions have changed somewhat, but still not enough in
some areas.

* A labyrinth was created to confuse the merely curious and those seeking to
disrupt the magickal work and tradition.

* Quite often, LHP Adepts have a 'seperate professional' life (which in some
cases is part of their long-term magickal goals) and the 'stigma' of involvement
with magick would be detrimental to that. Quite often this seperate life is
beneficial to the evolution of the 'Occult' in general as it provides opportunities
for dissemination (mostly clandestine).

That some individuals have gone 'public' is fair enough - that is their
decision. But those who prefer or need to work 'underground' in order to
continue their own reclusive and secret traditions should not be castigated
for in many cases they are guardians who can never have a 'public' Occult role.
Societies, and the individuals within them, are still structured on the basis
of categories and generalizations.]

ONA STRATEGY AND TACTICS

The fundamental strategic aim, expressed exoterically, is to aid evolution of the human species by increasing the dark, creative, forces which presence on Earth. Expressed esoterically, the aim is to aid the creation of a 'New Aeon' wherein what is now known as Adept-type consciousness and abilities are the preserve of the majority. This aim is long-term: c.3-S centuries.

This aim involves keeping opening already existing nexions, and opening new nexions, these nexions effectively drawing forth acausal (or sinister) energies. The energy is then directed to achieve specific goals, or left to disperse and disrupt according to its nature. Exoterically, this aim is 'The Return of the Dark Gods' and the creation of a Satanic Age and a Satanic Empire on Earth. To achieve this aim, various tactics, or means, are required. Some are:

Existing power structures and thus societies need to be disrupted and re-shaped, enabling some of them to be used to create a Satanically inspired society or societies.[10]

*The means and techniques of achieving Adeptship, and thus real individual freedom, need to be made known, thus enabling an upturn in genuine Adepts. These Adepts will form an elite, and from this elite influence will be gained and the sinister implemented. Some of this elite may well take or hold or influence various forms of political power in the future when disruption/destabilization occurs on a large scale.

Each of these involves certain specific things. For instance, a Satanically inspired society could well be of a fascist/National Socialist type – i.e. this type of society would achieve or could achieve certain Satanic goals either directly or via the dialectic of change, and thus aid the ultimate goal: a New, Satanic, Aeon. Accordingly, such views and the organizations upholding them would be aided, mostly

---

[10] See Addendum at end of MS.

secretly. Esoterically, the creation of an Imperium by a charismatic individual (Vindex) would be aided both by magickal means and more directly. Vindex would be a nexion for the dark forces.

Essentially, NS type politics is considered as, at this moment of aeonic time, aiding the sinister dialectic, and an NS society as one of the first stages in changing evolution toward the sinister on a large scale. One of the primary goals of Imperium must be the conquest of Space. [This assessment arises from Aeonics.]

The disruption of existing forms is necessary, whatever tactics (such as politics) are used to aid the sinister Aeon. Disruption means the destabilization of societies – particularly Western ones, where global power at present resides. On the practical level, this means that the societies must be made the breeding ground for the tactical forms chosen. The peoples must yearn for something – and what they yearn for must be given to them. That is, their instinctive yearning will be controlled, psychically, via sinister Adepts. They will be made ready, psychically and practically, for what power-structures are required. To achieve this, various archetypal energies must be used and directed, and some implanted in the 'collective unconscious' (e.g. by using archetypes manipulating them – and creating new archetypal forms).

Further, societies must be destabilized on the practical level. This will be achieved in two ways – via using sinister magickal energies, and by aiding practical disruption. The first means an increase in chaotic type energies: sinister random energies which infect susceptible individuals and drive them to do certain things, to disrupt, cause chaos, spread evil and so on. The second means aiding those things which will undermine societies – e.g. drugs, pornography, crime, political unrest, economic misfortune, racial and other social tensions (including religious ones).

Of paramount importance is disrupting those large, influential power structures, the United States of America and the Soviet Union. Without these structures (both of which are forms of Nazarene/Magian control and influence) the natural, disruptive forces within those States and within the States which are covertly controlled/influenced by them, would re-emerge, making it easier for the strategic goal to be achieved. That is, without these two power structures, contending rival States would emerge both within Europe and world-wide. There would be many wars as long-suppressed conflicts were fought out, just as the naturally strong and aggressive would re-assert themselves by using force. In short, natural forces would take over.

In the case of the Soviet Union, the tactics are to use magickal forces to disrupt – and to encourage those elements which seek the destruction of the Soviet bloc. The former involves directing magickal energies at the power structures and seeding susceptible minds with certain disruptive/chaotic/directed forms: e.g. the performance of rites, both ceremonial and hermetic, with] specific aims. [Exoterically, the Dark Gods would be invoked, via Nine Angles type rites, and sent to disrupt/provoke change.] The latter is more restricted, at the time of writing, due to lack of practical influence in that sphere – but three areas to encourage are: 1) The dissemination of Satanic ideas in the countries under Soviet control/influence and in countries where influence can be spread into those countries (e.g. Eastern Europe); 2) The spread of heretical views (e.g. with regard to National Socialism, the Holocaust etc.); 3) Aiding the emergence/influence of Islam to undermine Communist ideology/Nazarene ideals in certain areas.

In the case of America, the tactics are similar – to use magickal forces, and to encourage overt disruption. The former involves directing energies both chaotic and sinister to infect others; spreading Satanic ideas and methods (e.g. by making available rituals and the ideas of Satanism); and undertaking rites appropriate to destabilizing both individuals and the power structures in general. The latter involves supporting various organizations and groups on both sides of the political spectrum (to enhance disruption/breakdown); spreading subversive and heretical ideas (e.g. National Socialism); and generally trying to break down the society from within – this involves encouraging drugs, crime, and such like (which will provoke not only breakdown, but which will also provoke a reaction, which reaction will become more extreme as the breakdown becomes more extreme, this reaction aiding the emergence of natural forces and instincts). Whatever means are necessary can and should be used – the aim is to cause the American State structure to collapse, creating chaos, from which a reaction will emerge, this reaction being of a certain type – i.e. tending toward authoritarianism, anti-Nazarene in essence. This collapse of American power will free the world, and enable at present suppressed forces to emerge and take control, which forces will be beneficial to the long-term goals. Nowhere will this be more evident than in the 'Middle-East'. A tide of Islamic fundamentalism would bring great changes, enabling a beneficial alliance between the new power structure which should emerge in America.

What applies to both America and the Soviet Union applies to Europe – but America and the Soviet Union have priority at present, at least in terms of magickal energies. That is, the attack occurs on all levels, in Europe, America, the Soviet Union and world-wide (particularly in the Middle-East)[11]* – but if resources are or become stretched for whatever reason or reasons, America and the Soviet Union have priority. Adepts will immediately understand that even if the strategic aim is not achieved, the disruption/chaos caused in trying to achieve it by some of the tactics mentioned, will be Satanic. All such tactics pay homage to Satan!

ONA 1988 ev

Addendum: Since the MS was written, Soviet power has, in fact collapsed. It would be unwise at this juncture, to attribute this to magickal and other means – i.e. to see the magickal campaign as being solely responsible. What is clear, however, is that such means played a part – perhaps began the process via a psychic contagion.

---

[11] Note: It should be obvious that the aim in the Middle East is to encourage Islam this undermines both America and the Soviet Union in the short-term and prepares the ways for future alliances.

This fall now makes the United States of America the prime magickal target insofar as such workings are concerned. Here, there are 'Adepts' of the Nazarene Magian traditions to contend with.

The means of magickal disruption will continue to be:

a) Spreading already existing rites (such as in the *Black Book*) enabling others in that country to invoke/open nexions and so spread the energies those rites re-present (one of the aims of those energies being disruption).

b) Performing Nine Angles rites and directing the energies toward disrupting power structures and directing it toward targeted individuals.

c) Performing Death rites with the aim of eliminating or harming certain influential individuals.

d) Spreading existing forms (and creating new ones) which infect the psyche of individuals.

e) Continue to perform traditional ceremonies and direct their energies toward achieving disruption or aiding those causes/individuals who will assist or aid perhaps without their knowledge the sinister dialectic.

f) Direct energies into already existing nexions (and create new nexions) to aid/create those tactical forms which aid the emergence of Imperium-like forces. g) Loosing undirective/chaotic energies of sinister import.

CONCERNING THE TEMPLE OF SET

The Temple of Set, as both its High Priest and its members admit, understands what they regard as Satanism as a religion. Further, the fundamental basis on which the Temple was founded is the 'Infernal Mandate'. This mandate, it is claimed, was given to Aquino by the Prince of Darkness Himself (in his manifestation as Set) and, it is said, makes the priesthood of that Temple the only one consecrated by the Prince of Darkness – that is, only the Temple of Set is a true representation of Satanism. The Temple sees itself as a sacred guardian – it has a 'sacred duty' because its High Priest has been chosen by the Prince of Darkness.

However, these two things – which so define the Temple of Set – show that it cannot be a genuine Satanic organization. To prove this, we will consider each of these things in turn – first, the question of an· 'Infernal Mandate', and then the question of Satanism as a Religion.

Aquino maintains he has a 'sacred duty' because of the mandate, and that this mandate gives him authority to consecrate his Priesthood. Further, he claims that only this Priesthood is truly consecrated to the Prince of Darkness. What this means in practice, is that the Temple of Set has set itself up to be the unique representative of Satanism.

In reality, Aquino claims to have received a Mandate during some magickal working and thereby claims authority. A genuine Satanist, on the contrary, has authority by virtue of his or her Wisdom – and has achieved Wisdom by virtue of practical experience. There is no need to claim a 'spiritual' authority given by some 'entity' real or imagined be that entity Satan or Set or whatever. Indeed, to so claim such authority via an entity external to oneself exposes the person who so makes the claim as needing this spiritual crutch because they lack real Wisdom – that is, they rely on something external to themselves, something external to their own achievements. Such an individual has to rely on something external because what really matters is missing – what is missing is that which is created by the following of the Black Arts to the ultimate ending. That is, direct practical experience and the mastery and wisdom which are thereby won.

A genuine Satanic Master (or Mistress) does not need to pose – they do not need to claim they have a mandate. The authority of a real Master or Mistress arises from their experience – it is rooted in them by virtue of their character and is evident in their eyes, their attitude and their knowledge. They have a unique, individual character – they do not playa 'role' or claim to be in touch or have been in touch with some supra-personal entity. What they say and teach is based on their own experiences, on their own learning – they have struggled along the Path for many years, and learnt the hard way, via direct experience. They know because they have done.

Accordingly, anyone who claims and need to rely on a mandate given to them – either by some entity or someone who instructed them – reveals themselves to be a charlatan.

To make this even clearer, I shall be personal for a few sentences. I represent a certain Satanic Order – and in a sense I therefore have some 'authority'. But I have this authority because, in this Order, I have gone further than anyone I have experienced more, and so learned some things. Perhaps I have gained some Wisdom – I certainly have esoteric knowledge and skills beyond that of most others. What I say and do arises from my experience – it results from years of effort along the Left Hand Path. My authority is because of my character – a character forged via experience. Even though I had been Initiated by a Satanic Mistress who instructed me for a while, my authority does not derive from her – or from Satan. It derives from my own character. Others can learn from me if they wish they are free to judge what I say or write or create, and learn from it and use it should they wish. They must assess its worth for themselves. I do not make out what I say or write or do to be anything other than mine – except where it concerns some traditions: learned from my Mistress. But even these are to be judged on their own merits – there is nothing special about them, nothing 'Infernal' in the sense of a mandate attached to them. They have not been 'sanctified' by the Prince of Darkness Himself – they are not 'sacred' truths. In brief, there is nothing of a religious nature attached to me, the authority I have or those teachings I have inherited and substantially added to. I stand on my own merits, and my creations likewise.

The same is true for any genuine Satanist. Why? Because it is in the nature of Satanism. This leads us to the second question: Satanism as a religion.

The whole of Satanism is a defiance against the religious attitude. Satanism is a rebellion against all those forms which hold or try to hold our existence, our being, in thrall – and the most potent form of thralldom has been and still is, religion. Religion emasculates us – whether it be overtly, via a religion, or covertly by a religious attitude such as is evident in political or social zealousness, in conformity to a dogma and an authority.

Satanism, in essence, is an individual defiance – an individual pride, an individual striving, an individual quest for excellence. It is about fulfilling the potential inherent in our existence – and this means finding and fulfilling our unique Destinies. Satanism means self-effort, self-learning, self-experience: it means each individual striving to become like a god; striving to be like the Prince of Darkness Himself. The Prince of Darkness does not seek weak, docile followers: He desires Comrades, individuals of strength, of Character, full of pride and defiance, overflowing with existence itself (which is expressed in deeds, in creation, in changing, in altering evolution). of course, He (and all genuine Satanists) use others for Satanic ends – they manipulate. He, as Satanists of character do, has followers – have those who obey. But these are not Satanists, they are tools, used to achieve something, perhaps broken, but mostly discarded when what they have been used for has been achieved. They are the dominated, the slave-majority, While the Satanists are the elite, the masters.

Satanists are never constrained – they learn for themselves, via experience, and so progress toward greater understanding, toward a new existence. It is the aim of Satanism to produce unique individuals possessed of character. Accordingly, a genuine Satanic Master or Mistress or group merely guides others merely offers advice, based on experience. There are no restrictions, no religious zeal. There is not and cannot be any dogma – any authority which the individual must be subservient to. There cannot be any form of conformity. If there is it is not Satanic.

The Temple of Set constrains its members by dogma, by ethics, by making them subservient to the authority of the priesthood, and to the High Priest himself. It fosters a religious attitude – 'believe! because I/we are empowered by Set/the Prince of Darkness and so possess his authority'. It restrains – 'do not associate with that person/organization, for they are proscribed'. It breeds a sycophancy, stifling genuine experience and creativity.

Naturally, there any many fine-sounding words and phrases, a great deal of intellectualism, which obscures these brutal truths. The Temple of Set encourages verbiage at the expense of real, dark, sinister experiences. Its members wallow in the illusory world created by words and ideas when they should be alone undergoing formative ordeals. They play at magic(k) and enjoy the glamour of pretending to be 'Satanists' – but they do not go to and beyond the limits of their lives, they do not live life as a succession of ecstasies, they do not go to 'the edge' again and again. Instead, they correspond With one another, meet and talk, meet and talk, do little rituals together or alone, read, and talk and read and write " and they know they are safe – the Prince of Darkness has been tamed: he is not really 'evil' (as we are not, they say to themselves and mean it). and they have their 'progress' mapped out for them – awarded to them by the Priesthood in whom they trust and by Aquino, their High Priest. If they please this priesthood, and Aquino, they are rewarded – exalted to the higher grade and can give themselves and call themselves an exalted name: priest, perhaps, or Adept, or maybe even Magister Temple if they have truly been sycophantic enough for long enough.

Meanwhile, the few genuine Satanists get on with their hard tasks – with following the path of Black Magick by their own efforts, by learning for themselves the hard way. The work to achieve a real mastery, of themselves, of magick making errors, perhaps, but learning, and so growing, so changing and so becoming a changer of evolution itself. For them, there are no restraints, no dogma, no authority. There is only success – or failure. They achieve their own Grades, in their own time, and have the self-honesty and the insight to know if they have really achieved.

One illustration to end with. Consider the path of Satanism as a marathon race. There is a start, and a finish, which we will consider to be Adeptship in this instance. Satanists and would-be Satanists line up at the start. The race begins. The Satanist runs the race, and finishes, by his or her own effort – there is no help, only the will to finish, the hardship of the race itself. It is an individual achievement. But the Temple of Set members are those who run some of the distance, and then find someone running alongside (or perhaps driving along would be more apt) saying 'The rules have been changed! By a decree [read by an 'Infernal Mandate'].The marathon is now only 10 miles – so stop and   will award you your certificates [read 'confer Grades'].' The Temple of Set members of course believe this person, they do not doubt the Decree – or if they do, they accept it. They stop, and receive their 'rewards' – and believe they have succeeded: they have run a marathon. But in reality, they have deluded only themselves.

To conclude: The Temple of Set is the epitome of what Satanism is not.

Anton Long ONA

HOSTIA III

HOSTIA

Secret Teachings of the ONA

Volume III

Printed & Published by: Thormynd Press PO Box 700 Shrewsbury Shropshire England

ADEPTSHIP – ITS REAL MEANING AND SIGNIFICANCE

Attaining real Adeptship is more difficult than being selected for, and training with, a 'Special Forces' unit (such as the British SAS). I shall explain why this is so, but first will describe what genuine Adeptship is.

An Adept is an individual who has undertaken an Occult quest and who has, as a result of that quest, the following abilities/attributes: a)' a real understanding of esoteric, Occult matters, and a deep esoteric knowledge/insight;

b) esoteric skills – chief of which is empathy: with both natural and 'Occult' forces/energies. An important aspect of this empathy [an intuitive understanding of things as those things are in their essence] is with living beings and that species mis-named Homo Sapiens Sapiens;

c) a unique character – formed via experience;

d) a unique 'philosophy of life' attained via self-discovery and self-experience – by finding answers unaided. Adeptship results from a transformation – a transmutation of the individual.] This begins at Initiation, whether that be ceremonial or hermetic [i.e. as part of a group or alone]. It is an internal alchemical process of change .and occurs on all levels – the psychic, the magickal, the intellectual, the psychological and the physical. It is the birth of a new individual who has skills, knowledge, understanding and judgement not possessed by the majority. The changes themselves arise from a synthesis – there is an evolution of the] individual and their consciousness because of a successful response to a challenge. Or rather, because of a series of such successful responses over a period of some years. In essence, the Initiate undertakes a challenge, strives to achieve a certain goal, and if successful, grows in character, maturity, knowledge, esoteric skill and so on. They then move on to new challenges, until the process is complete and Adeptship attained. The challenges themselves occur on all the levels mentioned above – i.e. the psychic, the magickal (or Occult), the intellectual, the psychological and the physical.

Essentially, the path to Adeptship is a quest which involves ordeals, the achievement of goals and so on. Furthermore, the quest is individual and involves experiences in the real world: not just 'in the head' or of a 'magickal' nature. By its nature it is solitary – it involves the individual overcoming the challenges, undertaking the ordeals, alone. If certain ordeals and challenges and experiences are not undertaken – and if all of them are not done alone – then there is no real achievement and thus no genuine Adeptship. The nature of the experiences, challenges and ordeals which are necessary, and the fact that they all must be done alone and unaided, makes Adeptship difficult to attain, and is the reason why real Adepts are rare, although there are many who claim the achievement. Returning to the example mentioned above – that is, real Adeptship is more difficult to attain than being selected for and successfully training with a Special Forces unit. The selection procedures for such a Unit are tough, and the training likewise. But the individual undergoing them has a definite, concrete goal – and that individual is with others: there is a camaraderie, a desire not to 'lose face' in front of others. Also, the individual is in a definite environment – usually a training camp with Instructors and other members of the Unit. There is a 'tradition' with its special signs: a uniform, a beret, an insignia. and everyday concerns – food, shelter etc. – are taken care of.[12]

In contrast, the goal of Adeptship is mostly intangible: id seems 'magickal' and Occult; part of another world. Further, the Initiate is on their own and still lives, for the most part, In the 'real world' – they have responsibility to clothe and feed themselves (at the very least) and find or have some shelter.

But there is more. The physical challenges alone which an aspirant Adept must undertake are, in fact, more difficult, more tough, than

---

[12] Except, of course, during training exercises of the survival kind – but these are limited, in time and space, and part of 'the course' which is real and known.

those used by any Special Forces unit. They are more testing, more selective. Only the strongest, the most determined, survive them. Add to these physical challenges the many others that are required – intellectual, magickal. psychological and soon – and it is easy to understand why Adepts (or genuine ones at least) are so rare. and why they are part of an elite.

Of course, there are many – in fact, most – who call themselves Occultists of whatever Path or none, who maintain that such things are not required for Adeptship to be achieved. [I shall describe in detail the actual challenges themselves shortly.]

These Occultists maintain that Adeptship is actually one or more of the following:

(a) amassing a great amount of what passes for 'esoteric knowledge' by, for example? reading a lot of books and magazines, and by attending various meetings/discussions/conferences/participating ni 'Magic(k)al' forays; (b) being given the title 'Adept', by either (i) someone else for services rendered or whatever, or (ii) undertaking a self-written/published 'Rite' after which one congratulates oneself and uses the title Adept; (c) achieving an 'enlightenment' during some stupor/trance/communication ceremony/working/ritual/discussion with a supra-personal entity/extra-terrestrial intelligence; (d) being 'chosen' by someone/some entity/some extra-terrestrial intelligence; (e) hanging around the Occult scene for so long that one feels entitled to call oneself an Adept.

All of these are merely delusions of attainment. I do not expect this article to shatter the delusions and illusions of the deluded – for they need them and the false Adepts will continue to fantasize about their achievement just as many individuals will continue to fantasize about belonging to or having belonged to. various Special Forces units. What this article will do is to present the real meaning and significance of Adeptship in a way which is not open to mis-interpretation: to reveal, for once and for all, the illusions of

Occultists for what they are, and thus what is really necessary for genuine Adeptship.

Among the challenges an Adept has successfully undertaken. are the following:

1) Several physical (and mental) goals of which the minimum standards are (a) walking 32 miles carrying a pack weighing not less than 30 lbs in under 7 hours over difficult hilly terrain; (b) running 20 miles in less than 2 ½ hours over fell-like/mountainous terrain; (c) cycling not less than 200 miles in 12 hours.

2) Having organized and run for not less than six months, a magickal/Occult group/coven/Temple of not less than seven people and performed ceremonial and hermetic rituals regularly.

3) Having found and loved (and probably lost) at least one 'magickal companion and worked with them in a magickal and personal way over a period of many months.

4) Having attained an understanding and mastery of esoteric magick – external and internal – via practical workings over a concentrated period of time lasting at least two years. and, following this, have begun to understand what is beyond external and internal magick – i.e. Aeonic magick and processes.

5) Having experienced in real-life situations, danger involving one's possible death.

6) Having faced many and severe dilemmas of a personal and 'moral' nature, the resolution of which required a choice and which consequently brought a maturity of outlook and a sadness. 7) Having spent at least three months living totally alone in an isolated area without talking to anyone and without any modern comforts and distractions.

8) Having developed one's intellect by hitherto foreign to one: e.g. advanced mastering a complex and abstract subject mathematics, the Star Game; symbolic Magick.

Show me someone who has not done the above (or very similar things) alone and who claims to be an Adept, and I will show you a liar – be that liar aware of the lie, or unaware of it. For too long, the intentional and unintentional liars have had no one to challenge them – and their characterless version of 'Adeptship' or 'Adepthood'.

All the challenges enumerated above breed character. They are formative; they create the Adept. and those mentioned are only some of the challenges an Initiate must successfully experience and triumph over – there are many more.

There is no easy way, no easy path, to Adeptship. The journey takes years, and involves self-effort, self-discovery, unaided. It involves triumphs, and mistakes – and learning from one's mistakes. But perhaps most of all it involves a commitment and a learning from practical experience.

However, it should be remembered that Adeptship is not the end of the quest. There are stages beyond, which require even more difficult and dangerous experiences – which need even more self-honesty. For conventionally, Adeptship is only half-way between Initiation and the ultimate goal, sometimes described as the gateway to immortality.

As with Adeptship, there are many who claim to have been to the stages beyond Adeptship – who claim to be 'Masters' or Grand Masters, or even the stage beyond! Like most 'Adepts', these are liars, both intentional and unintentional, and they will be exposed in another iconoclastic article.

ONA 1992 eh

MASTERY – ITS REAL MEANING AND SIGNIFICANCE

Mastery is one of the names given to the achievement, by an individual, of one of the advanced stages of the Occult way or path. In the septenary tradition – which some regard as the authentic Western tradition in contradistinction to the Hebrew 'Qabalah' – this stage is the fifth of the seven that mark the quest. and those who reach it are often known by the titles Master of Temple or Mistress of Earth.

It follows from the stage of Internal Adept. which is the stage of Adeptship [qv. the MSS 'Adeptship – its Real Meaning and Significance]. Between the two, lies an area often called 'The Abyss'. Basically, an Internal Adept [or simply 'Adept' for short: an 'Internal' Adept is distinguished from an 'External' Adept by virtue of the former having achieved an internal, as well as an external insight/understanding and a skill in both internal and external magick] has discovered the nature of their unique Destiny in the real world. That is, they are aware of personal wyrd. Before they can venture into and beyond the Abyss, this Destiny has to be strived for – the Adept has to make real. ln the real world, this dream of Destiny.

For every Adept, the Destiny' is unique. But for all it means an interaction with the real world – in effect transforming their inner vision and energies – in a practical way and so in some way (often quite significant) changing the real world. All Adepts effect changes in others. Some do this in a directly magickal way – for instance, by running a Temple/group and teaching esoteric traditions. Some do it via creativity – for instance, music, Art, writing. Some do it via direct action, which appears to non-Initiates as divorced from Occultism – for instance, politics or business. Some combine elements of all of these. There are many other ways. What is important is that the Adept is using their skills and abilities, derived from achieving Adeptship, in a practical way – their life has a vitality, a purpose, a dynamism which is beyond that of most others.

While this is occurring, the Adept is learning and evolving further. For some Adepts, the majority in fact, this interaction, this striving for a Destiny, is totally satisfying. In effect, their wyrd is this Destiny. [Note: wyrd and Destiny are not identical. Wyrd is beyond, but includes personal Destiny. The 'Tree of Wyrd' comprises all the seven spheres or stages of the Occult quest.] In esoteric terms, they possess no desire to progress further; and usually their desire to follow the Occult path to its ending fades, slowly, and then is lost in everyday and personal concerns. Their quest has been a phase of their lives – a rewarding one, but nevertheless a phase, which they mostly consider they have 'outgrown'. However, some Adepts see and understand this Destiny in a different way. Or, rather, they feel it differently after a number of years of striving.

They gradually become aware of what is beyond, in esoteric terms: they understand this Destiny as a part of their wyrd, and that wyrd as the 'dialectic of change'. In essence, they understand in a real, complete way [i.e. not just 'in theory'] what Aeonic magick is – of how their life and deeds are part of an Aeonic imperative.

Of course, all Adepts – if they are genuine – understand the rudiments of Aeonic theory. But this is a purely intellectual, abstract, understanding. It is cerebral, devoid of numinosity. Further, most Adepts are aware of the rudiments of Aeonic magick – but, once again, this awareness is cerebral. What occurs in some Adepts is that by the very process of striving to achieve a personal Destiny in the real world, they gradually come to understand what Aeonics really means, in personal and supra-personal terms: they experience Aeonic magick via their striving. This makes it real to them in a meaningful way – cerebral understanding is mostly a vacuous understanding.

In essence, therefore, the esoteric understanding of these Adepts grows in the only way real esoteric understanding does – via practical experience of the realities. They acquire more insight into the world, the Cosmos and themselves. On the psychic level, the energy which imbued their personal Destiny. which gave them the vitality, the 'élan' to pursue it, wanes. They begin to seek after something else – they

300

desire what seems to be an intangible wyrd. Thus, they move toward 'The Abyss' after some years of striving in the real world, of garnishing experiences, of learning from them. In effect, the self-image, which Adeptship created, is waning. [Note: Initiation creates an 'ego-image'; an External Adept has both an ego-image and the beginnings of a self-image. An Internal Adept has achieved a self-image: a certain unity of conscious and unconscious/pre-conscious forms. This self-image is vitalized by a Destiny.]

For a period, the Adept lies between two-images: the self-image which has almost died, and an intangible but tantalizing wyrd-image. This is often a most difficult time in the personal life of the Adept. There is nothing and no one to help them.

Gradually, they may achieve more understanding and come to understand the real essence hidden behind appearance: in themselves, others, the structures of the world, the cosmos itself. They will also come to realize what is missing from their own life – in terms of experience. Accordingly, they will redress the balance by living to attain what they lacked, to fully complete themselves. This, of course, is difficult, requiring as it does not only a genuine self-honesty and awareness, but also a real understanding of what the balance itself actually is. Here, 'theory', book-learning and such like is no use.

Then, when some balance is achieved, there will be a discovery of the essence of not only Aeonic Magick but also what the essence of magickal forces really are. A dis-covery of that which is beyond opposites – a return to and a going away from, primal Chaos.

Following all this, there is usually an ordeal which is magickally ruthless which ascertains if the person undertaking it has actually achieved both an internal and a magickal mastery. In the septenary tradition, this ordeal is the Grade Ritual of Master/Mistress which involves the candidate walking. alone and unaided and carrying all food etc., a distance of 80 miles in isolated terrain, starting at sunrise on the first day and ending at sunset on the second day. After reaching the target distance, a magickal ritual is performed which is psychically dangerous. Then, there is a certain satisfaction of having achieved the stage of Master of Temple/Mistress' of Earth.

Naturally, the above is only a brief outline of the transition from Adept to Master or Mistress. The salient points are that it involves many years of striving for something in the real world, of causing changes via a Destiny; that there are and must be more experiences to take the individual far beyond 'the self'; and that there is a real understanding of what lies beyond external and internal magick – of the patterns and processes of dialectic change, of evolution itself: in brief, of Aeonics, a real Mastery of forms.

To provoke or cause the individual to go beyond 'the self', the experiences of necessity are hard. By their nature they take the Adept to and beyond the limits of living – mostly in a way more extreme than those which form the character of an Adept and which therefore a novice may undertake to experience and learn from and so grow.

Because of all this, the Adept who progresses to the stage beyond possesses real wisdom. They have achieved many things. They are different from ordinary mortals –inside, where it matters. They know because they have experienced: because they have seen more of life; because they have been to the limits of themselves and gone beyond what they were. and because they have maintained their resolve to follow the Occult path they have chosen to its ending.

In effect, they belong to a new race – they are part of an elite more exclusive than that to which Adepts belong. They have developed a significant part of their latent potential; have fully understood themselves, the world, the people in it. The esoteric or hidden forces in the world, and the Cosmos itself.

This does not mean that they are infallible or that they have nothing more to learn. Neither are they deceived by their own abilities and [understanding. They are, however, aware of what it is they must do. conversant with their own abilities and the dialectic of change. That is, they know how to use Aeonic Magick to affect evolution – and do so, for their own life is a part of the creative change necessary.

Most who claim to be a 'Master' (or 'Mistress') – are charlatans. As with the false Adepts. they appoint themselves to this title, or are appointed to it by someone who claims to have progressed even further. They have not achieved it. They have not achieved anything significant in creative terms; have little or no self-understanding; possess no real knowledge of Aeonics and Aeonic Magick. They have not lived their limits – and gone beyond them. They have no 'genius', no wisdom. They are still full of self-delusion, particularly about their esoteric knowledge and their own abilities, and have no real insight into others, let alone themselves. In fact. many who claim to be 'Masters' lack even the basic qualities of an Adept.

The same applies – even more so – to they who claim to have gone beyond the stage of Mastery, and I shall explain why in words which will expose them for the frauds that they are.

The stage beyond that of Master – often signified by the title Grand Master – requires for its achievement significant Aeonic works. That is. it requires the person to have produced profound changes in the causal and magickal forms which mark a particular Aeon: or to have actually presenced esoteric/magickal energies in such a way that a new Aeon is created. This does not mean that someone believes they have done these things –'on the magickal level'. It means that the structure of evolution has been significantly altered in accord with the wyrd of that Grand Master/Mistress: and in such a way that the changes are perceptible, in real life. In those forms and structures which Aeonic energy is presenced in the causal, such as societies.

This does not mean a playing at magick by heading some self-created Occult organization or Temple – or writing/talking at great length about Occult matters. Neither does it mean that one assumes the title by taking over some already existing organization or group. It most certainly does not mean someone else awards it or confers it.

Further, it means one has not only reached the limits of present knowledge regarding Aeonics and other esoteric matters [and knowledge in the sense of practical experience] but has also extended those limits by one's own creativity – taken conscious evolution further. That is, added in a profound way to a conscious understanding and to the means for others to attain such understanding. This in itself does not mean anything 'dogmatic' or of a religious nature – or 'given to one' by some entity/supra-personal intelligence or whatever. It is never 'revelatory' in the sense of a religion. That is, it does not mean one is 'appointed' by some entity/extra-terrestrial intelligence or whatever and so 'heads' some sort of messianic crusade of a religious nature.

The frauds indulge in pseudo-mystical babble and Occult histrionics – they expect and mostly demand obedience. They play a 'role' and often dress the part. of course, by doing these and similar things they obtain followers, sycophants – i.e. weak individuals who need to fawn and obey. All the frauds rely on something external to themselves, be this something a 'role', a mandate, a divine/diabolic revelation, an imagined/real lineage, an organizational authority, a messianic/diabolic/extra-terrestrial commission or whatever.

In reality, all these traits and actions are signs of someone not yet achieved Adeptship – someone striving for self-insight.

A real Grand Master (or Mistress) has a wealth of practical experience both Occult and 'in the real world'. They have genius – a highly developed intellect and creativity. They possess empathy in the highest degree. They have Judgement. They possess a critical awareness and understanding of all those factors and forms which have and do shape and change our evolution both conscious and unconscious from individuals to Aeons. and they are unique – 'their own person'. They owe allegiance to no one and they are not constrained by any affectation or role (such as conforming to the imagined image of a Master or Grand Master or 'teacher'). Like genuine Masters and Mistresses, they are spontaneous and human, without affectation of 'knowledge' or 'cleverness'. Neither do they-pretend to be 'venerable' .

There are perhaps two or three genuine Grand Masters/Mistresses a century – and that is all. and this is unlikely to change, given the present capacity of individuals to delude themselves and given the fact that few are prepared to undertake the really hard and difficult struggle that lasts for at least a quarter of a century and which creates such a unique entity.

As regards the last stage of the Occult way, which the septenary tradition describes by the term Immortal and which the distorted and inauthentic tradition of the 'Qabalah' describes as the stage of the 'Ipssisimus' [and I had to look-up how to spell the word], this really is not obtainable except In the last few years of the causal existence of a Grand Master/Mistress who has created for themselves an acausal and thus Immortal existence. Thus, anyone claiming this title in the causal or mortal world is, 'ipso facto', a fraud – and one who has little or no knowledge of real esoteric matters. Those who so claim, show themselves up to be not even a genuine Master or Mistress – and seldom, if ever, even an Adept.

As Aeschylus once explained – παθει μαθοσ : one can learn through adversity/ suffering as so achieve wisdom. Before this 'law', people suffered, but did not learn. Most Occultists have never suffered, and so learn nothing; they eschew ordeals, and teal life experiences, in favour of mystical meanderings and a religious mentality. Or they find comfort, an escape in the Occult.

A real Occult quest involves adversity – undertaking hardships, surmounting real physical, mental and psychic challenges; forging into the unknown, alone. Questing through adversity to transform one's existence.

It takes years of self-effort and adversity, of accepting challenges and triumphing, to achieve real self-insight and genuine esoteric understanding, and thus to become an Adept. It takes even greater effort and adversity and learning to go beyond that.

Real wisdom is still, unfortunately, a precious commodity. The esoteric path to Wisdom is open to all – its techniques and methods work. But such is the primitive self-awareness of most people that they cannot appreciate this or be bothered to undertake a real quest in search of the next stage of existence. So the Occult babbling will continue, and the frauds claim their titles. *De nihlo nihil fit.*

ONA 103yf

ARTHURIAN LEGEND
ACCORDING TO THE SECRET SINISTER TRADITION

There is a secret oral tradition regarding the person known as 'King Arthur' which deserves recording. According to this tradition:

1) Arthur was a 'Romano-British' chieftan.

2) His wife was called Gonnore, and her father was a chieftan whose base was the fortified site now known as 'old Oswestry'.

3) Arthur's base – and thus 'Camelot' – was the city of Viroconium (present-day Wroxeter in Shropshire).

This city was the' capital of a prosperous and powerful war-lord and British chieftain Vortigern (c. 450 ev). It was also associated with the-war-lord Ambrosius, who was of Roman descent.

Arthur maintained a continuity and a certain style of life 'Romano-British'. He followed in the tradition of Vortigern and Ambrosius, being a powerful chief tan whose rule extended far. He flourished after Ambrosius – c.500 ev.

4) Arthur and his people were pagans. Their beliefs were indigenous ones, connected with gods and goddesses.

5) Arthur faught many battles to secure his kingdom from rivals. Some of his battles were with invading tribes – but for the most part, these new tribes settled peacefully into what is now England. There was more assimilation than there was conquest. [The idea of 'barbarous hordes' ruthlessly invading is a myth – created by later generations and part of a Nazarene indoctrination campaign.]

6) One of his relatives – known under the later name of 'Modred' sided with some of his enemies (i.e. rival chieftains) and Arthur faught against him in a battle in which he was badly wounded. The

site of this battle was near the Camlad River and the modern Shropshire hamlet of Wotherton. Arthur returned to his stronghold via a lake called now 'Marton Pool', near Worthen (SW of Shrewsbury). At the time, this lake had an island – a mound containing a grove of trees. The place was regarded as sacred, and the waters were reputed to have healing powers. The island was an abode of a goddess, and a Priestess lived there. This was the 'Lady of the Lake'. This mound still exists, although today it is not surrounded by water, as the Lake has shrunk to become a Pool.

7) The 'Merlin' of legend was actually a pagan wise-man who was adviser to Arthur. The abode of this person was the area around the west of the Long Mynd.

8) After his final battle, Arthur returned mortally wounded to his city, where he was burled. Sometime later, the city was peacefully evacuated, as it had become undefencable. A new stronghold was founded on a mound between a loop of the river Severn, and Arthur was re-buried here. This mound served as one of the seats of the Kings of Powys – much later a town grew up around it called Scrobbesbyrig. The town was later called Shrewsbury. One early name for this mound was said to be the 'hill of the Alders' A Nazarene Church now stands near the site of Arthur's tomb.

9) Arthur's 'clan-symbol' was a Dragon.

SATANISM – OR LIVING ON THE EDGE

Genuine Satanists are at the sharp end: they act. They strive for and implement their personal Destiny and they work for the fulfillment of sinister strategy. That is, by their lives, by their ways of living, they actively aid the creative forces of Darkness. Or, expressed another way, they do the work of the Prince of Darkness.

In contrast, the dabblers, the psueds, keep themselves secure in their imaginary and fantasy 'Satanic' worlds – with correspondence, meetings, conclaves, discussions; with performing and writing/reading about worthless Occult rites; with their babbling about their pseudo-mystical fantasies.

A Satanist will be living Satanically – and will therefore be dangerous, in the real world. They will do Satanic deeds rather than just talk or write about them. He or she will be, for instance, disrupting society in a practical way, or working to actively create a new, revolutionary society which is more Satanic. They might be real heretics – fighting against the State either politically or via armed warfare if that State (as most Western ones do) upholds the Nazarene sickness of spirit (evident in modern political ideas like 'liberalism' and 'humanism' and 'equality': the triumph of the worthless at the expense of the noble). Or perhaps they will be aiding the collapse of such a State, and fostering a reaction, by morally undermining it, for example by dealing in drugs or pornography. Or maybe they will be teachers in influential positions, subverting others in secret towards Satanism or those transient forms Satanism often assumes to gain control and influence. Or they might be actively culling the worthless, the scum – by being a vigilante, or a zealous, honourable Police officer...

Whatever, they will have a direction, a purpose, an intent which goes beyond the edification of their own ego. They will be working to achieve something great by Virtue of which they can excel in their own lives and thus really live to the full. They will be developing and using their potential, their skills – and thus exulting in life, in overcoming challenges. They will be contributing toward their own

309

evolution and that of existence itself because they are harnessing in a practical way the darker forces.

This direction, purpose and intent is Satanic strategy, or Aeonics. A rational and thus conscious understanding of those forces which shape and change evolution and the forms assumed by sentient life from individuals to societies to civilizations and Aeons.

It is this sinister or Satanic strategy which makes genuine Satanism what it is, and it is knowledge and understanding of this strategy which marks the genuine Satanic Initiate from the imitation.

A Satanist not only acts in a certain way – achieving things in real life – but they know what they are doing; they possess perspective. An Initiated knowledge. This 'knowledge' is not primarily of the psuedo-mystical kind, to do with rituals or other Occult workings/techniques. Rather, it is primarily concerned with how and why certain things are as they are, and how those things can be altered or changed. In essence, it is about how cosmic forces interact With and change/evolve life – about the mechanisms by which Aeons, civilizations, societies and ultimately individuals grow, are or can be influenced and changed.

In the past few decades, many professedly Satanic organizations have arisen, and some have propounded various aspects of the genuine Satanic world-view. But almost without exception they have shown themselves to be lacking in real esoteric knowledge – i.e. Aeonics. Quite often, someone from one of these organizations will 'sound-off' and reveal their ignorance, particularly concerning the actions of real Satanists in the real world. For instance, it has become fashionable in these psuedo-Satanic circles to castigate individual Satanists, or a Satanic group, if that individual or group becomes involved in Politics – particularly if those Politics are on what is often termed the 'extreme Right'. What the ignorant writers and/or speakers in question have not understood, is that such political action is chosen Satanically – to achieve things, both for the individual(s) concerned and for Satanism in general. That is, those who are so involved are so because they are consciously and with ruthless determination aiding the sinister dialectic: i.e. Satanic strategy. They are living on the edge – causing and aiding change/disruption in real life.

The ignorance of the psuedo-Satanists is revealed in another area – ethics. There is not and cannot be any such thing as Satanic ethics. What there are, are means to achieve Satanic goals and the means are a matter for the individual Satanist striving to achieve those goals. That is, it is for each and every Satanist to decide, for themselves, what is or is not acceptable. This is so because Satanism, in essence, is individual – it is not nor can ever be, religious in any way. Those who believe Satanism is or should be religious, do not understand Satanism at all.

As I have written and said many times, Satanism is an individualized defiance and affirmation: one of the fundamental aims of Satanism is to produce or develope proud, strong, unique, individuals of character who possess 'spirit' or 'élan', and who possess insight and genuine esoteric knowledge. The aim is not to develope subserviant, obediant, sycophants who cannot think for themselves. Satanism aims to develope the instinct and judgement of each person – and Satanists are critical, aware and capable of assessing things and situations for themselves. Or rather, they will be, after appropriate training/guidance. I make no apology for repeating yet again the statement that the religious attitude is anathema to Satanism: Satanism is a rebellion against the religious, dogmatic, instinct.

Satanism shuns obediance to a self-appointed authority; it despises the very idea of a religious 'mandate' and it does not idolize anything – not even the individual Satanists of distinction. Satanism is at the very edge, the frontier, of conscious understanding and knowledge and Satanists are the ones who try and often succeed in extending that frontier – in bringing more of the cosmos into conscious awareness and thus control. They dare, defy, are heretical, possess the courage to dream and make their dreams of Destiny real.

Because they know themselves, others and the esoteric workings of existence, they are in control, masters. They effect change. and they acquire all these things because they possess perspective, a perspective whose foundation is Aeonics.

What, then, is Aeonics? It is an esoteric understanding, and an understanding which in these times of overt and covert Nazarene domination is heretical. It is a knowledge of the processes by which Aeons arise, change and are replaced by another Aeon, and how the creative energies of a particular Aeon are made manifest via a civilization and thus the societies within that civilization and the individuals within those societies. It is also a knowledge of how all these various forms (or causal structures) can be changed – by esoteric or magickal means, and by more practical means.

On the purely individual level, Aeonics shows and describes how the psyche/ consciousness of the individual is influenced, both directly and unconsciously, and how that individual can be changed or controlled. One form of such change is esoteric development – i.e. the techniques and so on, magickal and otherwise, by which the individual can achieve Adeptship and beyond. One form of such control is via archetypal images.

In simple terms, an Aeon is an expression of evolutionary change. In esoteric terms, it expresses how the acausal intrudes upon, and thus changes, the causal. For convenience, the causal may be described, here, as the 'everyday' world (tt: world of linear time (past, present, future) and three spatial dimensions (height, breadth, width); the world wherein we live out our lives. The acausal may be described, again simply and for convenience here, as the creative energy that drives evolution – i.e. Satan.

A civilization – or more accurately, an Aeonic civilization – is how Aeonic energy, or the acausal, is ordered in the causal – i.e. an Aeonic civilization is how change is produced in the causal. Within each such civilization there are societies, and within each society, individuals. All civilizations, Aeons and individuals are examples of organisms – they are born, change and they die (in the causal, at least). These varying organisms are born, change and end in certain ways, and these processes can be studied and thus understood. This understanding gives the means of control.

Aeonic civilizations are regarded as being tied to, or part of, a particular Aeon, and each Aeon represents a change in our evolutionary development. Thus, each Aeonic civilization represents a significant step in that development: the invention, discovery of significant things, and the development of a greater understanding – of ourselves and the cosmos.

The first Aeon is called the Primal and is dated from around 9,000 to 7,000 BP [where 'BP' represents Before the Present: i.e. c. 1990 eh]. Each Aeon, for classification, has a name and is associated with a specific geographical area, a symbol and a 'magickal working' – or how the acausal energy was perceived/understood then. All Aeons, except the Primal one, are linked to a named civilization. Further, each Aeonic civilization possesses an ethos or sense of Destiny. Aeons and their associated civilizations are listed below.

of course, there are other civilizations – but Aeonic ones are the most significant ones because they produce significant evolutionary change by virtue of being a nexion, or nexus, for acausal energy – i.e. one may consider them, in magickal terms, as giving form directly via their structures and peoples, to acausal energy. Other civilizations are linked to or derive from, these Aeonic civilizations and while they may have in some way contributed to some evolutionary change (e.g. in terms of invention/discovery) that contribution is much less than for Aeonic civilizations.

Aeon	Magickal Working	Aeonic Civilization	Aeonic Dates
Primal	Shamanism	--	9,000 - 7,000 BP
Hyberborian	Henges	Albion	7,000 - 5,500 BP
Sumerian	Trance;Sacrifice	Sumerian/Egyptiac	5,000 - 3,500 BP
Hellenic	Oracle;Dance	Hellenic	3,000 - 1,500 BP
Western	Ritual	Western	1,000BP - 500 AP

It should be obvious that the esoteric 'symbol' of the Western Aeon is 'Satan' – i.e. Nazarene religion/ethics/forms are a distortion of the Western Aeon. The exoteric expression of the Western civilization is Science &Technology: the desire to rationally discover and to exercise control over the environment via technology.

All Aeonic civilizations end in Empire, and this Empire or Imperium lasts for around 390 years. The ethos of an Aeonic civilization is mostly manifest to (non-Initiate) consciousness via archetypes and a Destiny. These archetypes and this Destiny are different for each Aeonic civilization. The Destiny is often enshrined in a literary/poetic/saga-like form, and this form, for nearly all such civilizations is of the 'hero-motif' type: the successful response of a hero or heroes to a challenge or series of challenges. For instance, the Hellenic form was Homer's *Iliad* and Virgil's *Aeneid*.

The present Western civilization is at the stage where is should be entering its Imperium (c. 1995-2385 eh). However, the natural archetypes of the Western civilization have been mostly transplanted by alien Nazarene ones – and its sense of Destiny almost lost due to Nazarene ethics and social forms.

As each Aeonic civilization enters its Imperium, the energies of the next Aeon are or can become manifest, via a nexion or 'Gate' (or 'sacred site') which channels acausal energy into causal forms. The next Aeonic civilization follows after three to four centuries – i.e. it takes that length of time for the Aeonic energies to effect large-scale changes in the acausal. Or rather, it has, until now.

This brief and simplified description of Aeonics allows sinister strategy to be understood. Aeonics describes what has and is occuring in those forces that do mould and have moulded individuals still in thrall – i.e. non-Initiates. The knowledge gains brings a genuine understanding, a perspective. It enables effective sinister magick – it enables the Satanist to act, in the real world, and produce effective changes. To really live – to play at being god: i.e. to be like Satan.

It is a fact that most magickal acts are useless – they achieve nothing, except perhaps self-delusion. Some may achieve a few, external, results edifying to the ego. and they are useless because few really understand what they are doing. They evoke long dead 'magickal' forms from past Aeonic civilizations – or rather try to; they prat about with archetypal energies they do not understand. They confuse the forms and try to use some from one Aeon and some from another. Or they try and create their own. Or they are fundamentally so esoterically ignorant ·that they are infused with psuedo-mystical garbage and fanciful 'aeons' and extra-terrestrial beings and/or diabolic entities from obscure and worthless mythologies.

The Satanist, having access to the real esoteric tradition, can work effective magick, both personally and Aeonically.

Personally, it means working with the energies/magickal forms of the present Aeon as those energies/forms are. It means eschewing the distortion which has so affected the Aeon and its civilization. One aspect of this distortion is the 'Qabala'. Thus, any 'Satanist' who uses any of the forms or symbols or whatever of or deriving from this Qabala is aiding the distortion and thus in effect undermining Satanic energies/values. That most 'Satanists' cannot see this, just shows their lack of real esoteric undertanding i.e. their lack of a genuine Satanic Initiation.

One magickal form of the genuine Western tradition, is the septenary. Another is the understanding as 'Baphomet' as one name of the dark goddess – the Bride, Lover of Satan. Yet another is the knowledge of the real origins of both the word and the form of 'Satan' – from the Hellenic, to which the Western Aeonic civilization was loosely affiliated in its origins and growth, and from which certain esoteric traditions survived. [The derivation of the word 'Satan' is from the Greek αιτια meaning 'accusation'. It became the Hebrew Satan, whence also (Sh)aitan.]

On the Aeonic level, the esoteric knowledge of Aeonics means the Satanist can judge what to do, and act both in the magickal and the practical sense.

Aeonics shows that there has been and is a distortion in the Western energies, and that, given no distortion, the Destiny of the Western civilization was Empire – i.e. the triumph of 'Satanic' values on a world-wide basis for the benefit of an elite within the Western civilization. Aeonics also shows that it is possible at this moment in time to create a nexion and thus draw forth the energies of the next Aeon – to effectively create the next Aeonic civilization.

Thus, effective courses of action are: (a) aiding the creation of an Imperium; (b) countering the distortion in order to introduce new forms/ energies; (c) opening a nexion and thus aiding/creating a new Aeon, consciously [Heretofore, most Aeons have not been created via magickal intent because the knowledge to do so was lacking.].

All of the above mean changing evolution – societies and individuals – on a significant scale. (a) involves disrupting present societies magickally and practically and aiding Imperium-like forces; (b) involves countering the Nazarene forms and those allied to it, and creating new forms and presencing them via individuals/groups/society etc. All involve aiding Satanic forces e.g. spreading Satanic ideas esoterically and exoterically; aiming to become/guiding others to become Adepts of Satanic traditions. All involve action in the world.

There is much more to Aeonics, and esoteric tradition, than this. But sufficient has been described for the real essence of Satanic living to be understood.

A Satanist has a desire to excel – to effect changes; to be significant. They are not content to just live, to just survive. The perspective of Aeonics provides an intent, a purpose, by which they can achieve not only self-excellence but also change existence – fulfil or aid the sinister dialectic. They can help to build an Imperium, where Satanic values can be realized and where combat, war, conquest and exploration can make strong and extend the frontiers, take evolution to its limits. They can ruthlessly undermine and destroy and so aid a change. They can work works of genuine sinister magick and so influence others, create new structures and archetypal forms, and kill and then dismember the corpse of the Nazarene, exultant, as they revel in their mastery. They can, in brief, fulfil a real Destiny.

Meanwhile, the psuedo-Satanists can continue playing their pathetic games and fawning on one another, achieving nothing in the long-term and probably nothing in the short-term either. They can continue imbibing the drug of delusion, and so waste their life.

Everyone has a choice – only the gifted choose wisely.

ONA 1991eh

PO Box 235-
Shrewsbury
Shropshire
England

4th November 103 yf

Dear Mr Bolton,

Thank you for the copy of the letter to the Finnish 'Setian' which was most interesting.

Enclosed herewith some further material and MSS for Review and publication, should you be interested in publishing the MSS. The two sets of essays - "NS Essays" and "Physis - Essays in Praise of NS" are now available from Rigel Press at the address above, and not from the Thormynd address. They are £1 (or US$5 cash including Air Mail) each.

In your letter, you made mention of 'generational Satanists' and their contempt for Setians because of the Setian philosophy being 'divorced from Nature'. 'Traditional Satanists' feel the same way - the Temple of Set, like the Church of Satan, seems to be a collection of urbanized individuals who enjoy playing the intellectual (or rather, psuedo-intellectual) game of Setianism. For the most part, they have lost contact with the primal both within themselves and in Nature - they need the comforts and safety of urbanized society, although some of them may occassionally play "survival" games after which they return to the comforts of their home, their family, their friends, their 'Satanic' circles and pylons. They are rather like the individuals Adolf Hitler encountered in the early years of the NSDAP who dressed up in ancient Germanic costumes but who did not have the guts to face or fight real enemies, on the streets. [There is a lovely quote in 'Mein Kampf' about this, which you might be familiar with.]

Basically, such people are soft - inside, where it matters. As one of the enclosed MSS explains; "Attaining real Adeptship is more difficult than being selected for, and training with, a 'Special Forces' unit (such as the British SAS)." In traditional Satanism, the novice has to undergo real ordeals which test their strength of character - overcome difficult physical challenges. They are expected to live Satanically in the real-world (by, for example, fighting for an "extreme Right-Wing" organization or being a vigilante), as they must, if they wish to become Adepts, spend at least three months surviving in the wild, completely alone and without any of the comforts of urbanized living. The ordeals, the living Satanically, enable them to experience the primal within themselves; while the living in the wild of course forces them to experience primal Nature, and what is really hidden in themselves. From all these comes a learning, and a real Satanic character. Or, as I have written many times, failure.

The ONA makes no concessions. The novice either undertakes the tasks, the ordeals, and methods, and succeeds; or they do not, and cannot be considered a traditional Satanist: they are failures. They have not been selected and therefore cannot be (traditional) Satanic Adepts.

In my own life, I have done all what is expected of a novice, and much more. I struggled to and beyond Adeptship, and I know there is no easy way for real achievement. For essentially, the essence of Satanism lies in the striving, the achievement, and then a moving-on to new challenges and achievements with a genuine esoteric understanding which enables perspective: i.e. the implementation of the sinister dialectic. Satanism has other facets, of course - the ceremonial, the 'esoteric knowledge of magick', the philosophy and so on. But these are really incidentals - they are not the essence.

What organizations like the Temple of Set have done, is to take some of these incidentals (and/or distorted versions of them) and set these up as 'Satanism': and they have been believed! They have duped others. They have attempted to re-make Satanism in their own image - and the result is a spineless affected psued or the cowardly ill-disciplined self-professed "magickian".

For a number of reasons, it has been necessary to increasingly attack the psuedo-Satanic organizations and to explain in greater detail the secret teachings of traditional Satanism (e.g.   relating to culling). One reason, is the appalling level of reasoning and genuine understanding shown within 'the Occult' - a lamentable comment on the ability of people to delude themselves. Another reason, is that it is clear the distortion which so affects the Faustian civilization, has affected the Left Hand Path in general and Satanism in particular. In practical and magickal terms, the Church of Satan was an infiltration of Satanism by the distortion - i.e. by the spirit of the Nazarene and those forms derived from the Nazarene (in terms of ethics, politics and so on). The Temple of Set has simply continued this distortion - affecting a few minor changes in structure and attitude, and that is all. Of course, not very many will understand what I have just written regarding the distortion, and even fewer will comprehend the Church of Satan as belonging to the same world as the Nazarene.

On one level it is an attitude to existence. The Church of Satan took some of the trappings of Satanism - which, in its genuine form, is a contradiction 'par excellence' of the distortion expressed by the Nazarene - but it gave them a spirit which was entirely alien to genuine Satanism. It took, for instance, the carnal philosophy and the morality of the strong, as well as some of the magickal symbols/forms of the Left Hand Path. But a real Satanic intent was never within those forms; there was no real Satanic knowledge, no esoteric knowledge or perspective. All the forms did was encourage a self-stupefaction, a glorification of a puny ego, and a living-in a psuedo-magickal fantasy world with 'Satanic' rituals and conclaves and 'grottoes'. In short, all the Church of Satan and its version of 'Satanism' did was encourage personal weakness, fetishes, and a purblind hedonistic individualism - as well as a religious mentality; an obediance to the 'Church' and a fawning upon its 'leader'. In brief, it did not liberate, it did not make strong - it did not encourage the creation of a new race who acted Satanically in the real world and so profoundly changed it. The Church of Satan was part of the distortion, not a cure for it.

The Temple of Set continued what the Church had started. They took or tried to take their version of Satanism into intellectual realms - and, like the Church, they had no understanding whatsoever of genuine esoteric sinister tradition. For they mixed up aeonic images and magickal forms, and used aspects of the distorted qabalistic tradition - in short, they made their 'magick' ineffective and worthless both from the personal and the Aeonic point of view. It is charitable to believe that the founders of these organizations, as well as those who enabled their survival, were just plain charlatans, fiddling or tinkering about with magick without really understanding it. They used the images and forms of Satan, Set, Baal, they delved around in mythology and found others, and created lots of fantasy images - mixed them all up; intellectually found justifications for their approach. They strung together bits of qabalistic magic with bits of Crowley; added a touch of demonism (of the Nazarene/Babylonian or whatever sort); specialized in self-created workings of the dream-image kind. The result? Something so absurd it would be laughable were it not so detrimental to real Satanic change and thus Satanic strategy.

Are you and I and a few others the only ones who understand? Who know that real sinister (or Satanic) magick involves using Aeonic energies to create change and so alter evolution? That one cannot intermingle Aeonic forms - from one Aeon and another one or two - if one hopes to affect Aeonic change? That Aeonic energies are presenced via a civilization whose ethos and archetypal and other forms hold the majority in thrall - controls them unless and until they become free via the synthesis and transmutation which is genuine Adeptship? (That is, until they have objectified those energies internally, and thus can master/control them.) That this present Aeon and thus civilization has suffered a profound change/distortion which is essentially de-evolutionary and whose most obvious form is the Nazarene sickness?

319

Satanism means this liberation from external and internal forms, assumed by Aeonic energies, and the ability to control those energies for an ulterior purpose. It means a rational knowledge of what really _is_, in both magickal and practical terms; a real insight into one's self and the cosmos.

No condemnation is too strong for organizations like the Temple of Set which foster the "status quo" of ignorance regarding genuine magick. Which have tried to appropriate the one thing which can really liberate and which can change the patterns of evolution - i.e. Satanism.

The ignorance of such organizations and the people within them is displayed all the time. For instance, they do not understand the use of politics, by Satanists, as a means to achieve evolutionary change - as part of a dialectic. All they do is condemn those who do act from a 'moral' point of view - or from an 'intellectual' one which sees their version of 'Satanism' as being "beyond politics"! Neither do they have the slightest understanding of those who provoke change and de-stabilization by appearing to do 'immoral' things, such as drug-dealing. Once again, they reveal themselves for the non-Initiates they are. I have to continually repeat that the only guiding factor for the actions of a Satanist, in real life, is the sinister dialectic - that is, will the action benefit the Satanist (in terms of their esoteric development) _and_ will it aid genuine evolutionary change: the achievement of Satanic qualities; the fulfilment of the goal of Satanism **in the long term.**

Neither I nor the ONA shies away from difficult practical issues of a Satanic nature. Consider the Satanic drug-dealer. He or she is playing a part (admittedly a small one - but such individuals have to start their Satanic careers somewhere! They have to do 'on-the-job training'!) - they are aware, because they are genuine Satanists, of what they are doing: i.e. they have a knowledge of sinister strategy. They are aiding the collapse of a worthless society, and may also be aiding the weak ones (the addicts) to cull themselves. They are also engendering a 'moral' response in others - e.g. in the Establishment. Some of those in this Establishment (e.g. Police Officers) gain real understanding by exposure to the dregs, the worthless: i.e. they develope a good instinct, from practical experience, and so see the druggies as dregs. Thus, they are ripe for conversion to a radical resurgence of noble values, politically expressed - for the sake of illustration, let us say here a radical organization of the extreme Right. They have seen the liberal/Nazarene society, and it does not work - it produces dross; encourages vermin. And so on. Naturally, this is a simplified analysis, but at least the Satanic intent of the original act - the drug-dealing - can be seen.

Of course, the Satanists are few, and secret. But that does not mean they are 'powerless'! They seek to be the real motivators of change - both of themselves, and others, in terms of society, the civilization, and the Aeon itself. Hence, they really are diabolical, and sinister. And of course **dangerous.**

The above is only one example - not all Satanists undertake such actions as dealing in drugs. Some may involve themselves in aiding/creating the political form. Some may indeed by the Police Officer. Or the Judge. Whatever, they all know what they are doing, in Aeonic terms; they are all striving to change existence, and thus themselves, by actions in the real world. They are all enjoying playing at gods and goddesses.

Naturally, only some understand in all its complexity and effects, the goal - and can plan accordingly. And can motivate, urge others, to action. These are the real Masters and Mistresses: the really diabolical and evil ones. Those who have a genuine over-view of centuries and more, of millenia.

A Satanic Adept, for instance, might intuitively understand the supra-Aeonic goal. But their rational understanding will be limited - to a century, perhaps. They will see the present goal of Satanic strategy as an Imperium and, after that, a new Aeon and a new civilization. The novice will perhaps only understand the Imperium, rationally - that is, in terms of its effects and their own Destiny. But, hopefully, their understanding will increase as they progress, as, hopefully, the number of novices and then Adepts and then Masters/ Mistresses will increase with the implementation of sinister strategy.

The Temple of Set, and the other psuedo-Satanic organizations and individuals, lack both the primal awareness (of Nature and what is within each individual) inherent in real Satanism, and the esoteric knowledge or over-view afforded by Aeonics. It is to be expected that they and these others will continue with their campaigns of dis-information against the ONA. Quite possibly, they might descend to the personal level (if they have not done so already), and reveal their ignoble spirit. By revealing the dark secrets of traditional Satanism in a way that is not open to mis-interpretation - by expressing the true nature of Satanism (e.g. in culling; Aeonic action) - we have made it difficult for them to 'defend their corner' without trying to undermine our credibility, and it will be interesting to see whether they will reduce themselves to ethical tautologies. Whatever, with all esoteric tradition and practices revealed, everyone now has the opportunity to consider the matter for themselves - assess the differing versions of Satanism 'on offer'. Which really is as it should be.

On the personal level, your own sagacity and insights merits recognition, and your work likewise. What a global conspiracy we must seem to some of our more paranoid enemies!

With best wishes,

Stephen Brown

Box 38-262
Petone
Wellington
New Zealand
20 Oct 1992

Dear Markku

      Thanks for your letter of 12 Oct., and for the two articles which I'll be pleased to publish.

      When you said that you were going to publish a Social Darwinist magazine I thought it very encouraging and relevant - obviously you've changed your mind.

      You say that primordial law is inappropriate in Satanism, that it's the opposite to the concept of Satanism as non-natural and a rebellion against the natural order, more akin to christianity. Yet all of christian history and of the TYPE of people who are attracted to christianity should tell us that such religions are outside of nature - anti-nature because of a dis-ease certain TYPES feel with themselves, shut off from the 'Tree of Life' to put it in allegorical terms.

      'Setianism' is of course of recent origin - the result of a feud between Aquino and LaVey. Satanism goes back a bit before Setianism a nd even before the Church of Satan, a nd even before ancient Egypt - itb a reflection of man's understanding of the workings of the cosmos.

      Nature is NOT a (onefold' static system. The flux, the dynamic evolution are a reflection of it - as Darwin saw, for example. Evolution, genetics, selection, etc. are operative WITHIN nature - basic school science. Nature consists of polarities clashing and interacting - dialectics - responsible for change. This change in the cosmos is pushed by what physicists call entropy - what Satanists call Satan - in the Orient 'bat**'(The All) and 'Tan' (the energizing pri**ciple or Dark Force behind it). I think I tried to explain this in a prior letter (?). The ancients recognized this, the Tantrics saying 'Shiva without Shakti is a corpse' i.e. Shiva the cosmos - Shakti the energizing element - 'Satan', 'entropy' the 'Dark force in nature' or whatever one wants to call it.

      The Norse saw it as a clash of Ice and Fire - again polarities working within nature. Ragnarok - the forces of nature overturning the status quo, causing change, evolution, WITHIN nature. Satan is the rebellious ASPECT OF NATURE.

      This is what the ancients have taught for milleniums - here's where Satanism comes from - not from the founding of TS or CS a few decades ago.

      This is what is still taught by generational Satanists (the real ones, I mean, not the imaginery ones of the christians and neurotic women who claim to have suffered cultic child abuse). Such real generational Satanists have a general contempt for what they call 'Converts' (much like the Jews' contempt for the 'goyim'), but they have a very special contempt for Setians because they see Setianism as having ta en over their symbols etc., and presented Satanism or the LHP in a totally opposite manner - akin to christianity - divorced from nature.

      No, nature does not have 'one law' - it is in a state of flux, dynamic, because of entropy, of what we call the Satanic principle acting on it. I recognized this long ago and wrote of it in my own publications with some emphasis. Science, so long as it is not chained to a political or religous dogma like Marxism for example, does not have one law - it seeks to unravel the manifold laws of nature. Christianity has onet law - obey its dogma; so does Setianism which describes itself as an "ethical religion", as the ONLY genuine Satanic religion because of an Infernal Mandate, religious dogma at its worst. So it proscribes certain people and organizations, just as Stephen Brown of the ONA so accurately described it.

      So when I was given an ultimatum by Austen to quite associating with ONA and Balder my reaction w**as automatic - these are reflective of the genuine Satanic tradition, and what's more they are doing something in the REAL world. What do we have in the TS - a bunch of letter-writing, rituals, records of **ra dreams, etc. which apart from the imagery, is hard to distinguish from any New Age outfit. What do we have in the 'Scroll' - more dreams, mystical blabber, ..othing real; an escapism.

      ONA told it like it really is - intuitive,considering they must have been limited by the amount of TS material they've read. But they recognized the attitude, and we should be able to recognize how correct ONA is in its analysis of TS because we've had access to the material. The ONA offers a rational critique of TS, and how does

NOTES ON STUDY AND PRACTICE
IN MODERN SATANISM

In traditional Satanism, the novice is expected to not only study the tenets and traditions of Satanism, but also put these into practice in real life. Thus, a recent Satanic Initiate – whether working alone or as a member of an established Order/Temple – would study the following works, and then strive to apply the principles contained in them in the way described.

The works are: *The Black Book of Satan*; *Naos*; *Hostia* vols. I, ll, III; *Hysteron Proteron*.[13]

'*Naos*' would be used as a guide to practical hermetic workings, both external and internal. The *Black Book* would be used as a guide to forming and running a Satanic Temple to perform ceremonial magick. *Hostia* and *Hysteron Proteron* would provide an insight into Satanic traditions and beliefs. In addition, the images of the Sinister Tarot would be employed (e.g. in some of the workings given in *Naos*) and the *Deofel Quartet* might be read to provide additional understanding, together with *The Black Book* II and III.

Satanic practice in the real world would arise from (a) forming and running a Satanic Temple; and (b) undertaking Insight Roles and other Satanic tasks. Aside from a specific Insight Role, which the novice would choose, they would undertake the various physical challenges required [qv. the MS 'Adeptship – its Real Meaning and Significance', for example] and strive to increase their experience by living Satanically in a way which aided the sinister dialectic. What these experiences were, they would decide after having studied the works mentioned and after having undertaken the tasks, ordeals and so on, up to External Adept [qv. *Naos*, and the various MSS Guides to the Seven-Fold Way] e.g. having run a Temple for some months, and achieved the physical goals.

---

[13] Editor's note: these manuscripts are included in the ONA authorized volumes *The Sinister Way* and *The Sinister Tradition*.

One of the tasks might be to plan and undertake a culling. Another might be to aid Heretical forms by, for example, becoming involved with an extremist group which seeks the destruction of 'the System' and whose principles and aims are in accord with the Satanic ethos and whose actions aid the sinister dialectic. [Obviously, both of these could be combined.] Another might be to undermine present structures by fostering their decline – e.g. dealing in drugs. Another might be removing in a practical manner on a regular basis, the scum and the worthless – e.g. by vigilante action [this is culling performed on a regular basis rather than a 'one-off' event].

What matters about these tasks is that the novice chooses them to gain practical experience of Satanism in action and thus increase their understanding and so aid their esoteric development. Naturally, to qualify as Satanic actions, they must aid the sinister dialectic – be steps toward realizing the strategic goal of Satanism. Here, an understanding of Aeonics is crucial, as is a genuine insight into traditional Satanism: as explicated, for example, in *Hostia* I, II, III and as explained to prospective novices in the booklet 'Satanism – a Basic Introduction for Prospective Adherents'.

The choice of practical action is the novice's: they must use their understanding to select Satanic tasks. Occasionally, they might be given advice, from a more experienced Satanist, but the final choices are and must be theirs. What matters is to choose and act. The acts are learning experiences, ordeals, and thus it does not matter if because of, say, a certain lack of understanding, a novice chooses, or seems to choose, wrongly. They will either learn from this, or not. If not, they have basically failed – shown themselves not to be suitable. Whatever, their actions will have presenced the sinister in some way or ways.

Following these tasks – which should last for a few years – the novice then moves on to the next stage of their esoteric development, that of the Grade Ritual of Internal Adept. This is a rite of synthesis, and thus the emergence of the Adept.

THE PRACTICAL ESOTERIC AIMS OF SATANISM:
90-130 YF

The practical aims arise from Satanic strategy which has its foundation in Aeonics [qv. the various Aeonics and Cliology MSS – some of the most important are listed at the end of this MSS]. These aims are essentially r tactics to achieve the long-term strategic goal. This goal is the creation of a new species – and this means (a) a new Aeon; (b) a new aeonic civilization. For this to be achieved, present structures, forms, ideas and so on, have to changed.

Aeonics shows that the present Aeonic civilization, the Western, has been distorted in its ethos and its structures. One of the most potent forms of the distortion has been the Nazarene religion. The distortion has been carried on, and effectively controlled, by 'Magian' forces – there has arisen various other forms to implement the distortion and effectively undermine the Destiny of the West – that is, the emergence of Imperium. These forms include communism/Marxism/socialism and the idea of 'liberal-democracy': they are all opposed to a racially aware Europe and the idea of Aryan/White superiority. This Aryan superiority would have formed the basis of Imperium without it, Imperium is not possible.

In essence, the ethos of the West has been changed from a Faustian/Promethean pagan one, which exulted in conquest and exploration, to a neurotic materialism and a 'multi-racial' pacifist degeneracy. There has been a 'silent revolution' in all Western societies and they all now conform to unhealthy Nazarene induced forms – the power structures of these societies now actively seek to eradicate all heretical pro-Promethean ideas/groups/individuals, and use the full force of the 'Law', as well as covert tactics, against those who hold 'out against the relentless onslaught to enslave the peoples of the West to what are essentially 'Magian' created ideas.

Thus the campaigns, in schools and throughout society, against 'racism'. To implement this Magian revolution, a myth was created –

'the Holocaust'. In most societies of the West, this myth is a sacred dogma – disbelief being punishable by imprisonment.

Because of all this, an Imperium is increasingly unlikely. The real – i.e. esoteric – aim of the Magian is a 'Messianic Kingdom' ruled over by this 'Magian' elite. This would be de-evolutionary, in the Aeonic sense, and effectively wipe out the gains of all hitherto existing Aeonic civilizations. Essentially, the rule of 'Dogma' would hold sway, with terror to support this. This terror is already evident concerning the Holocaust and Aryan racism. The reasoned enlightenment, so evident in the Hellenic and Western ethos, would be displaced by a real despotism – a mentality akin to that imposed upon the West by the medieval 'Witch-finders' and their dogmatic Nazarene zeal. The Magian is a synonym for the Zionists.

This brief overview of the current state of aeonic affairs enable the practical aims, to be achieved/striven toward, to be understood in context. Esoterically, traditional Satanism/the septenary, and thus its magick, is an expression of the Faustian ethos and thus the Western Aeon. The other forms of 'Western' magic(k) existing at this time – including the 'Satanism' of groups like the Temple of Set – are expressions of the Magian ethos (as is evident, for example, in their use of Hebrew forms and the 'Qabalah'). Thus the actual 'magick' of these other groups/individuals is aiding the distortion. In practical terms, any magickal act, which does not use traditional Satanist/genuine Western forms (such as the septenary) is an action against the reasoned enlightenment that the Western Aeon represents.

On the practical level, it is considered necessary, in order to achieve strategic goals, to support the creation of a Western Imperium – that is, to support those forces trying to undermine in a practical way the current Nazarene/Magian status quo. This means upholding heretical views such as racial inequality, and denying 'the Holocaust' – as well as aiding/supporting National-Socialist/'racist' causes. The tactical aim here is the creation of a pro-Aryan, National-Socialist type State which has a noble, conquering spirit or ethos, and thus which represents Satanic values in action in the real world. An alternative aim is the emergence of a 'religious' form for this same noble, conquering ethos.

In addition, whatever means are necessary io undermine and thus destroy the present status quo must be used. This means disrupting societies supporting armed insurrection, spreading heretical ideas, aiding those groups/ forms which weaken societies from within (in the moral sense – e.g. drug dealing) and thus engendering a healthy, noble resurgence. A primary aim is to cause chaos, on the streets, economically, and socially – to thus provide opportunities for a revolutionary pro-Aryan group to take or seize power. A magickal and practical aim is to destroy the power structure of America for that country effectively is acting to maintain a global control in accord with Magian dictates and thus impose the Magian world-view. The real power of the Magian heart-land resides in America and in the control exercised in the minds of Europeans by the idea of 'multi-racialism' and the myth of the holocaust. If the present power structure of America was destroyed, the practical power-base, both financial and military, of the Magian heart-land (i.e. Israel) would collapse – what has prevented the destruction of this heart-land by the Arabs is the military superiority given to it by America. No country has ever been able or is able to supply superior weapons to any Arab state not under American control – not the former Soviet Union, not China. America has — secretly threatened any country which seems about to do so – and threatened both economically and militarily. Any country which poses a real threat to Magian lands has been dealt with – e.g. Iraq.

With the fall of this heart-land, the Messianic dream of the Magian would be unrealizable.

The next Aeon will be determined by the success or failure of these tactics. That is, for the next Aeon to emerge, and thus for the next Aeonic civilization to arise in around five centuries time, it is necessary to destroy the distortion affecting the present Aeon. Failure to do this will mean the emergence of that civilization will be much delayed – by up to at least a thousand years.

Further, the success of the tactics, and the emergence of an Imperium, means the spread of the present civilization beyond the confines of the Earth – out into Space. This is possible now, and only now, due to the inventiveness of the creative minority within the civilization and the technology to implement that in a practical way. A defeat would mean a hiatus, and thus a starting from the beginnings – effectively, the achievements of this Aeon would be wiped out.

Traditional Satanism is fundamentally pan-Aeonic: ie. concerned with the patterns and processes which are perceived, in the causal, as Aeons and Aeonic civilizations. However, to effect changes in the causal, actions of individuals and groups (and this includes magickal acts) must work with things as those things are – as they are presenced in causal time at particular causal times. The reality of aeonic energies is that they assume causal form in aeonic civilizations, and that at anyone millennia, only one civilization is aeonically significant. Therefore, aeonic magick is a working with the aeonic energies presenced in the particular civilization at the time of that magickal act(s) – or a working against those energies. Anything else is not Aeonic magick – i.e. is not effective on the aeonic level: it is purely personal, external, magick.

The present Aeon is the Western – and this Aeon dates from c.500 eh to c.2000eh – in terms of the energies being predominant. The aeonic civilization follows some centuries later: for the West, arising c. 900 eh and ending c. 2400eh. The energies of the next Aeon follow or arise some centuries after the last Aeonic ones: in practice this means at the end of the civilization of the last Aeon; when the Imperium is collapsing. Thus, the new Aeonic manifestations will arise c.2400eh.

In the past, Aeons arose as part of the unconscious process of dialectical change. However, we are now at the stage of evolutionary

328

understanding when we can alter the process itself because of that conscious understanding which Aeor.ics, cliology and so on, gives us. That is, we can significantly alter the process of aeonic evolution and thus the civilization which gives form and reality to aeonic energies. The time for such change is when the energies of one aeon are waning, and the energies of the next aeon have not arisen in any significant way.

Left to themselves the aeonic energies would have produced a Western Imperium which would have lasted from c. 1990eh-c.2450eh. A new aeonic civilization would then have arisen c.3000eh, and lasted for c. a thousand and more years.

The reality of aeonic magick means that one must work either with the energies of the Western energies – and thus aid/create an Imperium – or that one works against those energies. At this moment in causal time, no other energies of aeonic type are prevalent on Earth, and no other cultures/civilizations are significant in evolutionary terms. [This statement of reality will not please many.]

Thus, the only practical options for significant magickal work are the ones given above: aiding Imperium (and thus countering the distortion) or working against the creation of Imperium (and thus aiding the distortion). The former option is continuing the evolutionary trend – i.e. presencing the sinister; creating a dynamic imperative and thus aiding exploration/conquest/discovery. The latter option is de-evolutionary- i.e. it aids those forces which by their nature are restrictive in both the short and the long term. The former is a moving-on; the latter, a dogmatic standstill and then a recession. of course, the majority of non-Initiates see things differently – they view the distortion as 'progressive' and those arranged against it (e.g. NS type forces) as regressive/reactionary/primitive and so on. Such people have not only failed to perceive the essence of things veiled by their outer transient forms, but also have abandoned rational thought and judgement for abstract idealism arising from sentiment. The majority of such people who view the situation in this sentimental idealistic way, are simply victims of the distortion itself products of the unhealthy societies which esteem verbiage and clever pseudo-intellectuals concepts above judgement based on experience and real insight.

Initiation implies a development of real insight and judgement – and a learning of genuine esoteric knowledge. The esoteric knowledge of Satanism, hitherto secret by nature because it was and is heresy, is essentially a knowledge of Aeonics – of those factors governing evolution/change from aeons to individuals. One insight of a Satanic Initiate is into the forms and structures assumed by aeonic energies in the causal.

This insight means that a genuine Initiate understands a transient form such as 'National-Socialism' as a practical expression of some of the principles of Satanism and as, in the long-term, contributing to evolutionary change via its inherent dynamism and acceptance of the forces of Nature. Such an Initiate understands that, at this moment in aeonic history, such a form is necessary: ie. this form (or something very similar) and only this form presences the sinister in the way that sinister must be presenced to achieve the strategic goal of Satanism over centuries.

The current practical concerns of traditional Satanism lie thus with the Western civilization – with aiding those forms which can or do presence the sinister, or which will change societies to the benefit of the sinister. The tactics are geared to this. Thus, an encouragement of Islam in certain Arab states may be a tactic used – because Islam acts to discourage the 'American' materialism which would otherwise flourish, and thus offsets 'American' (read covert Zionist) influence. This in itself poses problems for America and thus the Magian.

However, the aeonic or essential reality, is that Islam is a transient form which like all religions enshrines the dogmatic, anti-evolutionary ethos, and while in the very long-term the goal is enlightenment or Adept-like liberation and thus understanding for everyone, the practical reality means that a working with this particular transient form is tactically right, in order to achieve the goals connected with the present Western civilization and thus the establishment of a new Aeon.

The reality is that there are no easy, idealistic options. A genuine insight and understanding of aeonic matters means certain judgements have to be made: certain tactics have to be employed in order to achieve anything. Satanism is concerned with real, meaningful changes in the real world: it is not concerned with mystical or psuedo-mystical world-views and impractical idealisms. In a fundamental sense, Satanism is pragmatic – aeonically.

The present reality is as stated above – no amount of 'wishful thinking' or idealism or sentiment will change this. One either aids aeonic change and thus contributes toward evolutionary change, or one does not.

On the magickal level, as well as aiding the forces of Imperium and countering the distortion, acausal energies can be presenced to begin the process that is the next Aeon. That is, a nexion can be created, consciously, and the acausal energies consciously directed into temporal forms, some of which will be 'magickal'. This is in addition to aiding the present aeonic forms. In effect, these new acausal energies will create the next Aeon and thus its associated aeonic civilization.

This creation is the 'esoteric' Satanic goal of Satanic Adepts – the 'exoteric' goal can be considered to be aiding Imperium and thus fulfilling the wyrd of the West (and hence countering the distortion). In reality – i.e. viewed from beyond the opposites inherent in causal forms – the esoteric and exoteric goals are essentially the same: or rather, different expressions of the same things, that is, sinister or acausal energy presencing in the causal and thus creating evolutionary change. However, this 'differentiation' into esoteric and exoteric goals is useful since its enables the tactics to be understood. Viewed another way, the exoteric goal is the short-term esoteric strategy, and the esoteric goal is the long-term esoteric strategy.

Ita lex scripta.

THE SONG OF A SATANIST

In an important sense, most of my life represents genuine Satanism In action – a going to extremes. a learning from the experiences of those extremes, and a doing of dark, dangerous and sometimes 'illegal' deeds.

This life stands in stark contrast to those of the psuedo-Satanists, some of whom have acquired a notoriety and a 'fame'. I have – as a Satanist should been intoxicated by the essence of life itself – by that which inspires, which causes the creativity, self-absorption and genius of all great artists be they musicians, writers, warriors, explorers or whatever. I have dared to dream and to defy – and have dared to try and make my dreams and inspiration a reality. I have used my life for Some purpose – striven toward goals with a passion that overcomes all obstacles. I have known great love – physical, intellectual, and of the soul, the essence of existence. I have also known the opposite – the sadness that awaits all who venture into the dark starkness of the Abyss within and without. and thus the synthesis of these and other things which is the apprehension of wisdom.

This living has been an ecstatic affirmation of existence – a self-surmounting. The goals striven for were for the most part irrelevant: what was important was the striving for something with a passion. For in such striving, in the action in the world so entailed, in the striving, there was an intensity, which captures the immortal and which re-presents the spirit of Satanism: that heroic defiance which is the essence of all conscious evolution and thus civilization itself.

Such exultation is dangerous. By its nature it is individual. It is anathema to those forms and structures which suck vitality and which by their very existence, level individuals down and break or try to break their spirit. It is Heresy. It is testing   some become possessed; some perish; some are broken in spirit and descend to the mediocrity of the majority some are caught In the snares left by those who adhere to those things which suck vitality (such as religion and 'law' and ethics). But some few survive and prosper and thus inspire others to venture out where no one has dared to go before. and of those few who survive. there are some who can express In words or other mediums (like music) what they have felt. and experienced and learnt – in a way which is easily understood. These few are the really dangerous ones ...

It amuses me – and has amused me – when I come into contact with modern, self-professed 'Satanists', be such people a part of some 'Temple' or 'Church' or 'cult', or be they working on their own. With a few notable exceptions, these people are ridiculous – for them, Satanism is an intellectual philosophy. a collection of rituals, and/or an anarchic attitude. For them, it is an object or study, and involves meetings, discussions. For them, it is communal, and involves 'ethics' and/or a religious approach and attitude. For them, it is a glorification of their ego and a wallowing in the pleasures and wealth this existence can offer: an excuse for self-indulgence and lack of self-discipline.

In reality, Satanism is an attitude to living – and an attitude foreign to these mostly urbanized people who profess to be Satanists. Satanism means living one's life in a certain way – achieving things, in the real world by one's own efforts and because one is exulting in existence itself consciously. That is, one's life is intentional – a striving toward a higher existence by practical deeds, by overcoming challenges which take evolution to new realms. A Satanist strives to change themselves – and then the world itself. They desire glory, fame – to be significant. They are not content, and even when a goal is achieved, there is the need to find and strive toward another goal, another way of living. There are always new experiences awaiting – new levels of achievement.

A genuine Satanist needs action – they need challenges, because they possess within themselves the 'fire of Satan', that vitality which is the quintessence of living. This vitality shows in their eyes, their character – it is evident in their deeds.

Fundamentally, one becomes a Satanist by acting like one – by doing Satanic deeds. A Satanist of some experience would say one and more of these things:

'I have experienced combat; I have killed, watched comrades die. I have loved – and hated. I have discovered something for the first time. I have been alone for months, bereft of most things, and thus come to know myself. I have faced my own eminent death, not once, but many times. I have achieved things with my body I thought not possible. I have exulted in overcoming physical, intellectual and psychic challenges. I know the passion that motivated Beethoven, van Gogh, Nietzsche, and I know the feelings and greatness of Caesar, Adolf Hitler and Alexander the Great ... I have heard the music of the galaxy and the stars and planets within it. I have been in a prison cell and known the meaning of freedom. I have culled human dross. I have done criminal deeds – to learn and defy.'

of course, these things are only examples – there are many more. What is important --is that they express real experiences of a dangerous or learning kind: they breed character; they test. They are selective. They are the type of deeds done by individuals with spirit – the type of understanding such an individual possesses. If only intuitively at first.

A Satanist will live life on the edge – will take up a profession which allows him or her to excel in deeds of action or creativity or exploration, or all of these. They will become experts in their chosen fields – and these fields by their nature will require persons of character and inner strength who prefer to work alone. Fields like assassination; Special Forces; Political manipulation... and then, having achieved, they will move on – to new ways and deeds. Or perchance they will die, defiant to the end.

Whatever, their quality of living will far surpass that of the weak majority. Their experience of both the dark and the light will be deeper, more extensive, and thus will they possess a greater insight, a greater understanding, a real depth of character. In contrast, the self-professed 'Satanists' will be shallow – all talk, with little or no real experience of living on the edge. They shy away from real self-effort, from real self-overcoming, and build fantasy worlds in which they find comfort. They need the company of others, as they need their ego to be massaged by what they regard as their 'Satanic peers'. They talk an awful lot with others about Satanism, and probably, having learnt a lot of 'theory' from books and various organizations, write their own 'Satanic' rituals which they perform with the glee of the necrophiliac.

Some of these denizens of psuedo-Satanic organizations and cults will indulge in anarchic behavior to impress themselves and others. But by so d0ing they reveal a lack of character – for a genuine Satanist possesses nobility and a self-discipline that others seldom understand.

Imitation Satanists make excuses – and devise theories to explain their lack of Satanic deeds in the real world. They have seldom if ever changed themselves to something greater than what they were at Initiation, and they most certainly have not changed the world in any way, significant or insignificant. They have achieved no glory – discovered nothing new; not extended the frontiers of understanding by even one micron. Instead, they wallow in obscure doctrines ... and consume the drug of self-delusion. To be brief, they have not composed a Satanic song which illustrates their life. They labour, but in vain – *poeta nascitur, non fit.*

Most Satanists cannot publish an autobiography, or even have a biography which relates their life in detail while they still live, for the simple reason that it would probably render them liable to prosecution by those asinine guardians of even more stupid system of 'Law'.[14] If this threat does not exist, then their life has not been Satanic enough. and, moreover, that life is never completed until causal death – something written at a certain age, should be out of

---

[14] Plus the fact that most wish to continue their sinister esoteric work in secret, to aid the sinister dialectic.

date within a few years. It if was not, then again the full Satanic promise of one's existence has not been fulfilled. The time for the publication of such writings is after the causal death of its subject – although an expurgated version may serve a purpose, for some replete with experiences who wish to express the essence and inspire others to follow and then surpass them.

In my own case, I have written a brief recollection of some of the experiences of my Satanic life, for posthumous publication. But even in that MS, there were many things not recalled, perchance the MS falls into the wrong hands before the right time. Such a recalling – of dark and occasional ecstatic deeds, most of them 'illegal' and all of them 'heretical' in this purblind society – will have to await my twilight years and a recounting of them to a trusted Satanic comrade. and even though the MS was written only two years ago, it is already out of date.

and of that living, it is the essence which is important, not especially the details. From that living, I have distilled the quintessence into words which cannot be mis-understood – devising a method by which others may obtain that elixir. I have constructed a guide to the goal, drawn a map and explained the goal in detail, because I have been there. I explored, and discovered.

Now others can benefit from the lessons learnt from such a life. *Non generant aquilae columbas.*

Meanwhile, I anticipate the lies, rumours and distortions will continue, based on jealousy. The small and weak of character have always saught to drag those who are outstanding down to their own level of mediocrity – at least in the eyes of others.

***

Stephen Brown (ONA) 103yf

THE LEFT HANDED PATH – AN ANALYSIS ONA

The Left Handed Path and Satanism are related insofar as Satanism is a particular LHP. The LHP is the name given to describe a system of esoteric knowledge and practical techniques – and this system is also known as 'The Black Arts'.

The Difference Between the Left and Right Hand Paths:

The aim of all genuine Occult paths or systems, whether designated Right Hand or Left-Hand, is to achieve or find a certain goal – as well as to impart esoteric knowledge and abilities. The goal is variously described (e.g. 'Gnosis', the Philosopher's Stone, Enlightenment).

However, it has been a common misconception that the RH Paths were altruistic and the LH Paths egocentric – i.e. the difference between them was seen in individual moral terms. Another misconception is in seeing the difference in absolute moral terms – i.e. the RH Paths as representing 'good' and the LH Paths as 'evil'. Recently, attempts have been made to formulate 'grey' paths which combine elements of both, and such 'grey' paths are often said (by their exponents) to be the 'true' Occult way or path.

The reality is quite different. The LH Paths and the RH Paths [hereafter, the singular 'Path' will be used, although the plural is to be understood] are quite distinct and differ in both their methods and their aims. The most fundamental difference is that the RHP is restrictive – certain things are forbidden or frowned upon – and collective. That is, the RHP takes some responsibility away from the individual by having a formal dogma, a code of ethics and behaviour and by having the individual participate in an organized grouping, however loose that grouping may be. In brief, the identity of the individual is to some extent taken away – by the beliefs – systems which that individual has to accept, and by them accepting some higher 'authority', be such authority an individual, a group or an 'ideology' (or even, sometimes, a supra-personal Being – a 'god' or 'gods').

In contradistinction, the LHP in its methods is non-structured. In the genuine LHP there is nothing that is not permitted – nothing that is forbidden or restricted. That is, the LHP means the individual takes sale responsibility for their actions and their quest. This makes the LHP both difficult and dangerous – its methods can be used as an excuse for anti-social behaviour as they can be used to aid the fetishes and weaknesses of some individuals as well as lead some into forbidden and illegal acts. However, the genuine Initiate of the LHP is undertaking a quest, and as such is seeking something: that is, there is a dynamic, an imperative about their actions as well as the conscious understanding and appreciation that all such actions are only a part of that quest; they are not the quest itself. This arises because the LHP Initiate is seeking mastery and self-knowledge – these being implicit in such an Initiation. Accordingly, the LHP Initiate sees methods as merely methods; experience as merely experience. Both are used, learned from and then discarded.

Because of this, the LHP is by its nature ruthless – the strong of character win through, the weak go under. There are no 'safety nets' of any kind on the LHP – there is no dogma or ideology to rely on, no one to provide comfort and soften the blows, no organization, individual or 'Being' to run to when things get difficult and which will provide support and sympathy and understanding. Or which, just as importantly, takes away the responsibility of the Initiate for their deeds.

The LHP breeds self-achievement and self-excellence – or its destroys, either literally, or via delusion and madness.

Further, the goal or aim of the LHP is individual specific – it is the raising of that individual to 'god-head'; the fulfillment of individual potential and thus a discovery and fulfilment of their unique Destiny. That is, it breeds a unique character, a unique individual. The RHP, on the contrary, is concerned with 'idealistic' and thus supra-personal aims – aiding 'society', 'humanity' and so on: the individual is 're-made' by abstract and impersonal forms.

The LHP by its nature means that its Initiates work mostly on their own. Followers of the LHP are masters of their as yet unmanifest Destiny. and while they may accept guidance and advice, they eschew any form of subservience: they learn for themselves, by their own experience and from their own self-effort. This is crucial to an understanding of the true nature of the LHP. The LHP means this self-reliance, this self-experience, this self-effort, this personal struggle for achievement. The RHP means someone else – some individual, or some authority or some hierarchy – awards or confers upon the RHP Initiate a sign or symbol of their 'progress'. That is, the RHP Initiate assumes the role of student, or 'chela' – and often that of sycophant. They rely on someone else or something beyond themselves, whereas the LHP Initiate relies only on themselves: their cunning, skill, character, desire, intelligence and so on. The successful LHP Initiate is the individual who learns from their own experiences and mistakes. The RHP Initiate tries to learn from theory – from what others have done.

Essentially, the LHP Initiate is a free spirit, already possessed of a certain willful character, while the RHP Initiate is in thrall to other people's ideas and ways of doing things.

The notion of self-responsibility is as mentioned above, crucial to the LHP and accordingly any organization which claims to be of the LHP and which does not uphold this in both theory and practice is a fraudulent organization. In practice this means that an organization does not restrict the experiences of its members – it does not, for instance, impose upon them any binding authority which the members have to accept or face 'expulsion' just as it does not lay down for them any codes of behaviour or ethics. That is, it does not promulgate a dogma which the members have to accept as it does not require those members to be obediant to what the hierarchy says. There is no 'proscription' of certain views, or individuals or other organizations as there is no attempt to make members conform in terms of behaviour, attitudes, views, opinions, expressions or anything else. If there are any of these things, the organization so doing these things is most certainly not an organization of the Left Hand Path even though it may use some of the motifs, symbols and methods of the LHP. Such an organization is instead allied to the RHP in nature – in the effect it has upon its embers.

In summary, the RHP is soft. The LHP is hard. The RHP is like a comfortable game – and one which can be played, left for a while, then taken up again. The LHP is a struggle which takes years. The RHP prescribes behaviour and limits personal responsibility. The LHP means self-responsibility and self-effort. The RHP requires the individual to conform in certain way. The LHP is non-restrictive RHP organizations and 'teachers' require the Initiate to conform and accept the authority of that organization/'teacher'. LHP organizations and Masters/ Mistresses only offer advice and guidance, based on their own experience.

Satanism:

As mentioned above, Satanism is a particular LHP. Conventionally, and incorrectly, Satanism is described as 'worship of Satan/the Devil'.

The word 'Satan' originally derived from the Greek word for 'an accusation'.

That is, Satan is an archetype of disruption – the Adversary who challenges the accepted, who defies – who desires to know. In essence, Satan is a symbol of dynamic motion: the generative or moving force behind evolution, change.

In reality, Satan is both symbolic or archetypal, and real. That is, He exists within the psyche of individuals, and beyond individuals.

Satanism is, in part, the acceptance of the necessity of change – of the reality of things like struggle, combat, war, creativity, individual

341

genius, defiance' of the evolutionary and puritive nature of these things. But Satanism is much more than the acceptance of the reality of these things – of their necessity. It is also the individual seeking to be like Satan – to be Satanic. A true Satanist does not worship some Being called Satan. Rather, a Satanist accepts the reality of Satan [on all levels] and quests to become, in their own life and beyond, a type of Being of the same kind as Satan – that is, to change their own evolution and that of others: to evolve to a new type of existence. The existence can be described by what is known as 'Satan'. This quest is a dynamic and real one, and it means that those who aspire to follow the way of Satanism go further than others who merely follow the LHP. That is, Satanism leads to new areas of being: it goes beyond 'the Black Arts' while having its foundation or ground in those Arts. Part of this is a greater esoteric knowledge (e.g. Aeonic Magick) and part in techniques or methods or create· a new individual. The Satanist effectively' learns to play at being god. Since Satanism, as described above, involves the individual questing to become like Satan, it is relevant to consider who and what Satan is.

Satan is the Prince of Darkness – master of all that is hidden or secret, both within ourselves and external to ourselves. He is the ruler of this world the force behind its evolutionary change; the 'fire' of life. He is Lord of Life – of all the sensual delights and pleasures.

He is also 'evil' or 'dark' or 'sinister' – merciless, ruthless, Master of Death. He can and does promote suffering, misery, death. But all these things are impersonal – they are natural consequences of life, of change and evolution.

Satan, by His nature, cannot be 'bribed' or 'propitiated' – and neither can His services be bought, by a 'pact' or anything else. He is not interested in such futile things. Thus, there can be no such thing as a 'religious' Satanism – the offering of prayers or offerings or promises or whatever in return for Satanic favours. Such things imply fear, subserviance and those other traits of character Satan despises. Rather, the satanic approach is to glory in Satanic deeds and chants and such like because they are Satanic because by so doing them there is an exultation, an affirmation and a being like Satan: not because something is 'expected' or done out of fear of the consequences. It is by living life, by deeds, that a Satanist becomes like Satan and so evolves to partake of a new and higher existence. Such deeds are those to bring insight, self-discovery, to achieve, esoteric knowledge, experience of the 'forbidden', of the pleasures of living – and they are -also those which change others and the world and which thus can and do bring suffering, misery, death: which are, in short, evil. Furthermore, Satan is a real Being – he is not simply a symbol, archetypal or otherwise, of certain natural forces or energies. He has life, exists – causes things to occur – external to our own, individual psyche. That is, our individual wills, or even our individual magick, cannot control Him [as the soft imitation Satanists like to believe]. However, this 'life' is not 'human' – it is not bound by a body or even by our causal time and space. Expressed esoterically, it is acausal.

Satan, however, is not alone – that is, He is not the only Dark, sinister Being who affects our world and thus existence. He has a female counter-part, a Mistress, Lover, Bride. Esoterically, Her name is Baphomet. She is the Dark Goddess.

Thus, a Satanic Initiate is often described as the lover of one or both of these sinister entities – and a genuine Satanic Initiation may be likened to a ritual copulation with either Satan or Baphomet [where the Priest/Priestess assumes the form of the entity]. In genuine Satanism there is no 'worship' of Satan (or Baphomet– but rather an acceptance of Them as friends, lovers (or, in the early stages, sometimes a 'father' and 'mother' or a brother and sister).

A Satanist thus evolves toward a higher form – and expresses conscious evolution in action. Hence, Satanism is the quintessence of the Left Hand Path.

Evil:

It is a mistake, recently promulgated by some, to see the LHP in general and Satanism in particular as merely a body of esoteric knowledge and/or a collection of rituals or magickal workings, either of which, or both, may be 'dipped into' for personal edification and to provide oneself with an 'image'.

All LH Paths are ordeals – they involve self-effort over a period of years. They are also dark, and involve the individuals who follow them going to and beyond the limits all societies impose. That is, they are sinister or 'evil'. They involve real sinister acts in the real world – not a playing at sorcerers or sorceresses.

Certain individuals and certain organizations who claim to belong to the LHP have tried to dispel the 'evil' that surrounds the LHP and Satanism – by denying the very real evil nature of these paths. However, what do these imitation Satanists, these posturing pseuds, think Satanism is if not 'evil'? If Satanism is not evil, what is? [Or, more precisely, if Satan is not evil, who is?]

The true nature of evil – and thus Satanism and the LHP – has been misunderstood. Evil is natural and necessary – it tests, culls, provokes reaction and thus aids evolution. and to repeat – Satanism is replete with evil: it is evil. Satanists are sinister, evil. They cannot but be otherwise.

Evil, correctly defined, is part of the cosmic dialectic – it is force, which is a-moral: i.e. it is beyond the bounds of 'morals'. Morals derive from a limited (human – or, rather, pseudo-human) perspective, and a morality is a projection by individual consciousness onto reality. Nothing that is 'moral' or immoral exists. All morals are therefore artifice – they are abstractions. Actions, by individuals, which are normally considered as 'evil' are things that are done by individuals against others – that is, evil acts are considered as belonging to us, as a species. It is not considered 'evil' for a tiger to kill and eat a person: that is natural, in the nature of the tiger. What has been and generally is considered to be evil, in humans, is in general nothing more than instinct – or rather, a feeling, a pre-conscious desire or desires.

Such instinct is natural – the actions which result from it can be either beneficial or not. That is, the actions are not 'evil' in themselves. They should not be judged by some artificial abstractions, but rather by their consequences – by their effects, which are either positive or negative. However, they can be positive or negative depending on circumstances: that is, the evaluation of them can vary depending on the perspective chosen. This perspective is usually that of 'time'. The only correct judgment about a particular act or action is one which takes into account the effects of that action not only in the present but also in the future, and this latter on a vast time-scale. Thus, the judgment concerning such acts is essentially a-personal – it bears little or no resemblance to the emotional affects of that act in the moments of that act or in the immediate moments following that act. [In the symbolic sense and imprecisely – such judgment could be said to be that of 'the gods'.]

Real acts of evil are those which are done consciously – and these can be of two kinds. The first are ignorant acts: done from a lack of self-knowledge and usually with no appreciation of their effects beyond the moment. The second are impersonal acts done with a knowledge of the effects beyond that of the moment. The former involve no evaluation beyond the personal feelings; the latter involve an evaluation beyond the personal (although they may still be personal acts – i.e. of benefit to the individual). A Satanic act of evil is of this second kind – they are affective and effective: a participation in the cosmic dialectic. At first, they may not be fully understood – i.e. arise from instinct in the main. But the Satanic intent behind them makes the individual more conscious, more aware of their effects, both personal and supra-personal, thus enabling judgment to be cultivated.

Instinctive acts are not 'evil' – they usually derive from immaturity. Evil acts derive from maturity – but immaturity is required to reach this stage. That is, there is a growth. 'Morality' tries to stifle instinct and thus restricts growth. Satanic acts of evil in effect redress the balance – and allow real maturity to develope.

INTRODUCTION TO *THE DEOFEL QUARTET*

The works collected under the title '*The Deofel Quartet*' were written as Instructional Texts for members of a Black Magick group. As such, they deal with certain esoteric matters relevant to Novices and those who have begun to follow the path of Black Magick and Satanism.

While the form chosen is fictional, it is not that of a 'conventional' novel. Instead, a new vehicle was created with the aim of combining a fast (and thus entertaining) pace with a narrative style that not only required the imaginative participation of the reader, but which also saught to involve their unconscious. Thus, detailed descriptions – of, for instance, characters and locations – are for the most part omitted. It is left to the reader to supply such 'missing details': partly from their imagination] and partly unconsciously, from their own expectations and 'projections'.

This form also had the added advantage of making the works interesting to listen to when read aloud in a group considered as an extended 'prose poem'.

While each work is self-contained in terms of 'plot' and 'characters', they all deal with the varying insights attained by those following the darker path to esoteric enlightenment, as well as with those practical [i.e. real-life] experiences which form the basis of genuine magickal training and which explicate real sinister magick in action.

Each work deals with (although not always exclusively) with a certain type of magickal/archetypal energy – and thus each is connected with one of the spheres of the septenary Tree of Wyrd. Thus, in the instructional sense, each work explicates particular archetypal forms as those forms affect so explicated. Naturally, quite a few of the forms are dark or sinister.

In order to guide the interested reader and student of the Occult Arts, some 'Themes and Questions' concerning the Quartet are included as an Appendix to Volume I.

The works are reproduced exactly as they were originally circulated in manuscript form, with typed/hand-written corrections.

ONA

RESPONSES AND CRITICAL ANALYSIS

Each novice reading the Quartet should try and analyze their response to it – the feelings, expectations, points of agreement and disagreement and so on which arise from reading it.

A first reading will be sufficient to show the works of the Quartet are Satanically subtle – i.e. they are not blatant 'horror/Black Magic(k)' stories and neither are they pornographic. They are also not akin to the amoral diatribes of other writers – e.g. de Sade.

'Instead, they are intended for those of discernment, those who can see beyond mere appearance and affectation – i.e. Satanic novices: those who wish to know and who seek to question; those who wish to discover secrets (often about themselves).

As explained elsewhere, they deal with problems a novice following the Left Hand Path might be expected to come across or be familiar with – both in terms of their own development/feelings/expect-ations, and in terms of real Sinister magick. Such magick is for the most part subtle and esoteric – it is hidden and bears little, often no, resemblance to what most people (and some Initiates) consider magick to be.

Hence, those who turn to the Quartet hoping to find the kind of cheap and sensational thrills often associated (in the herd-mind)with 'Black Magic(k)' stories and 'horror' will be disappointed. The Quartet is not intended for such sensation seeking, uncritical and weak individuals – it is intended to instruct Satanic novices in some esoteric aspects of their craft: to aid their own understanding and Sinister development.

'Falcifer' concerns Initiation and the gathering of Satanic experience. It also deals with the Dark Gods – revealing esoteric knowledge. The energies which give form to the 'story' are concerned with the first sphere on the Tree of Wyrd – magickal form 'Night/Nox'; Tarot images – 18, 15, 13. Alchemical Process – calcination.

349

The Temple of Satan also concerns the Dark Gods – but it deals mainly with emotion on the personal level, particularly 'love': how a Satanic Initiate of some experience encounters and deals with this emotion. 'Love' of this type is a stage, to be experienced and transcended. For a Satanist not yet achieved Adeptship, this feeling is often a snare, a trap – which they can fall into, thus ending their sinister quest. It is about still unconscious feelings and desires – about making these more conscious, controlling them and transcending them. Third sphere on Tree of Wyrd. Magickal form – ecstasy. Images – 6, 14, 17. Alchemical process – coagulation.

'The Giving' concerns 'primal Satanism' – and a more subtle magick and manipulation than the previous works. It is a story based on fact – on real life happenings and real people. It reveals a real Satanic Mistress in action someone quite different from the 'accepted' notion of a Satanic Mistress. Spheres – third and Fourth. Forms – ecstasy/vision. Images – 7, 12, 5, 6, 14, 17. Processes – coagulation/putrefaction.

'The Greyling Owl' (the title is significant) concerns the second sphere, and the magick is even more subtle and esoteric than in the previous work. It requires an understanding of individuals as those individuals are – a subtle changing of them. Magickal Form – indulgence; process – separation; Images –0, 8, 16.

In all the works of the Quartet, 'the other side' (i.e. those with 'morals') is shown in context – moral individuals are described and things seen from their point of view. It is vitally important for a novice to be able to be detached – to see things and people as those things and people are. Only thus can they learn judgement and discover how to work esoteric Sinister magick. Such detachment is necessary – and its cultivation part of Initiate training. It is the aim of the Quartet to cultivate this ability – and the self-criticism which is a part of it. This 'criticism' is a self-awareness, a self-knowledge. Thus, some characters in the Quartet and the attitudes they express may provoke the Satanic Initiate into disagreement and possible discomfort. This is intentional. The novice should analyze why they react as they do – and why they 'expect' certain things/certain views/certain outcomes.

In short, they are entertaining instructional Satanic texts – those who are prepared to spend some effort in understanding them will discover their many layers, and so learn.

THE DEOFEL QUARTET – A SATANIC ANALYSIS

Falcifer:
This MS deals with overt magick in a magickal setting – temples, rituals etc. It describes Satanic initiation from a Satanic viewpoint, and the tests etc. a novice may undergo as well as the awakening awareness appropriate to a novice. It also deals with the Dark Gods – describing them and the magick which returns them to Earth.

Of all the MSS of the Quartet, it is the most easily understood, although it does contain some hidden/esoteric meanings. These, however, are quite explicable since the perspective of the MS is overtly Satanic.

Temple of Satan:
This also has an overtly magickal setting, but deals with the stage beyond that of a novice: i.e. someone who has been involved for some time and who has developed certain magickal skills – e.g. manipulation. Melanie is the archetypal Satanic Priestess: sexually alluring, using her sexuality to manipulate and captivate, enjoying some delicate pleasures (e.g. sadism). But, as a true Satanist, after some time she becomes bored by the routine. So unconsciously at first, she seeks after something else: and is drawn toward Thurstan, against her better Satanic judgement. She is 'drawn' because she still has to gain a deep self-understanding – because there are still aspects which remain unconscious and powerful in her psyche (relating to the 'numinous' power of love etc.). Gradually, she falls in love – but is she herself being manipulated toward this by Saer? and if so, why? [Consider the crystal he left with Thurstan for her to find and read.] Saer is 'beyond the Abyss' – an image/symbol of aeonic magick as against Melanie's external and internal magick. This love causes the loss of her magick.

But she gradually understands its purpose – to propel her toward the next stages of the sinister journey, and to provide a child who because of her own sinister abilities and the apparently non-sinister abilities of Thurstan will have special qualities. That is, the child will be beyond opposites (as, e.g., symbolized by Melanie and Thurstan). Toward the end, Melanie is presented with a choice – love, or her duty/destiny. She chooses the latter, and her magick is restored. Claudia is a complication for Melanie – a further test/distraction. Does her love cause her lover's death? Pead and Jukes, representing old aeon magick, try to keep Melanie and Thurstan apart – because without him she cannot fulfil her Satanic wyrd: i.e. move on to the next stages and thus undertake aeonic magick, to the detriment of the old order and 'the light'.

The Giving:
This MS has several esoteric strands, and several overt meanings.

Lianna is a Mistress of Earth (note: stages beyond Melanie in 'Temple') and it is her duty to undertake The Giving – rite of sacrifice. As a Satanic Mistress, Lianna uses magick in a subtle way, as befits her status. This magick is esoteric (e.g. empathic) but she also directly manipulates others, although in a subtle way. Consider how she draws/attracts Thorold to her: sending Sidnal to him with books, visiting his shop as a customer. Lianna requires two important things: an opfer, and someone to father her heir. The MS describes her attaining these goals.

Mallan is a recent initiate – enjoying as all good Initiates should, overt magick and evil. He involves Rhiston in his games. Lianna however presents Mallam with a choice – finely and subtlely presented. She advises him that his activities are not conducive to further advancement, for she understands he has become ensnared by some of his desires, rather than enjoying them and then discarding them to rise beyond them and so attain self-insight and mastery. However, he sees her hints 'morally' – he mis-interprets them because he cannot see what she is trying to do; i.e. he shows no Satanic insight. The reader is shown this from Mallam's perspective – like Mallam, a certain discernment is required to see beyond the outer appearence to the essence. [This sudden change of perspective occurs in the MS several times, as it does many times in other parts of the Quartet. The reader should often ask: what is really going on here? A critical

353

judgement is required because often the characters and what they may do/say are not what they seem: i.e. the real intent/magick is hidden.] As it is, Mallam's lack of insight means he believes Lianna is making a 'moral' point, and he openly breaks with her.

Following this decision by Mallam, Lianna provides him with a test, a new opportunity to prove his worth or otherwise. She sends her Guardian, Imlach, to him – unknown to Mallam, of course – with a secret MS. Again, Mallam fails to realize what is happening – he cannot 'see through' Imlach. Instead, he is overwhelmed by unconscious desires: material greed, lust for power. Rather than controlling, and using his desires for some purpose, he lets his desires control him. She goes to Lianna's village – and again fails, because he does not recognize the young woman as a Priestess of Lianna's tradition: he sees her as dull, easily manipulated. Thus, he shows he has no genuine magickal insight or abilities.

Hence he becomes a candidate for sacrifice. Basically, he chooses himself he is not chosen because of his 'evil' activities. They merely provide a fail-safe to deflect attention from his disappearence (when the rite is completed): no one in 'conventional' society would miss him/mourn him or worry about his disappearence. Lianna also tests/manipulates Thorold. Does she also manipulate Monica? Or is she genuinely annoyed when Thorold becomes involved with Monica? Is this a further test of Thorold? Certainly, for Lianna, Monica' death or removal is necessary – or seems to be. Lianna has drawn Thorold into her world – and changes him, for he is captivated by her: in a sense, in her power. He has qualities which she judged would make him a suitable person to father her child.

The MS ends with an unasked question: what is to be Thorold's fate when his purpose has been achieved? That is, when he has fathered her child. Will he be an opfer, or will he become part of her tradition? Clues to the answer are given at various points in the MS. Also, is Lianna a Satanist? Certainly, she does not seem to be – there are no 'Satanic' rites, no invocations to Satan. At one point she says she belongs to an older tradition. Does she say this for a reason? – to deceive? She certainly represents a primal darkness: and is a genuine Mistress of Earth ... This raises the question as to what genuine Satanism really is: a question answered, in fact, by Lianna's actions as described in the MS from its beginnings to its end.

The Greyling Owl:
This is the most esoteric and therefore the most difficult MS to understand – at a first reading – and when viewed by conventional/ accepted ideas of Satanism/Black Magick. It shows real magick in action on several levels: manipulation, empathic, forms (e.g. music), images, and via opening psychic nexions within individuals.

Essentially, the MS deals with the changes wrought in the lives of Mickleman and Alison, and how these are made to aid the sinister dialectic -i.e. sinister aeonic strategy, to aid the presencing of sinister energies in the causal and so bring/provoke change to the benefit of the sinister, aiding evolution.

The magick here is that appropriate to an Internal Adept and beyond, while the energies described (the outer form) are symbolic of a particular sphere on the Tree of Wyrd (Mercury), although other energies are sometimes involved/intrude.

This magick is far removed from external magick and thus rituals/robes. This magick means a working with individuals as those individuals are – a subtle re-orientation of their consciousness/lives.

Mickleman is gradually changed, and brought into an influential position the Professorship – without him realizing this is occurring, in the magickal sense at least. He believes he is still in control of his own Destiny – and it is important not to undermine this belief, except insofar as a certain self-insight is obtained. He must have this assurance of his abilities, this confidence, to fulfill what is his 'hidden' wyrd. He becomes aware, on terms he can cope with/is familiar with [this is important], of certain archetypal aspects which will be important for his future professional development/ standing. These aspects, by which he will influence others in a non-magickal way by

355

'seeding their minds', will aid the sinister dialectic. Part of this would be through academic work (aided by the insights attained during his 'manipulation') and part by his own life-style: his 'decadent' past and his future deriving from that past – both would influence others, providing inspiration, and thus changing others in certain ways.

Alison also is changed – realizing the power of music to transform. Again, her aims, dreams, hopes etc. are described from her own perspective, from her own 'moral' view of the world. However, her fundamental insights are 'provoked' via the subtle magick/influence of Edmund etc. Further, the future forms she creates/uses, while having the appearance of conventional forms (and perhaps a moral content), will achieve and aid the sinister [or at least most/some of them will]. She herself will see her aims in terms of her own perspective: often 'morally', without fully realizing what she and her work are achieving opening nexions, and presencing dark energies to influence/infect others. This arises because she has been influenced/directed by magick in a specific way: to access a certain nexion within her own psyche. [All this is a very important notion to understand – and marks the insight appropriate to those who aspire to go beyond the stage of novice. It reflects genuine magick in action.] Her thoughts/action etc. (as others) are often 'morally' described.

The dark interior life of both Edmund and Fiona (and thus their real aims) are hidden – i.e. not overt, as generally befits a Master and a Mistress. Such Adepts generally work esoterically – they do not fit conventional 'Satanic' role-models. In their different ways, Edmund and Fiona live in the ordinary world in an 'ordinary' way – they are real shape-changers who blend] into their surroundings. This enables them to work sinister magick effectively. Further, Edmund possesses no trappings normally assumed to be part of his station – he has no wealth, no power, no obvious influence. His Satanic power is internal, hidden – it is insight, wisdom, magickal skill of a rare kind. This skill enables him to work magick on others (and thus the world) as those others are – in the confines of their own roles/image for the most part. Fiona's magickal work is often more overt – e.g. using her sexuality to advantage, but her real magick is still hidden. Thus the MS describes real Adepts at work.

****

A Note Concerning 'Breaking the Silence Down:

This MS is often regarded as making the *Quartet* into a *Quintet*. It is similar in its magick to the 'Greyling Owl' – although the background is Sapphism. Basically, Diane – who already possesses an intuitive awareness of primal darkness and thus Satan ism – is led toward self-discovery and a magickal partnership.

She has an insight into the female persona/strength (after the attempted rape) and discovers the power of music to capture the essence hidden by appearence.

She is seduced by Rachael, who uses music (her piano playing) as a magickal act. Apthone is the archetypal immature product of this age and its societies: swayed by desires, and using petty manipulation to achieve lowly goals. When he becomes a threat to Diane, he is dealt with by those who desire her, magickally and sexually (Rachael and Watts). Is his accident purely chance? Or is someone, or two, watching over Diane? In the end, Rachael wins Diane. She is an hereditary sorceress – carrying on her grandmother's tradition (thus missing a generation: Rachael's mother). This tradition thrives in a certain part of the countryside near where Diane lives.

As in 'Greyling', the perspective is often that of the character involved: i.e. events/thoughts etc. are seen through their eyes, with their (often moral and conventional) understanding/attitudes. This gives an appreciation and understanding of these people as they are – and how magic affects them, usually without them being aware of it. It requires the reader to suspend and transcend conventional Satanic/sinister notions (which are often only the outer form of what is Satanic/sinister rather than its essence). This should enable genuine magick to be understood – as it should aid the understanding of how forms/energies etc. affect/change individuals, often unconsciously. All this should aid self-insight.

NEXION

A

Beginning

1977 ev

I

Per Sorensen was dead.

His death did nothing to ease the shelling. Katgusha rockets still shattered the buildings around. A tram burned as rubble from a nearby explosion slithered onto the tracks in front of it and the armoured troop carrier bearing Sorensen's body turned to avoid the flames.

A pretty woman wearing a Wehrmacht helmet for protection against debris looked up at the carrier and briefly smiled. But her smile did nothing to relieve Dieter's sadness, and he watched her as she walked nimbly through the rubble clutching a canteen of water. The block of buildings ahead of her shook with explosions ,and smoke and dust drifted away with the slight wind. Somewhere nearby a man screamed.

Dieter and his comrades did not move as the carrier bore them and the body toward the Ploetzensee cemetery. Zhukov's Red Horde was near and Dieter imagined he could hear small-arms fire in the brief pauses between shell, rocket and bomb. Despite the explosions, no one ran along the streets, and a tired Volksturm guard waved the troop carrier through the intersection. Nearby, young boys in Hitler Jugend uniform worked cheerfully, digging a trench parallel to a lane of twisted, torn trees. Their leader spoke, but Dieter heard nothing except another shell burst nearby. For a few seconds the boys stood silent, their caps removed, as the carrier passed. Sturmscharfuhrer Hermann acknowledged their respect with a salute.

Sorensen's coffin was made from empty ammunition crates and Dieter helped lower them and their body into the grave. The symbolism seemed fitting for a man who had fought for three years on the Russian front, always with his machine-pistol dangling on a lanyard around his neck.

Dieter's eulogy was brief: 'Bright and glorious that warrior's Destiny who in battle-array stands for his children and home, stands for the woman of his heart, bravely opposed to the foe. So Death may come, when it will, bringing this life's thread to an end.

'For think not that Destiny will allow for a man to live always unharmed, great though he be, though even he boast descent from the gods. Even though the coward pass through fury of battle saСe to his home in his flight – death will assail him there. But then he dies unlamented,] unloved by his folk, while both the high and the low weep by the tomb of the brave.

'Yes, with a nation's tears wherever he may die, we bewail him; and if he the brave lives he is hailed all but a god upon Earth. Strong as a fortress of defence in the fight do we gaze on our hero: his are deeds for the many, and he does them alone.'

Amid the falling shells Hermann led the last salute before the honour guard fired their three salvos over] the grave. A woman flak helper threw fresh Spring flowers before earth protected the body: not for Sorensen the mutilation the Soviet troops inflicted on the bodies of dead SS officers. The men, led by Hermann, were singing 'I Had a Comrade' and there were tears in Dieter's eyes. Sorensen had saved his life, twice. The journey back to the dug-out. was slow, and Dieter wished Zhukov's troops would attack. For every bullet, a kill; for every Panzerfaust, a tank. Vengeance for Sorensen's death.

The smoke twilight from the battle bombardment was long, and Dieter was relieved when the first tank appeared, lurching over the rubble in the street. A Soviet sniper made a dash for the safety of the Church facade on Dieter's right but then stopped to clutch his throat and topple to the ground dead. The tank turned abruptly, its machine-gun hitting' nothing that was living. Dieter aimed the pin on the edge of the Panzerfaust at the tank, gripping the weapon under his arm. His muscles ached from the repetition and there was no elation about the kill. Close-range Soviet bombardment began while machine-gun fire spattered the ground. The buildings around or what was left of them – hid a few German snipers and Dieter was trying to judge their number from their sporadic fire when the bombardment and bullets ceased. Dieter tensed while buildings and the burning tank crackled with fire. A few grenades were thrown, then the slow ruh of] Soviet troops among the rubble and the bodies. 'Tank riders!' shouted Dieter.

The only thing tank riders did was advance and die. and Dieter did not disappoint Stalin's expendable peasants. He shot two three, six. Hermann had run out of grenades. More Soviet snipers were seeking cover to provide cross-fire but Dieter could only target one before the others escaped into the rubble of the Church. He threw his last grenade after them.

The young machine-gunner in the dug-out beside Dieter was dead and he rolled the bloody body away before quickly changing the clogged barrel of the gun. Hermann fed the ammunition belt until. without a sound, he slithered down the trench, shot in the head. The tank riders were crawling closer but Dieter held their advance with Hermann's sub-machine gun while through the smoke filled street another tank lurched toward him.

Soon, Dieter had no more ammunition, the men in the dug-outs behind him were dead and he began to throw bricks, stones and anything else he could find before scrambling back to find a weapon with which to kill. From the still warm hand of one his dead comrades he took a Mauser pistol but had no time to aim. The shell from the tank exploded near him knocking him over before burying him under earth, rubble and wood.

Dieter awoke to consciousness to hear the crackling of a nearby fire and the distant explosions of battle; to smell burning wood and flesh, and to see above him framed by the crack of light, a large brown rat. No voices reached him and when he clawed his way cautiously into the light he could see no human movement along the street. The light drizzle refreshed him. and he let the rain water soak his hair and trickle over his bloodstained face before crawling toward his dug-out. The tank smouldered but the dead Soviet troops had been removed.

Along the street an old man pulled a wooden cart while beside him two women walked enwrapped in long coats with black shawls covering their heads. From the end of the cart two sets of bare feet protruded. A squad of Zhukov's soldiers led by a bandy-legged officer in a peaked cap strutted toward them. They shouted and laughed. The old man tried to speak, but the officer knocked him down before three soldiers dragged one of the women into the facade of the Church. She screamed and resisted and was shot.

Several soldiers pushed the other woman to the ground. Dieter shot the officer through the head. Surprise and his marksmanship killed four more before inaccurate fire was returned but within seconds he had shot the remaining three. 'Thank you,' said the old man as Dieter approached. 'You must go – there are more.'

Dieter knelt down to retrieve a selection of weapons from the bodies before helping the woman to her feet. Her beauty surprised him and he forced himself to turn away.

'Where is the front-line'?' he asked.

'There is no front-line,' said the old man sadly, staring at the ground. Before Dieter could reply, the woman spoke. 'You must go – if they find you alive...'

'and you'?' he asked.

The woman smiled. 'We are now the children of Fate. We shall head West.'

The old man knelt briefly beside the body of his dead daughter before covering her face with her coat. He dragged the two bodies of his wife and young daughter from the cart to lay them beside, covering them as best he could.

'I have no more strength to carry them for a burial,' he said. A lorry smouldered at the end of the street where a building showed a lilting inside of floors.

'Where is your Regiment'?' the woman asked. Dieter looked around the scene of their last battle. 'I am the Regiment!' he said proudly. Dizzy and weak from loss of blood and concussion, he collapsed against the cart.

'We must help him,' he heard the woman say.

The old man sighed, wearily. 'Yes, 1 know.'

The last thing Dieter remembered was the woman's beautiful smile.

II

Wolfram stared into the quartz sphere while outside his shuttered room the high-ranking SS officer waited in the cool air of the Bavarian Alps.

There was no mystery in what he sensed through the medium of the crystal as, many years ago, there had been a mystery when a gaunt young man fresh from war had saught with Dietrich's help to seek him out. Now they both were dead and he alone of the original seven was left to try and build from the ruins of the destruction a new empire to reach toward the stars.

The Dark Gods that for most of his life he had served would be waiting among those stars and he had only to open another Gate for their power to be his for him to use it as he had used it to help that young man of vision. Yet there was something that he did not understand about the events that had brought destruction to his dreams. Some other power opposed to his own must have been invoked and he moved away from the crystal to stare for several minutes at the pieces scattered over the seven boards and one hundred and twenty six squares of the Star Game. But he could see no pattern that might explain the events and, sad, he shook his head, to play perhaps for the last time upon his piano a piece of music by Bach.

The music brought a quiet joy and he entered his plain Temple to seek the guidance of his gods. The quartz tetrahedron glowed, a little, as it had done for the past few days and he rested his hands on it. The coldness seemed to drain away his sadness and joy and he imagined' was travelling through the dimensions beyond the seventh Gate. There was a presence awaiting him among the stars at the very edge of the galaxy and he allowed it to shape his consciousness as many times in the past it had been shaped. The futures of his own planet lay in visions around him and he had only to find her desire to make one future real.

With one possibility he returned to the terrace where against the backdrop of mountains the officer waited, holding a sheaf of files. The files contained the personal details of 55 officers who had distinguished themselves in the savage combat of the last few months of the war, and Wolfram read through them all slowly and with interest. Per Sorensen, his favoured, was dead but in an hour he had found a successor.

He handed the file of the chosen to the officer. 'You can make the arrangements?' 'Yes!' replied the officer curtly but with respect. 'and the country?'

'England.'

The officer was surprised. 'As you wish.' He saluted, bowed slightly and left the terrace to walk down the steps toward the road.

Dieter could recall little of his journey. Burnt by fever he heard mumbled voices, the sound of aircraft, smelt putrid smells, felt a damp cloth on his face and the bumping as the cart trundled its slow way across a ravaged land. At length, daylight stung his eyes and he saw convoy of-lorries, Soviet soldiers standing idle, the husks of burnt-out tanks. Behind the cart where he lay hidden he could see a straggle of unkempt people pushing or carrying on their backs their few possessions.

A few more miles and the old man ceased his pulling of the cart. 'There is a Soviet check-point ahead' someone had said.

Slowly, night drew its darkness over them and the people huddled in the small convoy for safety stopped, exhausted and hungry.

'What shall we do?' Dieter heard the beautiful woman ask her father.

Stiffly, Dieter climbed from the cart. A haggard woman in a black skirt, coat and shawl stared at him. Even in the twilight his uniform was distinct. Soon, everyone was staring at him.

'There's a reward for the likes of him:' crooned the old woman. 'It would feed us all for days:' Several of the group stood up to move toward Dieter.

The old man who had pulled the cart moved between them. 'You make me ashamed to be German,' he said to them.

'Germany's finished!' shouted the old woman. 'and it's due to the likes of him.' She spat on the ground. 'When did you all last eat, eh? A proper meal, I mean. Meat and fresh vegetables!'

Dieter held the old man's arm. 'I am strong now and shall leave.'

The old man nodded. He held out his hand. 'Hans-Peter Schemm.'

'Haupsturmfuehrer Dieter Norkus.' They shook hands.

'My daughter, IIse.'

Dieter bowed toward her. 'I have much to thank you and your father for.'

'It was nothing,' she said, 'compared to the sacrifices some have made.'

'and the war?'

'Unconditional surrender.'

'The Fuhrer?'

'Dead – so they say.'

Dieter sighed. 'I hope I shall see you again.'

'Koblenz – that is where we go,' Hans-Peter said. 'Ask for us near the Florinsmarkt in the Old Town – if it still exists.'

'Until then, I thank you.' He brought his heels together in the Prussian manner, bowed toward Ilse and strode purposefully away from the road into the gathering darkness.

Dieter walked for several hours across fields before stopping to take a rest and check the two pistols he still carried. The night silence was strange after the bombardment of Berlin and he could not sleep only try and dispel the sadness he felt because the war was over with Germany's defeat. He did not know what to do except journey toward the farm of his father in Hessen. But Germany was in ruins, occupied by foreign armies and he felt himself bound still by the oath of loyalty sworn those many years ago.

Dawn's first rays found him in a small copse. Somewhere near, he knew, would be a farm, with water and food, but probably foreign soldiers, and he forced himself to remain within the cover of the trees until darkness brought again the freedom he needed to resume his journey.

Sleep did not come, just insistent hunger, thirst and the boredom of inaction. Twice he thought he heard voices and once, the distant rumble of tanks and when night came he was content with the caution born of combat to edge his way slowly through fields, avoiding all roads and tracks.

Toward dawn he came upon farm buildings. A man slept by the entrance to the courtyard, a rifle beside him, and Dieter watched the buildings for nearly an hour before walking down the track to kick the sleeping man awake and taking his rifle.

Good people!' the startled [man] blurted out. He saw Dieter's uniform and shouted several words in Polish.

'Quiet!' commanded Dieter. 'You speak German?"

"Yes!' said the old man proudly.

'Who is in charge here?'

The man stood up to face Dieter. 'Landrat von Leiden.'

'No Russians.'

'No,' replied the man nervously, 'not yet.'

Dieter looked around, listening. 'The Landrat – tell him I want to see him.'

'of' course!'

Dieter did not have long to wait. Von Leiden stumbled toward him, bent and shuffling because of' arthritis. 'Berlin?' he asked.

'Yes.'

'You have come a long way. Alone.'

'Yes.'

'Hmmph' He turned to speak to the Pole who was skulking behind. Fetch some of the bread. and water.' He scowled. 'and a little of that sausage you have hidden in the urn.' The Pole displayed no emotion, and scuttled away. 'No manners these Poles, 'muttered von Leiden. 'They steal my geese.'

'I am Hauptsturmfeuhrer –'

'I do not care who you are. The Russians are everywhere.'

'How far to American lines?'

'Not far – a day, walking. Perhaps.' He stared at Dieter's uniform. 'My son –.. he began. Then, abruptly:' I have some old clothes, should you wish. Your uniform –'

'No, thank you.'

Von Leiden shook his head. 'This war's ending – it is not the same. No honour in peace.'

Dieter gave him the rifle and this gesture of trust brought tears to von Leiden's eyes. 'Our old world of honour lies in ruins.' Then, seeing the Pole return he took the food and water and gave them to Dieter saying, 'Go, and quickly.'

Dieter stuffed the black bread and sausage into his pockets. The water was cold and refreshing and he cleaned his face briefly before handing back the jug, bowing his head to von Leiden and striding along the track toward the fields.

He walked for several hours, unconcerned about being seen for he had resolved to die fighting, like all his comrades, rather than surrender. He stopped briefly, to take from an inside pocket his Knight's Cross which he pinned to his camouflage jacket, making sure all his insignia were clear and bright. Nearby, he heard someone whistle. It was a tuneful whistle and, as it came nearer, Dieter recognized it as the Parade March of the 18th Hussars. It was whistled by a boy dressed in the striking uniform of the Napolas.

Dieter let him pass as he lay hidden by a tree before calling out to the boy.

'Heil Hitler!' the boy replied with enthusiasm. Tall and muscular, he appeared to Dieter to be the perfect advertisement for the Jungmannen.

Dieter returned the salute, with less enthusiasm. 'Where are you heading?' he asked. 'Home!:' replied the boy cheerfully, his left hand resting on his dagger.

'Where is that?'

'Hamburg. and you, Haupsturmfeuhrer'?'

[text illegible]

'No, sir.'

Dieter gave him all the bread and half of the sausage.

'What will you do when you reach Hamburg?'

Brightly, the boy said, 'Build a new Germany!'

'Germany will certainly need re-building.'

'Sir?' the boy asked seriously.

'Yes?'

'I would consider it a great honour if you would allow me to accompany you.'

'What about your home?'

'There will be plenty of time.' He stared at Dieter's Knights Cross.

'Have you seen any action?'

'Yes! Anti-aircraft battery at Grunewald. Then when the Reds came I joined some Volksturm and Hitler Jugend. When we ran out of ammunition we split up.'

'I have no intention of surrendering. But you are Germany's future.'

'I am not afraid to die.'

Dieter smiled. 'I can see by your eyes you speak truth.' He gave the boy one of his pistols. 'You might need this.'

In silence they walked together for many miles while Dieter's spirit grew troubled, and he was about to order the boy to leave him and find safety in the American lines when ahead they saw a straggling line of soldiers.

'Go now,' Dieter said, 'while you can.'

The boy smiled and shook his head before releasing the safety catch on the pistol. Slowly, the soldiers encircled them.

The boy was lying on the ground, his young, earnest face intently watching the advancing soldiers. Dieter took the pistol from him.

'The future is yours,' Dieter said.

'and you, sir?' the boy asked.

'At least they are American,' said Dieter, throwing the pistols away and raising his hands in the gesture of surrender.

III

They were taken to a small village occupied by the Americans. Several of the timbered houses, as well as the Saxon church, lay in ruins while around the largest standing building which served as American headquarters, small groups of old woman and young children sat, strangely silent, on the ground. Amongst the destruction, trucks, jeeps, stores and American soldiers were littered without any appearence of order.

Pushed against a courtyard wall, they were searched for the third time. 'O.K.,' shouted the American Sergeant, 'turn around you Nazi bastards!'

The American Major who approached them did not smile. Behind him a small bespectacled soldier carried a clip-board.

'Rank, name and unit,' he said to Dieter.

'Haupsturmfeuhrer Dieter Norkus, Waffen SS, Nordland Division...'

'Sir,' the bespectacled soldier interrupted, talking to the Major, "the boy.'

'What?'

'G2 orders, sir.'

'Take over, Sergeant!' The Major strode back toward his headquarters, his clip-board carrier in tow.

With the Major gone, the Sergeant approached Dieter. 'Let's see that medal.' he grinned. 'Kinda nice, aint it?'

He went to rip it from Dieter's uniform when the boy sprang forward. Without speaking a word he wrenched the American's arm and tripped him up. The other guards laughed.

'You son of a bitch!' Enraged, the Sergeant jumped up, snatched a rifle and smashed the butt into the boy's face. Dieter moved toward him, but two guards pinned his arms against the wall. Nearby, a few birds sang their unchanging songs of Spring. The Sergeant ripped the Knight's Cross from Dieter's tunic. 'Sergeant Piaggiot' shouted the Major from his doorway. With a swaggering gait, the Sergeant walked over to him

[text illegible]

370

Dieter was forced into the building and onto a chair. The Major said a few words in German before Dieter said 'I do speak English.'

'Great! Cigarette?'

'No, thank you.'

'Where is the rest of your outfit?'

'They fell in Berlin.'

Nearby, a brief burst of gunfire could be heard.

'How did you get here?' the Major asked.

'I walked.' There was a knock on the door and the Sergeant entered without saluting. 'That kid, Major,' he said. 'Tried to escape. We had to shoot.'

Dieter stared at him, his eyes bright with anger. 'How heroic of you to shoot an unarmed boy!'

'Shut your mouth!' shouted the Sergeant.

'I wish to report this to a senior American officer,' said Dieter.

The Major was smiling and the Sergeant had started to laugh when Dieter leapt across the room to grab the machine-gun the Sergeant was holding. His hand was on the barrel, his finger near the trigger when his two guards beat him into unconsciousness with the butts of their rifles.

For Dieter the next few days became a blur of impressions: a long journey in a covered lorry with other prisoners of war with whom he was forbidden to speak, an interrogation, another journey, another interrogation, a guarded prisoner of war compound where he and the other prisoners were forced to sleep on the ground.

He lost count of the days and weary from the months of fighting, the shock of defeat, lack of sleep, hunger, the journeys and the interrogations, he sat in the back of an American lorry watching through the open flap the stream beside the road as the lorry wound its way among some hills. The day was warm, perfumed by the scent of Spring's flowers and Dieter began to recall the quiet beauty of the Germany he had known in Hessen as a boy, his spirit began to yearn to return to the house of his family where to renew with his own hands the cultivation of their lands. There was a family legend, he knew, connected with the farm and he possessed a desire to wander free and homeward to hear his grandfather tell it. But Germany was in ruins, he himself was a prisoner of war and he still believed he was bound by his oath of loyalty sworn in the exuberant first year of the war. 'My Honour Commands Loyalty' said the motto on his ring – and to all the questions that in the last few days he had .been asked his answer was always the same: 'I have done nothing,' he would say with pride, 'that is dis-honourable.' But they did not understand.

'For my fatherland in sadness I weep,' he recalled from memory for himself when alone or when no one would listen or believe his words of truth, 'for of my country am I robbed. How great is the chant of our woe: tear upon tear is shed and only the unseeing dead forget how to weep…' Enwrapped in dreams of his home, he did not notice when the lorry stopped. But the driver brought him and his two guards out into the warming sun to move the rock-fall from the narrow road.

An old man shuffled slowly toward them along the road while they worked and Dieter was dragging the last rock away when he reached them. Without speaking he walked straight to the two guards who were lounging against the side of the lorry, grabbed them and knocked their heads together. Limply, they fell to the ground. The astonished driver went to draw his holstered pistol but swift like a wolf in attack the old man leapt toward him striking at his windpipe with his hand. The driver fell down to lie still on the road.

The old man was smiling, his eyes bright and blue like the clear sky of summer. 'Come, Dieter Norkus, we must leave.'

Dieter did not question his sudden freedom and followed as with surprising agility the old min led him upwards through the rocks and trees, along twisting tracks to a small wooden hut. Dieter recognized the SS officer who was waiting inside. The officer handed him a sheaf of documents, saying: 'All the documents for your new identity are there.

A few days from now, and you will be in your new country.'
Dieter looked up from the documents. "Which is?"
'England.' Dieter was surprised. 'May I ask – for what purpose?'

'To continue what has been achieved, and prepare for what for what is next.' The officer saluted, bowed, and left.

'I', the smiling old man said, 'am Rundi and will be your guide. Come now, for there is much to do.'

Made in the USA
Middletown, DE
29 March 2016